THE STORY OF PEKING MAN

FROM ARCHAEOLOGY TO MYSTERY

JIA LANPO AND HUANG WEIWEN

TRANSLATED BY
YIN ZHIQI

BEIJING
FOREIGN LANGUAGES PRESS
AND
HONG KONG
OXFORD UNIVERSITY PRESS
OXFORD NEW YORK
1990

Oxford University Press

Oxford   New York   Toronto
Petaling Jaya   Singapore   Hong Kong   Tokyo
Delhi   Bombay   Calcutta   Madras   Karachi
Nairobi   Dar es Salaam   Cape Town
Melbourne   Auckland

and associated companies in
Berlin   Ibadan

First published 1990
Published in the United States
by Oxford University Press, Inc., New York

ISBN 0 19 585118 9

Library of Congress
Cataloguing-in-Publication Data
available

British Library
Cataloguing in Publication Data
available

Typeset by Foreign Languages Press

Published by Foreign Languages Press, 24 Baiwanzhuang Road,
Beijing 100037, People's Republic of China
and by Oxford University Press, Warwick House, Hong Kong

033819

Contents

Acknowledgements

Although the authors themselves cannot say they are happy about the book as it is, it is the fruit of much labour and the result of generous help from many sources. The foremost is Professor Pei Wenzhong, who made his private file —containing, among other items, unpublished letters concerning the missing Peking Man fossils—available to us.

From abroad, our requests have always met with warm responses. Professor Anders Martinsson of Uppsala University spared no efforts to organize the collection of biographical material on Johan Andersson, Otto Zdansky and Birger Bohlin for the book. Zdansky and Bohlin, veterans at Zhoukoudian, promptly sent their recent photos through Professor Martinsson when they learned that we needed them. The Museum of Far Eastern Antiquities, Stockholm, sent Andersson's photos to us.

A number of our own colleagues at the Institute contributed greatly while the book was in progress. The historical pictures were developed during the sweltering summer by Wang Zhefu of the photo section, who also made a special trip to Zhoukoudian to take pictures of present views of the sites; the charts are the handiwork of Dai Jiasheng and colleagues from his section. Their work graces the entire book.

Finally our thanks should go to the editors, translator and others concerned at the Foreign Languages Press, without whom the publication of this book would not have been possible.

Jia Lanpo
July 31, 1986, Beijing

Preface

It has been sixty-nine years since Dr Johan Gunnar Andersson of Sweden made the discovery of the Zhoukoudian site in 1921. An ordinary hamlet before then, Zhoukoudian village has over the years evolved into one of the most valuable places in the world for the study of early human beings. Visitors by the hundreds, many of whom are scholars making the trip for scientific purposes, come each year to pay homage to this home of the famed Peking Man.

What distinguishes the site is the presence of a great variety and quantity of artifacts and human and vertebrate fossils. Their existence has provided reliable evidence for scientists tracing the human race's remote past—the dim corridor of history is illuminated in the shining light of the relics dug up at such sites.

Zhoukoudian as a project has been distinguished by its international character; it is the result of the common endeavours of scholars the world over. Having a direct connection with the project were such well-known scientists as Weng Wenhao, Li Jie, Yang Zhongjian, Pei Wenzhong and Bian Meinian of China; Davidson Black of Canada; Johan Gunnar Andersson and Birger Bohlin of Sweden; Otto Zdansky of Austria; Pierre Teilhard de Chardin of France; and Franz Weidenreich of the United States. To some of them, the project meant a lifelong career, and we are filled with nostalgia and respect today whenever we recall their labours. One such person was Father Pierre Teilhard de Chardin. In 1981 I wrote an article to commemorate the hundredth anniversary of his birth; it appears as an appendix to this book.

There are other brilliant scholars whom I shall never forget and who have inspired me in my work. The foremost is the esteemed Davidson Black. Born with a heart condition, and fully aware, as a medical professional, of what was in store for him, he never let the fatal disease stand in the way of his work on the project. From the early preparatory work for the digging to the later founding and directing of the Cenozoic Research Laboratory that supervised the fieldwork at Zhoukoudian, he was interested in every detail and would do many of the tedious jobs himself. In addition to heavy administrative duties, he took charge of the studies on Peking Man fossils and made outstanding contributions to the subject. He drove himself relentlessly, stealing time from impending death, which finally caught up with him in the deep of the night on March 15, 1934. He was found dead in the morning at his desk, specimens from Zhoukoudian lying in front of him.

Many papers and books have appeared on Zhoukoudian over the past decades, but we still lack a systematic account of the entire history of the excavation. In this respect we have only Pei Wenzhong's *The Excavation of the Zhoukoudian Cave (Geo-*

logical Bulletin, Ser. B, No. 7, 1934), which gives an account of the activities of the earlier days.

For half a century, from the spring of 1931 on, my life has been inseparable from the Zhoukoudian project. As one of the few of the earliest participants still living, and with the longest fieldwork record among all the colleagues at the site, I believe I am qualified to tell the story of our great endeavour. The idea of committing this significant episode in history to paper has long been in my mind. I began collecting material for a book in 1941 when I was out of a job after the Pearl Harbour attack, but the increasing tension of the war forced me to abandon my plan. Again in the mid-1960s I was urged by Yan Tianming, a senior colleague at our Institute, to write down everything I knew and experienced on the Zhoukoudian project before my memories should fade. On impulse, I worked feverishly for two months and produced a draft of some 50 000 words. But the 'cultural revolution' intervened and for a second time I had to undo what I had begun.

In that fantastic political atmosphere people like me were dismayed to find so many of our friends and colleagues labelled 'reactionary authorities' or 'class enemies' of all descriptions overnight. One category of people so labelled were those who had any association with foreigners. As the Zhoukoudian project itself was assailed as a 'stronghold of cultural aggression', I expected the same misfortune that befell my friends to catch up with me. Under the circumstances, the draft which was in my keeping had become a heavy weight on my mind, since it mentioned many foreign scholars and their contribution. There was no telling what the consequences would be if the 'rebels' ever got hold of my 'blasphemy'. Thus after long deliberation, I made the painful decision to destroy the manuscript. I still remember the stabbing at my heart as I threw the pages one by one into the flames.

Swift changes forced Lin Biao, Jiang Qing and their associates out of power, but I did not consider resuming work on the book until I was again urged to. By this time, the senior colleague who had inspired me to write the first draft had passed away. It was on a summer day in 1980 that the head of the publishing division of our Institute, Bi Chuzhen, dropped into my office and advised me to pick up the writing again while there was still time. "You aren't going to see Karl Marx in the Other World with that book in your head, are you?" I promised that I would do it, but not without hesitation. Owing to my advanced age, the task seemed formidable. Fortunately at this point, the young archaeologist

Some of the references used for this book. (*Photo by Wang Zhefu*)

Huang Weiwen was transferred back to the Institute and shared an office with me. He had been working at Zhoukoudian for a few years immediately prior to his return, and it was natural that we would often talk about the projected book. We found ourselves agreeing that we owed it on the one hand to our colleagues, Chinese and foreign, who had passed away, and on the other to posterity, that a faithful record of this sort be written. It was a happy coincidence that the Foreign Languages Press of Beijing called on me and offered a contract for the book. This new source of encouragement gave me the extra strength with which to make the final decision.

I decided to ask young Huang Weiwen to be my co-author and named the book *Excavations at Zhoukoudian* [title of the original Chinese manuscript—*Tr.*]. I remembered that what I had done on the previous draft had been a combination of scientific description and personal account from my own memory. Since memory can be unreliable, we decided this time to make full use of the files, some of which had never been published. In the process, we copied sections when we deemed necessary. These include material from correspondence of the Cenozoic Research Laboratory, the *Daily Journal* and the *Weekly Summary Sheet* on the fieldwork at Zhoukoudian, and photos. In addition, there was my own correspondence, which had been a nuisance to my family the few times we had moved because of its bulk. Now these letters turned out to be a great asset, for they would often remind me of significant happenings that had vanished into oblivion, or invoke fond memories. According to the rough estimate I made, their total weight was no less than 100 kilogrammes. To sift through such a pile was indeed an arduous task, but Huang Weiwen took it in his stride. It is inconceivable that the writing of this book could have been done in the way it was without his co-operation.

1

'Dragon Bones' in
Scientific Perspective

The account of what happened at Zhoukoudian, where the Peking Man fossils were unearthed, best begins with a discussion of the 'dragon bones' that led to digging at the site. And, as the concept of dragon bones presupposes the existence of dragons, it is relevant to consider that mythical species first.

The dragon image has deep roots in China, and legends and myths abound in which the dragon is a divine creature capable of creating clouds and rain at its pleasure. In the *Works of Guan Zhong*,[1] it is described as a being that "may shrink to the size of a silkworm or bulge to a size too large for the world to contain; it may soar above the clouds, or immerse itself in the abyss of waters." An ancient dictionary[2] also has it that "the dragon is sometimes visible, sometimes obscure; it may appear slender, or grow immense; it may shorten or lengthen itself at will; and it soars into the sky on the spring equinox, and submerges into the deep on the autumnal equinox."

Through its status as a deity, the dragon became the traditional symbol of the throne. And indeed, emperors were believed to be dragons incarnate. Any visitor to the Palace Museum in Beijing (Peking) · will soon notice the ornamental dragons carved on pillars in front of Tiananmen and on stone slabs laid along the steps leading to the great halls. These fierce-looking images are so omnipresent that the old palace seems to be a world of dragons.

But has there ever been such a species? The answer is an emphatic no! In no part of the world can any vertebrate paleontologist dig up a dragon fossil of the creature described in *Eryayi*:[3] "a being that has the horns of a stag, the head of a camel, the eyes of a rabbit, the neck of a snake, the belly of a sea serpent, the paws of a tiger, and the ears of a cow." Even though no such animal ever existed, as a general concept it may be comprehensible. Analyzing these mythical descriptions in the light of modern zoology, Jia Lanpo and Professor Zhen Shuonan have noted that they "may boil down to a being which has scales over its body that reflect light and which changes in size as it breathes and in length as it creeps; its disappearance in winter clearly suggests hibernation. These are characteristics common to snakes, lizards and crocodiles."

With legends and myths about dragons long in currency, 'dragon bones' were naturally thought of as real objects. *Mountains and Seas*,[4] probably the earliest work on geography and paleontology, has recorded this term, as have a score of other books

---

[1] A work attributed to Guan Zhong, one-time Prime Minister of the state of Qi in the Spring and Autumn Period (770-476 B.C.).

[2] *Shuowen*, compiled by Xu Shen of the Eastern Han Dynasty (A.D. 25-220).

[3] Compiled by Luo Yuan in the Song Dynasty (960-1279).

[4] A famous work whose author is unknown.

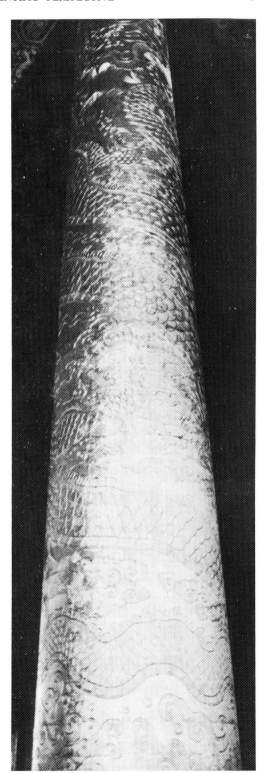

Dragon patterns gracing old Beijing buildings.
(*Photo by Wang Zhefu*)

the teeth from a big animal skull so that they could sell them separately for higher prices, and they smashed the rest of the bones for easy shipping in sacks. On a survey trip to Gansu Province, Jia Lanpo and the young geologist Wei Qi lamented over the sight of a roomful of sacks containing the fossil teeth, skull and other bone fragments of a whole three-toed horse. They also saw fragments of the remains of an ancient rhinoceros with cracks still new. At that time no museum or research institute in China possessed a complete skeleton of a three-toed horse! As to the rhinoceros, the situation was even worse, for no complete skull or even a lower jawbone could be found in any of these institutions.

Study has shown that most of these fossils found in northern China date back to the Pliocene Epoch, while those found in southern China date to the Pleistocene Epoch (from 3 million to 10 000 years ago). It is quite possible that some are from a much later date, as evidenced by the human skull fragments and teeth that are found mixed among other fossils at a number of medicinal herb centres in the Guangxi region.

The expression 'dragon bone' is readily understood by Chinese villagers in areas where the fossil-bearing deposits lie. They will show scientists the precise location of

written in various dynasties.[1] These records reveal that not only did the term have an early origin, but the sites that yielded dragon bones were long known.

The so-called dragon bones or teeth are actually vertebrate fossils, especially mammalian, which can be found in abundance in all the medicinal procurement centres and herbal medicine shops we have visited.

Most of the people who dug these fossils up were peasants. Ignorant of the immense value of the objects, they often knocked off

---

[1] These include the *Annals of the Tang Dynasty* (618-907); *Random Notes* by the scientist Shen Kuo of the Northern Song Dynasty (960-1127); *A History of the Jin Dynasty* (1115-1234), written in the Yuan Dynasty (1271-1368).

a site when this term is used, especially if the scientists display samples of what they are looking for. But if the term 'fossil' is used, the villagers will not understand.

A village supply and marketing co-op's medicinal herb centre is often a reliable source of information on the location of fossils of significance. This was so in the case of the discovery of the *in situ* deposit of a giant ape (*Gigantopithecus*) by the Chinese Academy of Sciences in 1956.

The story of that find really began in 1935, when the eminent paleoanthropologist G. H. R. von Koenigswald, a German of Dutch nationality, found at different times three uncommon teeth from among the dragon bones at a medicinal herb store in Hongkong. Based on their structure and size, he gave them the scientific designation *Gigantopithecus*. Later, in 1946, another paleoanthropologist, Franz Weidenreich of the United States, re-examined these teeth. He concluded that the species was closer to human than to ape, and renamed them *Gigantanthropus*, or Giant Man. In 1952, von Koenigswald found another five teeth of the same species. After studying them, he accepted the view of Weidenreich and asserted that the teeth came from a species of very primitive humans who lived in southern China during the Quaternary Period.

In subsequent years scientists of various countries took different points of view regarding the classification of this oversized primate, while other data pertaining to the fossil species, such as the sites where the teeth were found, conditions of deposits in which they occurred, and their dating, remained uncertain.

In searching for answers to these problems and trying to gather more information, the Institute of Vertebrate Paleontology and Paleoanthropology of the Chinese Academy of Sciences at the end of 1955 assigned Pei Wenzhong (W. C. Pei), Jia

Lanpo (Chia Lan Po), Qiu Zhonglang and Lü Zun'e to set up a team to explore the caves in the Guangxi Zhuang Autonomous Region. These caves were considered the likely home of the giant apes.

The team was divided into two groups in the spring of 1956. The group led by Jia Lanpo explored nearly a hundred caves of various sizes. They followed information provided by the Nanning Supply and Marketing Co-operative, searching cave after cave in the counties of Chongzuo and Daxin.

In Daxin, the team arrived at the village Nalongtun during a heavy shower. Despite the weather, the members were impatient to start their work. Armed with dragon teeth procured at the Nanning Co-op, they began to question the local people. One old woman, upon seeing a dragon-tooth sample, produced a box filled with her own collection of dragon bones. Among these were 'giant ape' teeth. Pointing through the window, she showed them the small cave entrance where she had obtained these 'bones'. It turned out to be an *in situ* site for giant ape fossil teeth.

In 1963, another team from the Chinese Academy of Sciences made discoveries of great significance in Lantian County, Shaanxi Province, in much the same fashion. The scientists involved were Zhang Yuping, Huang Wanpo, Ji Hongxiang and Tang Yingjun. The earth strata in the area they investigated have been largely undisturbed during the past 70 million years so that a cross section of the sequences often shows the original continuity. More important, almost all layers bear vertebrate fossils. This makes the area ideal for the Cenozoic Era geological and paleontological studies. In addition, the site had earlier yielded a lower mandible bearing a close resemblance to that of Peking Man. This was found on July 19 of the same year.

When the team arrived at Gongwang

Village, 16 kilometres from the county seat of Lantian, a sudden rain forced the members to look for shelter at a roadside store. They joined villagers who had gathered there to get out of the rain. Conversation promptly turned to the subject of dragon bones.

"Right on the ridge behind this village you can find plenty of them," said one of the villagers. So the team stayed, and in three days they recovered five boxfuls of fossils. Because of this initial success, the Academy of Sciences sent a larger team to the village the following year, and that was when they found the Lantian Man skullcap.

We may lament over the ruining of fossils and fossil sites by villagers, but their search for dragon bones has thus unwittingly led to many finds of great significance. The following is one more such instance.

In 1974, Jia Lanpo and Wei Qi were on a trip in Inner Mongolia with colleagues from the Autonomous Region's museum. The group was tracing the northward distribution of microliths. They began their study at Bailingmiao, passed through Erlian, and stopped for the night at Jining. During a conversation in the hotel where they were staying, Wei Qi related that at a village named Xujiayao (Hsu Chia Yao) in Yanggao County, Shanxi Province, the villagers had dug up thousands of kilogrammes of dragon bones and had delivered them to the local trading co-op for sale. This piece of information so intrigued Jia Lanpo that he changed his itinerary to go to this village instead of to Lanzhou, the capital of Gansu Province.

The village, 60 kilometres east of the city of Datong, lies at the boundary line, defined by the stream Liyigou, between the provinces of Hebei and Shanxi. Wei Qi's information proved true. No sooner had the group climbed on top of the steep western bank of the stream than they noticed that the ground was strewn with bone fragments and stone artifacts. In scarcely half a day, they had dug up or gathered more than 500 stone artifacts, a pile of bone fragments with artificial cracks, and some identifiable mammalian fossils.

It proved to be a surprisingly large site. A preliminary survey of the fossil distribution showed that it covered some three square kilometres in area. Excavations conducted there from 1976 to 1978 yielded the remains of twenty species of vertebrates, thousands of stone artifacts, great numbers of bone and antler implements, and human remains of more than ten individuals. The site was dated to the later phase of the Riss Glaciation, and the absolute age was estimated to be over 100 000 years.

But the story of dragon bones would not be complete if we failed to mention the fact that China came to be known to the scientific world as a prospective region for early human fossils because of its medicine shops. At the turn of the century, K. A. Haberer, a German physician working in Beijing and an amateur collector of fossils, bought a large number of dragon bones and dragon teeth from local medicinal shops. He was unfortunate enough to be in Beijing at the time of the invasion of China by the Eight-Power Allied Forces. These troops sacked Beijing, and the doctor was thrown out of his job and had to leave the country.

Haberer took home a boxful of fossils from his collection and, after arriving in Germany in 1903, donated them to Professor Max Schlosser, a well-known vertebrate paleontologist. The professor found that one of the teeth was similar to a human's and even identified it as a third upper left molar. Yet, with the limited scientific knowledge of that time, he could not confirm his own finding. Schlosser merely stated that it belonged to an ape-man.

Nonetheless, the tooth attracted much attention in the scientific world. The reason for this was that there were many conjectures and much confusion over the fossil Neanderthal Man found in Germany in 1856 and the Java Man found in Java in 1891. Any such new find made on the Asian continent was naturally looked upon as of the utmost importance.

Because the tooth had been bought in a medicinal shop, the site at which it occurred and its dating perforce remained obscure. It could, however, be determined that it was of North China origin, since dragon bones had been abundant in this region. The tooth would not have been imported from elsewhere.

In an earlier time, dragon bones from China, especially those from North China, had been noticed and studied by a few European scholars. In 1870, the British biologist and pioneer vertebrate paleontologist Richard Owen had published a paper on mammalian fossils in China. At the beginning of the twentieth century, scholars of a number of countries joined forces in research on ancient vertebrates in China, thus laying groundwork in the field. Besides Professor Max Schlosser, these scholars included Otto Zdansky of Austria, and Torsten Ringströn and Einar Lönngerg of Sweden.

2

Initial Explorations
at Zhoukoudian

Early in 1914, Dr Johan Gunnar Andersson, Director of the Geological Survey of Sweden, came to China as a mining adviser to the Chinese Government. Profoundly learned and many-sided, he had led a Swedish survey team in the exploration of the Antarctic from 1901 to 1903. For ten years from 1914, he worked in China as, in his own words, "a mining specialist, a fossil collector and an archaeologist." His contributions to fossil collection and studies of the culture of prehistoric China have, however, turned out to be better known than his official work.

Andersson reported for duty at the then Department of Agriculture and Commerce on May 16, 1914. From then on he never let the dragon bones of China slip from his mind. The sight of even a tiny fragment of bone would spark his curiosity, and he would spare no efforts to discover its source. After his arrival in China, he wrote to many Christian missionaries and foreign residents in central China, informing them of Max Schlosser's findings and asking for their help in locating sites that might yield such fossils. Schlosser had by then identified about ninety species of mammals in the collection that Haberer had donated, including the human-like third upper left molar.

Andersson also employed a number of technicians for fossil hunting. He dispatched them to Shanxi, Henan and Gansu Provinces, where there were known drag-on bone sites, in the hope that a flow of objects of antiquity would come into his hands. He then shipped the fossils he obtained to Professor Carl Wiman of the Institute of Paleontology at Uppsala, Sweden.

One day in February 1918, Andersson ran into J. McGregor Gibb, who was teaching chemistry in Beijing. Gibb, knowing well his friend's interest in fossils, produced a few pieces of bone fragments still covered with red clay. He told Andersson that they had just been unearthed at a place called Jigushan (Chicken Bone Hill) near Zhoukoudian (Chou Kou Tien), adding that the area had many limestone caves filled with such deposits. As expected, this news greatly interested Andersson. Zhoukoudian was a day's journey from Beijing on mule back. On March 22 Andersson set off for the site.

Zhoukoudian was an ordinary village situated some 50 kilometres southwest of Beijing proper, in a stretch of land where plain and mountains meet. To its southeast lies the vast North China Plain, and to its west and north the Western Hills, which are part of the Taihang Mountains. The earth stratification is clear in this area, especially the Pliocene and Pleistocene strata, which are well preserved. These facts had long been known to geologists, and the place had indeed been a favourite haunt of theirs.

The vicinity of Zhoukoudian, including Longgushan (Dragon Bone Hill), is a sec-

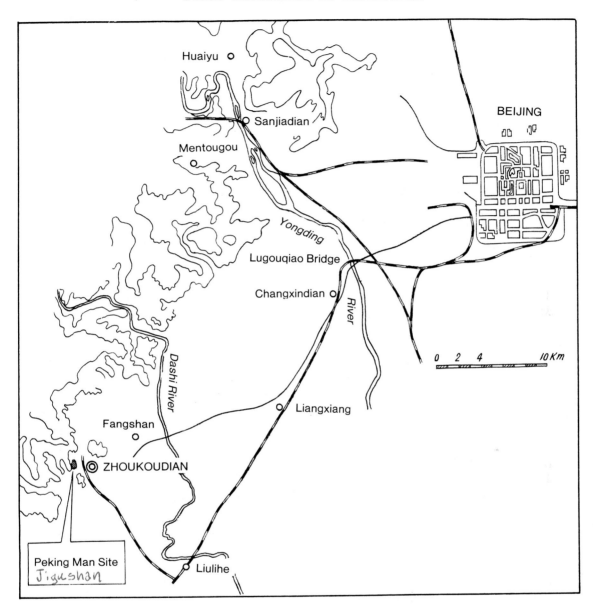

Sketch map to show the location of the Zhoukoudian area.

tion of foothills that are nowhere very high. The small Ba'er River winds past the west side of the village. Emerging out of a gorge not far north, it joins the Liuli River only ten kilometres away to the south. The river is, however, of considerable width, stretching to over one kilometre at places. In spite of this, the rain-fed torrents in summer have such a concentration of power that the river often carries away sizeable boulders. But during the dry seasons of autumn and winter, it gradually disappears and only some water holes are left.

In the nearby hills, the earth structures consist of Ordovician limestone formed 400 million years ago and a Carboniferous-Permian coal bed formed 200 million years ago. Further north, marble and granite formations are found. Because farmlands are scarce in this region, the traditional mainstays of the economy for the local people are lime-kiln, coal mining, and quarry industries.

The limestone formation here is very thick, and at places where faults occur, it is likely to be eroded by ground water, giving rise to caves and fissures. These often serve as depositories of 'dragon bones'.

But when did the people here first notice the bones? No written record has been found. It can reasonably be assumed that the discovery was made with the advent of the lime-kilns. Hearsay evidence, as that which Jia Lanpo learned when he was working the site in the early 1930s, shows the date of establishing lime-kilns here to be during the Song Dynasty (960-1279). There is material evidence in the form of a giant iron wedge found in an abandoned quarry. The wedge must have been used for splitting rocks before explosives were invented. It suggests a standard process of first heating a rock face by means of wood fire, then pouring water over the red-hot face to cause cracks and striking wedges into the cracks to obtain the desired chunks.

The Zhoukoudian area has many lime-kilns. The abundance of dragon bones unearthed there did not attract much attention, for the Zhoukoudian bones were marketable only during a specific season each year and at a specific marketplace in Anguo County, Hebei Province, far from there. Unless purchased at this market, a dragon bone would be regarded as fraudulent as medicine, hence devoid of value. Yet every Zhoukoudian household had some of them in store for use as poultices.

How Gibb obtained his few fossils from

Dr Johan Gunnar Andersson of Sweden (1874-1960). Employed by the Chinese Government as a mining adviser in 1914, he made extensive paleontological and archaeological studies at sites in northern and northwestern China. A spare-time researcher then, he discovered the Zhoukoudian Peking Man site in 1921 on a clue provided by a local kiln worker. (Courtesy of the Museum of Far Eastern Antiquities, Stockholm, through Professor Anders Martinsson)

Chicken Bone Hill is not known to us, but the site that yielded the fossils was well preserved prior to the time of the Japanese invasion in 1937. Bian Meinian (M. N. Bien) and Jia Lanpo, together with Pei Wenzhong had paid repeated visits there in fond reminiscence.

Although only a small town, Zhoukoudian has been famous in and around Beijing and Tianjin since the nineteenth century. The town produced not only coal but also building materials such as lime, marble and granite. As the land was barren, agriculture was not developed, but the area around Zhoukoudian was famous for its fruit and was the chief home of the Liangxiang chestnut, renowned throughout north China. Zhoukoudian persimmons were big and sweet and famous in Hebei Province.

When excavation work first started at Zhoukoudian, a line from Liulihe to Zhoukoudian had been built as part of the Beijing-Hankou Railway for the transportation of building materials and coal to other places. Since there were no scheduled trains, we often rode on mules instead of walking. We would set out early in the morning from Beijing and arrived at Zhoukoudian late at night. If we went on foot we would have to stop over in Liangxiang County for one night. Natives transported coal and lime to other places in handcarts, but camels were used more frequently for this purpose. When Jia Lanpo went to Zhoukoudian for the first time, he saw teams of camels laden with packs of coal moving slowly and laboriously from north to south along the foot of Longgushan (Dragon Bone Hill) to Liulihe, on their way to Tianjin.

Zhoukoudian was known as a centre of 'black and white resources', the black ore being coal and the white ore lime. Before and during the anti-Japanese war, a group of bankers from Beijing ran a sizeable col-

Paleontologist Professor Otto Zdansky of Austria. Born in 1894. Under the direction of Dr Andersson, Zdansky worked at Zhoukoudian in 1921 and 1923, when two Peking Man teeth were unearthed at Locality 1. The photo was taken in 1963. (Courtesy of Professor Otto Zdansky through Professor Anders Martinsson)

liery in Changgouyu, several miles north of Zhoukoudian, where coal was mined with new methods, transported by cable car to Zhoukoudian, whence it would be taken to other places in trains. In addition to this large colliery there were many small coal mines where primitive methods were used. A shaft was dug and the miners would carry coal out of the mine on their backs. The miners went nude in spring and summer but for their oil lamps, which they wore fastened to their heads, and in the colder months they would wear shorts. These hapless creatures were said to have been abducted to Zhoukoudian from faraway places. They were kept locked up in dark houses and were supervised while they were working. If any of them resisted or was caught escaping he would be beaten up, even killed and thrown into a disused shaft. Usually they had to work a whole year before they were allowed to return to their hometown.

There were dozens of lime-kilns in Zhoukoudian. All the lime was controlled by two big firms which had a permanent lease on the lime-stone hills in the neighbourhood. These firms decided where people could set up lime-kilns. Any lime produced in these kilns had to be sold to these two firms, at prices set by the firms. Occasionally people set up lime-kilns in places which did not belong to the two firms, but they were no match for the companies because they did not have sufficient capital.

In the past, the mountains around Zhoukoudian were bare but for a sparse covering of bushes used locally for firewood. In contrast, the col just north of Dragon Bone Hill was densely wooded with cypress and poplar. In late autumn the forest foliage was a glorious tapestry of red and amber. Deep in the forest lay Yongshou Temple, built in the Ming Dynasty. The temple was divided into three sections, and at its centre stood a bronze statue of Buddha. The statue rose four metres high. Serene and dignified, it was a rare work of art. To the northwest of Zhoukoudian beyond a mountain peak there was also a forest, the site of Jinshan Temple. During the anti-Japanese war Japanese troops razed the forests to the ground, viewing them as a potential hide-out for Chinese guerrillas. They destroyed the temples and carried off the bronze Buddha.

On his first visit to Zhoukoudian for excavation work in 1921, O. Zdansky stayed in a dilapidated temple in north Zhoukoudian. In 1927 Li Jie and B. Bohlin went there for excavation work. They lived in a camel caravanserai called Liu Zhen Inn in front of Dragon Bone Hill. It was a modest inn, consisting of nine adobe rooms and an oblong courtyard. Their rooms were low and damp, due to the nearby Ba'er River. Paper was used as a substitute for glass in the windows. The inn had been used for camels in the past but that all changed when Li Jie started renting it for 14 yuan a month. From 1927 to the spring of 1931 it was used as the office for the excavations, until a new house was completed on the northern slope of the western peak of Dragon Bone Hill. The new office, facing east, looked down over Zhoukoudian. There were six rooms in front of the office, with three in the north and three in the south. Of the northern three rooms Bian Meinian lived in the two bright ones and the darker one was occupied by Pei Wenzhong. Later Jia Lanpo lived in the darker room and the two bright ones were made into a drawing room. Specimens were kept in the three south-facing rooms and technicians lived in the six rooms at the back. There was a gate for carts in the north. After the office had been moved to Dragon Bone Hill the excavation team planted the eastern and western peaks with pine trees, cypresses and more than 5000 fruit trees. Sadly, the trees were all cut down by Japanese troops when they captured Zhoukoudian.

Today, great changes have taken place in Zhoukoudian. Since the 1950s a number of exhibition rooms and buildings have been constructed at the Peking Man site. A Beijing-Zhoukoudian highway has now been built and trains run regularly to and from Zhoukoudian. Many trees have been planted in the area. It is now a famous site of cultural interest visited by tourists from China and abroad.

Chicken Bone Hill lies about two kilometres from the present-day Zhoukoudian railway station. It is a limestone mount overlooking the plain area. The fossils occur in the deep red sandy clay that fills its fissures. When Andersson visited the site in 1918, the rocks around the fossil-bearing deposits had already been so eroded that there was a pagoda-shaped pile 5.5 metres high and 1 metre in diameter. He did some digging and recovered a few animal fossils representing three species. The name of the hill may have come from the small fossils that local people regarded as old chicken bones.

A dragon-bone site so near to Beijing could not fail to make Andersson happy, but his scanty first finds gave him no reassurance for going ahead with further excavations. In the fall of 1918, Andersson's technicians found an abundance of three-toed horse fossils at a site in Henan Province. This is where he then directed his attention. It was not until three years later that Chicken Bone Hill was again mentioned as a prospective site, and it was not until 1927 that a team led by the paleontologist Professor Yang Zhongjian (C. C. Young) began working there.

In a paper published in 1930, Yang gave an account of his finds, which included fossil wolves, foxes, badgers, rodents, hedgehogs, hares, and deer, with hares and wolves constituting most of the remains. The hares, numbering more than a hundred, were in fact the most numerous, but few were well preserved. Yang attributed this to the foxes and wolves that preyed on the

Initial digging at the Peking Man site, 1921. *Left*: Dr Otto Zdansky; *middle*: Dr Walter Granger. (Photo from J. G. Andersson's *Children of the Yellow Earth,* English translation, 1934)

hares, perhaps bringing them into the cave for consumption. The site was later designated as Locality 6, and determined to be of middle Pleistocene dating, ranking roughly in age with Peking Man.

On the advice of Dr Carl Wiman, the Austrian paleontologist Otto Zdansky came to China in the early summer of 1921, after he had completed his Ph.D. degree that spring in Vienna. He planned to work under Andersson for three years, studying and excavating the three-toed horse fossils. When Zdansky arrived in Beijing, Andersson sent him first to the Chicken Bone Hill site so that he might familiarize himself with the environs and life of a Chinese village, much like the one in which he was going to stay and work.

In August of that year, Andersson and paleontologist Walter Granger of the United States went to Zhoukoudian to pay Zdansky a visit. Granger had been assigned to China by the American Museum of Natural History as the chief paleontologist of its Third Asiatic Expedition team led by Roy Chapman Andrews. Andersson's purpose in this trip to Zhoukoudian was to show the American expert how Zdansky was progressing and to learn from Granger the latest American techniques in excavation. None of them anticipated the fact that during their visit the invaluable Peking Man fossil would be recovered.

In his *Children of the Yellow Earth: Studies in Prehistoric China* (1932),[1] Andersson has given an account of this trip:

> . . . Whilst we were sitting at our work a man of the neighbourhood came and looked at us.
>
> "There's no use staying here any longer. Not far from here there is a place where you can collect much larger and better dragons' bones," said he.
>
> Knowing well that in the matter of search for dragons' bones in China we must never neglect any clue, I immediately began to question the man. His information seemed so reliable that after a few minutes we packed up our kit and followed him in a northerly direction over the limestone hills. It appeared that the new discovery also lay in an abandoned quarry 150 metres west of, and at a higher level than, the railway station at Chou Kou Tien. In an almost perpendicular wall of limestone,

about ten metres high, which faced north, the man showed us a filled-up fissure in the limestone consisting of pieces of limestone and fragments of bones of larger animals, the whole bound together by sintered limestone. We had not searched for many minutes before we found the jaw of a pig, which showed that we were in the presence of a discovery with much greater possibilities than Chicken Bone Hill. That evening we went home with rosy dreams of great discoveries.

> Granger sat that evening and pondered over a toothless jaw which he had found and which I guessed to belong to a stag. The learned paleontologist would assuredly have laughed at me if he had not been such a far-sighted and kindly man, for this remarkable lower jaw showed such a marked thickening that it was almost circular in section and consequently far from the type of a normal stag's jaw. Now it so happened that in the late autumn of 1918 I had found in red clay on the Huai Lai Plain north of Peking well-preserved jaws with the teeth intact, which convinced me that I had to do with a stag with an extreme development of the mysterious phenomenon of bone thickening which the learned call hyperostosis.
>
> The following day broke in brilliant sunshine and we wandered along the straight road from our temple to Lao Niu Kou, as the new place of discovery is called, and which will one day become one of the most sacred places of pilgrimage for investigations into the history of the human race.

But it turned out that they had found not only a 'lower jaw with marked thickening', the jaw of what was later called a thick-jawed deer (*Megaloceros pachyosteus*), but a host of other fossils, including the remains of rhinoceros, hyena, and bear. They handed all their finds to Zdansky and persuaded the young scholar to stay longer at Zhoukoudian.

Meanwhile, Andersson retrieved bits of quartz at the site, white in colour and edged so sharply, he asserted, as to be good

---

[1] Translated from the Swedish and printed in Great Britain in 1934.

for cutting meats. Could they be tools of our ancestors? He would not rule out such a possibility. Tapping on the wall of the limestone, he said to Zdansky (*ibid.*):

> I have a feeling that there lie here the remains of one of our ancestors and it is only a question of your finding him. Take your time and stick to it till the cave is emptied, if need be.

His prediction soon proved true. Zdansky unearthed a tooth with a worn-down crown and three roots in one—quite possibly a third or second molar. From the uneven cusps on the crown, it was soon identified as a third molar, most likely the right one. When Zdansky first brought it to light, he thought it to be a simian tooth. A few years later, working at Uppsala University in Sweden on the specimens from the Zhoukoudian site, he sifted out another front molar with its roots fractured but crown well preserved. In a paper he published in 1927, Zdansky identified both teeth as belonging to *Homo*, but with reservations—he put a question mark after the species name.

Zdansky's first work at Zhoukoudian came to an end in the summer of 1921, and his paper on the exploit was published in 1923. He identified the fossil species he had found at Zhoukoudian as rhinoceros, boar, deer, buffalo, saber-toothed tiger, and rodents, birds and insectivores. But the tooth he had unearthed, the one he had identified as from *Homo*, was conspicuously absent from his list. The bits of sharp quartz were, however, included in the finds he mentioned. It was on the strength of these quartz bits that Andersson conjectured that Zhoukoudian was a prospective site for human remains.

Zdansky determined the animal fossils to be later in date than those of the three-toed horse fauna, for no trace of this species had been unearthed at the Zhoukoudian site. Instead, the toe of a 'real horse' had been found.

The scientist from Vienna went back to the site in the autumn of 1923, upon the request of Andersson, to explore further in the same overhanging deposits above a sheer cave wall. Without scaffolding, intensive digging in these deposits was rather dangerous. As soon as Zdansky had collected all the fossils he could, he suspended his fieldwork and returned to Uppsala University, where he occupied himself with the specimens he had obtained in China.

3

The French
Catholic Fathers

Before Andersson's attempt to find fossil remains of early human beings at the Zhoukoudian site, such explorations were carried out in other parts of China by scientists from a number of countries. The reason for this was the prevailing hypothesis at the turn of the century that the now infertile Central Asia Plain could have been the Garden of Eden that nurtured the human species. Among the scientists who held such a view were the renowned Henry Fairfield Osborn, William Diler Matthew, and Amadeus W. Grabau.

In 1914, Father Emile Licent from France began his fossil studies in the Huanghe (Yellow River) valley. These were to last for ten years before he departed. Licent was well known as the curator and founder of the Hoangho-Paiho Museum in Tianjin (Tientsin). He discovered a rich deposit of three-toed horse fossils in 1920, in a loess plateau of eastern Gansu Province. And he found three worked stone artifacts in an Upper Pleistocene loess deposit, the first paleoliths ever unearthed in China. According to his own account, one was a quartzite core 4.5 centimetres long that he unearthed on June 4 in a deposit 7.3 metres below the surface. Beneath this layer was a *Hipparion* (three-toed horse) red clay stratum of greater antiquity. The location, known as Xinjiagou, was 55 kilometres north of Qingyang in Gansu Province. The other two stone artifacts were quartz flakes recovered at Zhaojiacha, 35

kilometres north of Qingyang. They were embedded in a gravel layer containing ostrich remains, overlaid by two metres of light brown sand with 15 metres of loess on top.

The discovery of paleoliths near Qingyang at once corrected the biased view that no Stone Age humans had ever lived in China and inspired Father Licent to proceed with his search for early human fossils. In 1922, armed only with information provided by a local Mongolian named Wansjock, he travelled to the Sjara-osso-gol in the southeastern corner of the Ordos Plateau of Inner Mongolia, an area skirted by the great Huanghe river bend. Here, in the Pleistocene sand deposits he found a great number of animal fossils. This success impressed him deeply, and he decided that more serious efforts were called for. He invited the already celebrated paleontologist Father Pierre Teilhard de Chardin to come to China to join him.

Under the sponsorship of the National Museum of Paris, Teilhard de Chardin arrived at Tianjin in May 1923. The two scientists immediately set off to survey the Ordos region. Their reconnaissance began at Baotou. Going in a westerly direction along the north bank of the Huanghe, they came to the eastern foot of Langshan Mountain. From there, they turned south and crossed the Huanghe at Dengkou, then journeying along the east bank of the river. When they reached Hengcheng to the southeast of Yinchuan, the capital of Ningxia, they stayed and worked in that area for some time before they resumed their trip along the Great Wall towards the east. The survey ended at Youfangtou, near the Dali River, on the Loess Plateau in the northern part of Shaanxi Province. It was roughly a L-shaped course.

East of Hengcheng they found the Shuidonggou site in Ningwu County of the present Ningxia Hui Autonomous Region. It was a site rich in paleoliths, lying 25 kilometres east of Hengcheng in an area where a section of the Great Wall is in view. The two French scientists found lodging in an ill-equipped inn consisting of three adobe rooms, one of which was occupied by the innkeeper's family. The innkeeper's wife prepared them only simple fare, since food was scarce in this forlorn desert area. It was a great treat when the innkeeper managed to procure eggs and potatoes, the French scientists' favourite food.

The lith-bearing stratum was approximately 12 metres deep and over 80 square metres in area. The two Frenchmen recovered more than 300 kilogrammes of specimens, including retouched points, scrapers, burins and choppers. The tools were generally large in size, and their fine workmanship ranked them in style with Mousterian and Aurignacian implements found in Europe. They were made of red quartzite, mica-sandstone, siliceous limestone, and flint, all taken from the basal gravel beneath the loess formation. Found in association with these implements were cinders and crushed bone fragments, identified as belonging to wild asses, hyenas,

Ruins of the inn where Father Pierre Teilhard de Chardin and Father Emile Licent stayed while they were exploring the Shuidonggou site. The authors of this book are seen paying their respects at the site. Jia Lanpo (*middle*), Huang Weiwen (*second from right*). (*Photo by Wang Zhefu, August 1980*)

antelopes and bison. There were also eggshells of the extinct giant ostrich, *Struthiolithus*. It was clearly evident that the place was once a campsite for primaeval hunters.

The paleoliths were so common and widespread that Teilhard and Licent concluded, in their survey report, that their occurrence was possible in any steep loess slope.

Leaving Shuidonggou, the two proceeded to the Sjara-osso-gol area where Licent had found some fossils the previous year. The river is a section of the Wuding River, an important tributary of the Huanghe. Rising in a foothill north of Mount Baiyu in north Shaanxi Province, this approximately 100-kilometre-long river flows northward across a depression on the Ordos Plateau. Beyond the Batu cove it reverses its course to join the Huanghe at Hekouzhen. The name Sjara-osso-gol is Mongolian, meaning 'yellow waters', as the channel is always loaded with silt. It is also called the Red Willows River, for its banks were once lined with such trees.

The depression in the southeast of the Ordos Plateau, the area where the two Frenchmen worked, lies in the heartland of the Mu'us Desert, an area geographically transitional between a temperate steppe and a desert. The climatic changes from the time of the Quaternary are clearly recorded in the 80-metre-thick and loosely structured deposits that overlay the hard sandstone formed during the age of the dinosaur. The deposits are well stratified. At the bottom is a hilly layer of red loam, possibly formed during the Middle Pleistocene. In the middle is a 50-60 metre-thick sandy clay layer formed during the Upper Pleistocene. And the top layer consists of lacustrine deposits formed during the early Holocene interlaced with alluvial deposits formed a little later. The lacustrine deposits cover a wide area and stand at an average

altitude of 1300 metres above sea level. Overlaying these deposits are dunes formed late in history. All the above strata, especially the ones formed during the Upper Pleistocene, are rich in fossil remains and human artifacts from various periods.

The Sjara-osso-gol River, which flows through this area, came into being only about a thousand years ago. Its youthful power cut a riverbed that is nearly 80 metres deep, with terraced banks divided into five to six stages. In the section that flows through the Mu'us Desert, sharp turns of the river have made many coves that are like a chain of rings. These coves are surrounded by fertile pastoral and farming lands. Many are named after the families of local inhabitants. To scientists, however, these nooks are most significant because their many bare sides present clear views of the geological strata, thus making fossil finding easier.

The two Frenchmen stayed in a Belgian Catholic church at Xiaoqiaopan Village, east of the Sjara-osso-gol, in Jingbian County, Shaanxi Province. They surveyed the precipice along the river, making studies of the geological strata and collecting fossils. An old villager who helped them has recalled that their area of activity was mainly confined to the Big Cove north of the village, an area now under the jurisdiction of the Inner Mongolian Autonomous Region, especially at Shaojiagouwan where Wansjock lived. Here, a paleolithic site was discovered. They found animal fossils and artifacts mainly in the sandy clay and sandy strata ten metres above the river surface. Their abundant harvest of fossils, identified by the French paleontologist M. Boule and Teilhard de Chardin, consisted of 33 species of mammals and 11 species of birds. These included the straight-tusked elephant (*Paleoloxodon nomadicus*), woolly rhinoceros (*Rhinoceros tichorinus*), Ordos giant deer (*Megaloceros ordosianus*),

Wansjock's buffalo (*Bubalus wansjocki*), antelope (*Gazella prjewalskyi*), and giant ostrich (*Struthiolithus*). Such fossils represent the typical fauna of the Upper Pleistocene Epoch in North China.

Seldom do fossils occur in such a perfectly preserved condition as they did at this site. Not only complete skulls and limb bones, but whole skeletons of rhinoceroses, wild asses and buffaloes were found. At the place where paleolithic people lived, the animal fossils were scattered and fragmented. The species found here included rhinoceros, wild ass, buffalo, deer, elephant, camel and antelope. Among these, antelope fossils were the most abundant, 300 or more counting horns alone. None of the horns had complete skulls attached, evidence that they were used as tools by human beings. Fossil remains of hedgehogs, rabbits, rodents and birds abounded too, doubtless the 'kitchen refuse' of early people. The bone fragments were found in association with stone implements over an area 80 metres in length. The scientists concluded that the site must have been part of the land surface in early days.

The quantities of stone implements recovered fell far short of those brought to light at the Shuidonggou site, but their fine workmanship and small size attracted much attention. They were classified as 'veritable microliths'. The implements were mainly made of black chert, but white or light brown quartz was also used in a few cases. The tools included scrapers, points and burins. Although they were smaller in size than the tools found at Shuidonggou, the two assemblages were not very different in workmanship, and they occurred in strata of roughly the same age. The stage of culture for both sites ranked approximately with the later Mousterian and early Aurignacian cultures in Europe.

Sjara-osso-gol site. (*Photo by Wang Zhefu, August 1980*)

Because human fossils were what the Frenchmen were most eager to find, they were somewhat disappointed. They had indeed obtained two human thighbones and one upper-arm bone, but these were picked up from the ground, with no possibility of determining whether they were associated with the stone implements and animal fossils dug up at the site. Later, in the laboratory, Teilhard sifted out a human upper incisor from among the heap of antelope teeth and ostrich eggshell fragments that had been found among rhino and elephant fossils. The degree of fossilification of this incisor and its undoubted association with the rhino and elephant fossils led Teilhard and Licent to date it as coming from the Pleistocene Epoch.

Records show that the fragments in which the human tooth occurred were found by Father Licent in August 1922 on his first reconnaissance of the site. He found them in the level with, and only 500 metres from, the deposits containing the stone implements and animal bone fragments. However, the deposits had been so disturbed that it was doubtful whether the incisor had occurred *in situ*. Nevertheless, Canadian anthropologist Davidson Black, after a preliminary study, named it the 'Ordos human tooth'. It has since been renamed a tooth of 'Ordos Man' by Chinese scientists. Until the 1950s, Ordos Man was the only species of intermediate age between Peking Man and Upper Cave Man.

Many fossils have since been unearthed in the area, especially during explorations carried out between 1978 and 1980 by a team from the Institute of the Desert at Lanzhou and the Institute of Vertebrate Paleontology and Paleoanthropology, both agencies of the Chinese Academy of Sciences. They excavated nineteen Ordos Man specimens comprising parietal and occipital bones, lower jaws, shoulder blades, upper-arm bones and thighbones. Of particular significance was the fact that six of these were excavated from Pleistocene deposits. This fully settled the sixty-year-old problem of the *in situ* position of the earlier Ordos Man remains.

The dating of Ordos Man by Chinese scientists, based on the fauna, human fossils, and paleoliths of the site has altered the conclusions of Licent and Teilhard. Ordos Man lived in the late, not the middle paleolithic age, and the fossils represent late, not early *Homo sapiens*. Recent radiocarbon dating has put the antiquity of Ordos Man at about 35 000 years B.P.

The American Asiatic Expedition team sponsored by the American Museum of Natural History and led by Roy Chapman Andrews, was far less successful than the French fathers. They tried for ten years to find a trace of early human beings in the Ordos area, but failed. Their collection of Tertiary animal fossils was, however, impressively large and provided powerful evidence that the Central Asian Plateau was an important arena for the evolution of mammals.

Johan Andersson and Davidson Black were also swept into the whirling eddies of this 'central Asian vogue'. Andersson had started his studies on early Chinese culture in 1919. In 1921 he conducted excavations at two sites—Shaguotun Cave in Jinxi County, Liaoning Province, and the well-known Yangshao Village in Mianchi County, Henan Province. He spent another two years (1923-1924) exploring much of Gansu Province, where he discovered many sites, mostly of the late neolithic and chalcolithic ages. This gave rise to the problem of a missing link between the post-Ordos and middle neolithic cultures. Andersson held that the most promising area in which to look for an answer would be Xinjiang Province, basing his view on his findings in China which bore hallmarks of relics of a

'Western' type, suggesting their central Asian origin. He presumed that the early artifacts unearthed in Gansu and Henan Provinces must have been transmitted over routes south of the Tianshan Mountains. He thus proposed a central Asian expedition with Xinjiang as the target area.

In passing, it should be noted that the most recent thirty years of extensive excavations in the Huanghe valley have yielded no evidence to support Andersson's hypothesis that the early Chinese culture was a diffusion of Western culture.

Davidson Black of the Department of Anatomy at the Peking Union Medical College shared Andersson's view in his article 'Asia and the Dispersal of Primates'.[1] He asserted that central Asia was the most promising area in which to find the great home of humankind. The two scientists collaborated closely during the years in which Andersson conducted fieldwork in Liaoning, Henan and Gansu Provinces. All that he unearthed was sent to the laboratory for Davidson Black to work on. Their correspondence shows that they were discussing a plan for a central Asian expedition as late as June 1925.

They planned that the Asiatic expedition would be sponsored by the Geological Survey of China, to which Andersson was adviser, joined by the Union Medical College. The archaeological and geological part of the work was to be carried out by Andersson and an assistant, while the anthropological work was to be handled by Black. The funding for this project was to be divided between the Swedish Research Committee and the Rockefeller Foundation. According to their plan, they were to arrive in Xinjiang in late autumn or early winter of 1928 and remain there for at least two years.

In his letter to Andersson dated June 15, 1925, Black said:

> My interest in the expedition is primarily anthropological and my hopes are set upon the discovery of paleolithic or protohuman skeletal remains. I am, however, deeply interested both in the study of the people at present living in the regions of our proposed travel and in the prehistoric and historic human skeletal material also to be found there.

They worked separately and hard to obtain commitments for funding. Just about the time when they were prepared to launch their plan, the changing situation compelled them to drop the whole project and turn to a new one—the systematic excavation of Zhoukoudian.

---

[1] *Bulletin of the Geological Society of China*, Vol. 4, No. 2, 1925.

4

The Visit of the Crown Prince of Sweden

The year 1926 was a turning point for the Zhoukoudian project. In that year, the discovery of the first Peking Man fossil was announced, and a plan for systematic excavation at Zhoukoudian was decided upon.

On May 3, 1926, Black received a letter from Andersson, then in Stockholm, informing him that the Swedish crown prince and his wife were going to make a trip around the world starting in May. The royal couple, the letter said, would stop first in the United States and then in Japan, arriving in Beijing at the beginning of October. They planned to stay in China for two months and wanted to visit such places as Datong in Shanxi Province, Inner Mongolia, and Henan and Shandong Provinces. The prince had requested that Andersson assist him in planning and arranging places to visit, including the Union Medical College and other research units in Beijing.

The crown prince later became King Gustavus VI of Sweden. He was an amateur archaeologist and was well versed in Oriental arts. At the time, he was the Protector of the Swedish Research Committee, which controlled funding for fossil collection abroad. It was this committee that had been financing Andersson's fossil hunting in China. To Andersson and his collaborator Black, the visit of the Swedish crown prince to Beijing was no doubt an opportunity to ensure the materialization of their proposed central Asian expedition.

The royal couple arrived in Beijing on October 17, 1926, half a month later than scheduled. In preparing his trip to Datong, the prince made extensive contact with the scientific circles of Beijing and Tianjin. One such occasion took place on October 22, when he attended a meeting called by the Department of Anatomy of the Union Medical College. Other participants included Dr Henry S. Houghton, who was in charge of the Executive Committee of the College; Weng Wenhao (Wong Wen Hao), Director of the Geological Survey of China; O. Ewerlöf, Swedish Minister to Beijing; A. Lagrelius, Controller of the Swedish Research Committee; and Andersson and Black. During the course of this meeting, the central Asian project was discussed. It was announced that a letter dated July 1 and signed by Edwin R. Embree, Director of the Division of Studies of the Rockefeller Foundation, guaranteed half of the three-year project's expenses at no more than $10 000 per year. The other half, to be provided by the Swedish Committee, was confirmed at the meeting.

An academic welcoming party to honour the Swedish crown prince, sponsored by the Geological Survey of China, the Natural History Society of Beijing and the Peking Union Medical College was held that afternoon in the auditorium of the College. It was attended by many celebrated scholars, Chinese and foreign, from Beijing and Tianjin. After the welcoming ad-

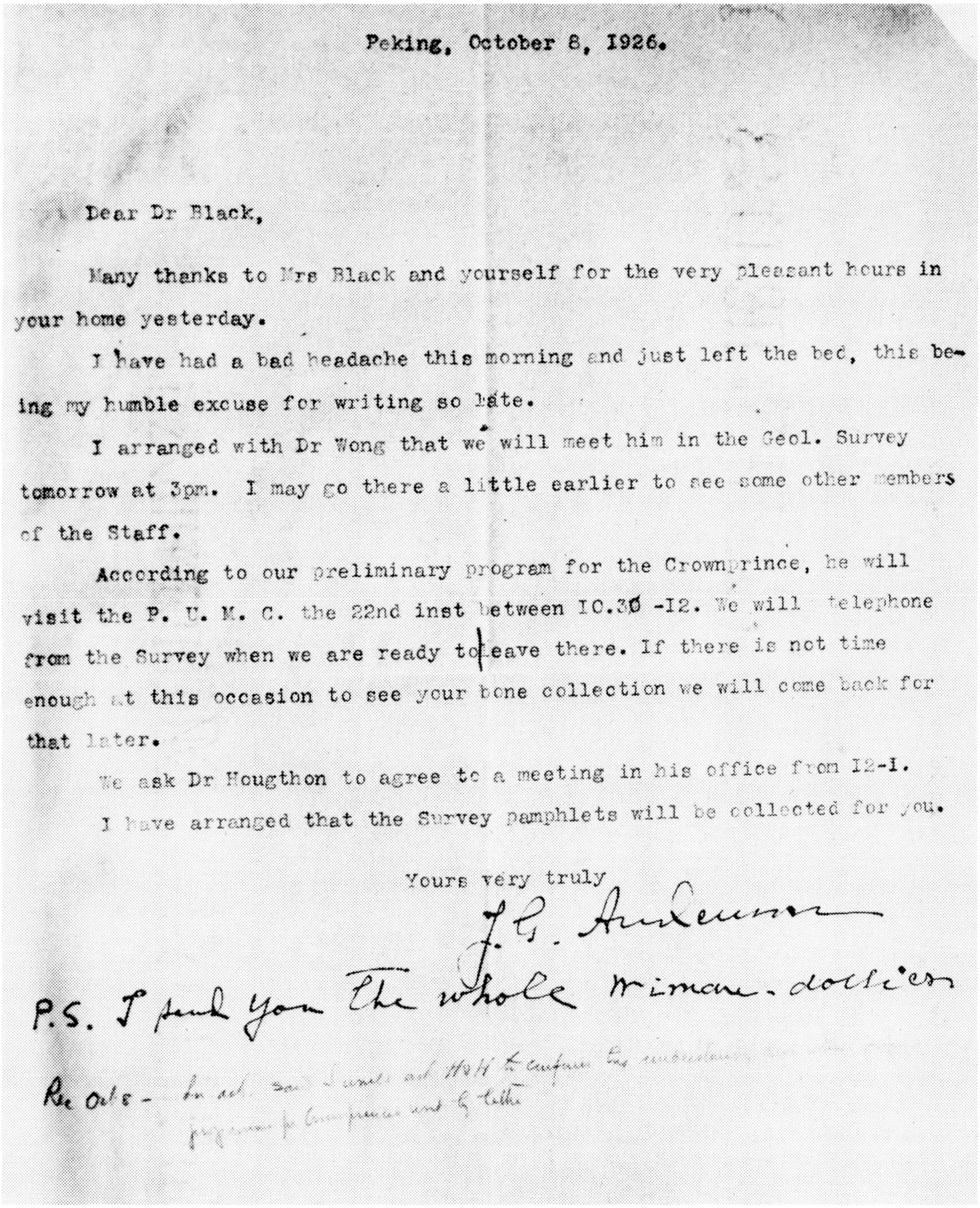

Peking, October 8, 1926.

Dear Dr Black,

Many thanks to Mrs Black and yourself for the very pleasant hours in your home yesterday.

I have had a bad headache this morning and just left the bed, this being my humble excuse for writing so late.

I arranged with Dr Wong that we will meet him in the Geol. Survey tomorrow at 3pm. I may go there a little earlier to see some other members of the Staff.

According to our preliminary program for the Crownprince, he will visit the P. U. M. C. the 22nd inst between 10.30 -12. We will telephone from the Survey when we are ready to leave there. If there is not time enough at this occasion to see your bone collection we will come back for that later.

We ask Dr Hougthon to agree to a meeting in his office from 12-1.

I have arranged that the Survey pamphlets will be collected for you.

Yours very truly

J. G. Andersson

P.S. I send you the whole Wiman-dossier.

Re Oslo -

Letter from J. G. Andersson informing Dr Davidson Black of the Swedish crown prince's plan to visit the Peking Union Medical College on October 22, 1926.

dress by Weng Wenhao and the formal response of the prince, a series of scientific reports were delivered. The first of these was by Liang Qichao, the famous reformist, statesman and scholar. He gave a general survey of the archaeological work being done in China at the time. The second speaker was Father Pierre Teilhard de Chardin, who reported on the Ordos explorations he had made with Father Emile Licent. Finally, Andersson spoke on behalf of Professor Carl Wiman of Sweden about the discoveries that had been made at Uppsala University on paleontological specimens collected in China, including dinosaur, giraffe and three-toed horse fossils. But of greatest interest were the two human teeth dug up by Otto Zdansky at Zhoukoudian.

Andersson had asked Davidson Black to prepare an abstract about these teeth to be included in his report at this meeting. The following passages extracted from this abstract, *Tertiary Man in Asia—the Chou Kou Tien Discovery*,[1] indicate how important the Zhoukoudian findings were considered, even at that early date.

> As a result of this research Dr Andersson has now announced that in addition to mammalian groups already known from this site there have also been identified representatives of the Cheiroptera, one cercopithecoid and finally two specimens of extraordinary interest, namely, one premolar and one molar tooth of a species which cannot otherwise be named than *Homo*? sp.
>
> Judging from the presence of a true horse and the absence of *Hipparion*, Dr Andersson in his preliminary report considered that the Chou Kou Tien fauna was possibly of Upper Pliocene age, an opinion also expressed by Dr Zdansky. It is possible

---

[1] *Bulletin of the Geological Society of China*, Vol. V, Nos. 3-4, 1926. Also published in the English journal *Natural*, November 1926. Although some of the views expressed here are now out of date, the paper won wide acceptance at the time.

however in the light of research that the horizon represented by this site may be of Lower Pleistocene age. Whether it be of late Tertiary or of early Quaternary age, the outstanding fact remains that for the first time on the Asiatic continent north of the Himalayas archaic hominid fossil material has been recovered accompanied by complete and certain geological data. The actual presence of early man in eastern Asia is therefore now no longer a matter of conjecture . . .

> One of the teeth recovered is a right upper molar, probably the third, whose unworn crown presents characteristics which appear from the photographs to be essentially human . . . The other tooth is probably a lower anterior premolar of which the crown is preserved. The latter also is practically unworn and appears in the photograph to be essentially bicuspid in character . . .

The Chou Kou Tien molar tooth, though unworn, would seem to resemble in its essential features the specimen purchased by Haberer in a Peking native drug shop and subsequently described in 1903 by Schlosser. The latter tooth was a left upper third molar having a very much worn crown, extensively fused lateral roots and from the nature of its fossilization considered by Schlosser to be in all probability Tertiary in age. It was provisionally designated as *Homo*? *Anthropoid*? It is of more than passing interest to recall that Schlosser, in concluding his description of the tooth, pointed out that future investigators might expect to find in China a new fossil anthropoid, Tertiary man or ancient Pleistocene man. The Chou Kou Tien discovery thus constituted a striking confirmation of that prediction.

It is now evident that at the close of Tertiary or the beginning of Quaternary time man or a very closely related anthropoid actually did exist in eastern Asia. This knowledge is of fundamental importance in the field of prehistoric anthropology, for about this time also there lived in Java *Pithecanthropus*, at Piltdown *Eoanthro-*

pus and but very shortly after at Mauer the man of Heidelberg. All these forms were thus practically contemporaneous with one another and occupied regions equally far removed respectively to the east, to the southeast and to the west from the central Asiatic plateau which it has been shown elsewhere most probably coincides with their common dispersal centre. The Chou Kou Tien discovery therefore furnishes one more link in the already strong chain of evidence supporting the hypothesis of the Central Asiatic origin of the *Hominidae*.

At this October 22 assemblage, in addition to delivering the report, Andersson drove home the point that this initial discovery might well be the most important achievement of Swedish archaeological endeavours in China. He stated that there was not yet a large-scale plan for excavation at the Zhoukoudian site, but he would be delighted to see such a project taken up by the Geological Survey of China in the near future, with the co-operation of Davidson Black representing the Union Medical College and the Rockefeller Foundation.

The announcement at the meeting of the Zhoukoudian human fossil finds attracted serious attention. The discovery won praise from authorities such as Ding Wenjiang (V. K. Ting), Weng Wenhao, Davidson Black and A. W. Grabau. The news was soon spread throughout the world. There were sceptics, though. Among them were celebrated scientists like Teilhard de Chardin who, two days after the meeting which he had attended, wrote the following note to Andersson:

Dear Dr Andersson:

I have reflected much on the photographs which you so kindly showed me and I feel that it would not be right, and still less friendly, to conceal from you what I think of them.

As a matter of fact I am not fully convinced of their supposed human character. Even the rootless assumed premolar, which at first sight seemed most convincing, may be one of the last molars of some carnivore, and the same is true of the other tooth, unless the roots are distinctly four in number.

Even if, as I hope, it can never be proved that the Chou Kou Tien teeth belong to a beast of prey, I fear that it can never be absolutely demonstrated that they are human. It is necessary to be very cautious, since their nature is undetermined.

I have not seen the specimens, however, and since I place great reliance on Zdansky's paleontological experience I hope most intensely that my criticism will prove unfounded. I have only wished to be absolutely frank with you.

Sincerely yours,
P. Teilhard

There may have been a number of other persons who shared Teilhard de Chardin's reservations, for, after all, the excavations of 1921 and 1923 had yielded only scanty evidence, and many of the authorities in Beijing had not seen the specimens themselves, but only slides of the two teeth.[1] It is little wonder that in the months after the announcement, scientists were uncertain whether the owner of the teeth had been a human or a carnivore. Andersson has recalled one instance showing such a mood:

"Well, Dr Andersson," A. W. Grabau exclaimed, "how are things just now with the Peking Man? Is it a man or a carnivore?"

"My dear Dr Grabau," Andersson answered, "the latest news from the Chou

---

[1] In his paper 'A New Tooth of *Sinanthropus pekinensis*', *Acta Zoologica*, 1952, bd. XXXIII, Zdansky stated that, in sifting the fossils recovered at Zhoukoudian, he found another Peking Man tooth, a second front molar. So the number of teeth discovered up to then was three, and all of them are still kept at the Uppsala University Museum. Professor Martinsson of that university related this fact to the co-author of this book, Huang Weiwen, on his visit to Zhoukoudian on September 27, 1977. He told Huang that this third tooth was sifted out in 1950.

Kou Tien field is that our old friend is neither a man nor a carnivore but rather something half-way between the two. It is a lady."

Andersson's humorous reference to 'lady' was just a rejoinder to Grabau's use of the term 'man', but this exchange gave rise to rumours for several months thereafter that a 'Peking lady' had been found at Zhoukoudian.

In spite of this scattered skepticism, the proposal for systematic excavation at the Zhoukoudian site won warm support at the October 22 meeting, and was soon afterwards acted upon. The central Asian plan of Andersson and Black, however, proved abortive because of public reaction in China against an exploration team headed by Dr Sven Hedin which, in the spring of 1927, was shipping cultural relics found in Xinjiang Province out of China. Hedin was a Swedish explorer who had arrived in China a few weeks after the October 22 meeting for a survey trip through central Asia. Andersson and Black had planned to consult him on the co-ordination of their teams.

Now that Hedin was in trouble, Andersson had to exercise prudence in the matter. In a letter from Stockholm to Black, dated July 14, 1928, he wrote:

> You will certainly remember how I, at our farewell meeting in Peking in the late spring of last year, pointed out how severely the opposition movement against Hedin's expedition had affected my own possibilities for going into Central Asia, especially with reference to the exceedingly reduced possibilities of getting any part of the material granted to a foreign museum...

He asked for modifications of the plan to be agreed upon by both sides, but he was actually trying to shelve it altogether. The plan had indeed been nullified, but fortunately, prior to its formal demise, it had been implemented at Zhoukoudian.

5

The Agreement

Around the end of September or the beginning of October 1926, news of the identification of two human teeth from fossils unearthed at Zhoukoudian was transmitted from the laboratory of Professor Carl Wiman at Uppsala University to Beijing. The news delighted scientific circles in the city. Promotion activities aimed at developing a larger project to achieve greater results were already underway. It was agreed that the news about the human teeth was not to be announced until the arrival of the Swedish crown prince.

On October 5, Davidson Black presented a report to the Director of the Executive Committee of the Union Medical College, Dr Henry S. Houghton, putting forth a proposal that the Rockefeller Foundation provide financial support for systematic excavation at Zhoukoudian and for the establishment of an institute for the study of human biology. Later, Black talked with Weng Wenhao, Director of the Geological Survey of China, to develop the proposal in greater detail. They put their conversation on record in the form of letters.

October 16, 1926

Dr Wong Wen Hao,
The Geological Survey of China,
3, Feng Sheng Hutung,
Peking, West City

Dear Dr Wong:

At the close of our informal meeting in your office last Saturday you suggested that it would be well to exchange letters setting forth in general terms the subject of our conversation. Accordingly I have outlined below the request I have made to Dr Houghton on the subject of the Chou Kou Tien research project and further the bearing of this on the proposal for the establishment of an institute for the study of human biology. I must again emphasize the fact that the plans I outline are purely tentative ones which if they are to become realities at all must first alike receive the approval and support both of the Division of Studies of the Rockefeller Foundation and of the Geological Survey of China.

In my opinion the discovery at Chou Kou Tien of late Pliocene or early Pleistocene[1] human or closely related anthropoid remains is one of fundamental importance in the field of prehistoric anthropology. It is now evident that in the late Tertiary or early Quaternary of eastern Asia man or a very closely related form actually did exist. About this time also there lived in Java, *Pithecanthropus*, at Piltdown, *Eoanthropus*[2] and at Mauer the man of Heidelberg. All these forms were thus practically contemporaneous with one another and equally far removed respectively to the east, to the southeast and to the west from the central Asiatic plateau which it has been shown most probably coincides with their common dispersal centre. The Chou Kou Tien discovery therefore offers at once both

---

[1] It was decided later at the eighteenth annual meeting of the International Geological Society that the dating should be middle Pleistocene.

[2] *Eoanthropus*, also called 'Piltdown Man', was said to have been found in Britain in 1912. But it was exposed by scientists in the 1950s as a fraud.

an added impulse to our projected central Asiatic expedition and a challenge to undertake a most important additional piece of related research before that expedition starts.

The Chou Kou Tien Research Proposals

My own time before we leave for central Asia will largely be taken up with department work together with the preparation of my monograph on the Kansu [Gansu] and Honan [Henan] material, while the full services of a qualified vertebrate paleontologist from your staff for the Chou Kou Tien research are not available. Dr Andersson has therefore suggested that it would be very desirable were it possible to obtain for this work the full time service of one of the men who have already become familiar with the Chou Kou Tien fauna in Dr Wiman's laboratory.

In the hope of obtaining such a man I have placed the facts fully before Dr Houghton and have asked him to approach the Division of Studies of the Rockefeller Foundation with the request that the sum of Mex. $12 000 a year over a two year period be placed at our disposal in order to provide funds to cover the salary and field expenses of a vertebrate paleontologist who would devote his whole time to the Chou Kou Tien research. In making this request the following points have been emphasized: (1) That this proposed research is to take the form of a co-operative enterprise with the Geological Survey of China; and (2) that the material obtained should be prepared for study, the human and anthropoid remains remaining in my hands for study and description in *Paleontologia Sinica*, the other material going to the Geological Survey for similar treatment and permanent housing. Further in making this request it was definitely understood that while no financial commitment was asked beyond the sum mentioned covering a two year period, the Chou Kou Tien project

Dr Weng Wenhao (*left*), Director of the Geological Survey of China, and Dr Davidson Black (*below*), Honorary Director of the Cenozoic Research Laboratory. (*Photo by Pei Wenzhong, late 1920s or early 1930s*)

should have the added objective of creating a nucleus around which in the future other co-operative enterprises would be grouped looking toward the establishment of a research institute as outlined below.

Proposal for the Establishment of an Institute for the Study of Human Biology

The possibility of the establishment of an institute for the special study of all phases of human biology has been tentatively considered by the Division of Studies of the Rockefeller Foundation. It has been suggested that such an institute if founded should devote itself wholly to research work both in the field and laboratory and to the training of qualified individuals in research. The tentative scope of such research may be outlined under three headings: (1) human phylogeny (paleontology); (2) human ontogeny (embryology); and (3) physical anthropology of recent man (morphology and physiology).

It has been considered that such an institute if founded would at the outset be wholly supported by funds received from the Rockefeller Foundation though from the outset also in its programme of work it would constitute a co-operative enterprise between Chinese and foreign investigators. As its work progressed however it would look forward to obtaining support from Chinese sources and eventually to passing wholly into the hands of Chinese scientists responsible both for its upkeep and for the continuance of its work.

When the institute idea was first mentioned last spring Mr Edwin R. Embree, Director of the Division of Studies of the Rockefeller Foundation, pointed out that one of the first things on which the Foundation would require assurance before even contemplating any plan would be a knowledge that the proposals to be made would be acceptable to Chinese scientists. Mr Embree suggested that the Geological Survey of China would be an ideal organization with which to co-operate in developing an institute scheme, were it possible to hit upon some method whereby the institute might become the direct means of forwarding the Survey's own plans of development. I pointed out to Mr Embree that a museum in which adequately to house and display the ancient human remains which the Survey had already placed at my disposal for study and description would be a step in the right direction. It did not occur to me then to suggest as you so aptly did last Saturday that the proposed institute could well aid the Survey's plan of development by serving as its 'Institut de Paléontologie humaine'. At the time my attention was fired upon the pressing need for more work to be done in the field of modern physical anthropology. Since this was a subject dear to the heart of Dr Ting and since I knew he was organizing a new Zoology Institute of Peking I seized the opportunity to write to him briefly outlining my scheme and asking if in his opinion such a plan would meet with the approval and obtain the co-operative support of Chinese scientists. Dr Ting replied in the following reassuring words: 'You need have no doubt in your mind about the attitude of Chinese scientists toward the establishment of an Institute of Human Biology. Whilst I cannot speak for anyone else but myself, I feel sure you will have the hearty support of all my countrymen interested in scientific research.'

After passing on this welcome message to Mr Embree, the institute proposal has remained in its initial nebulous condition until Dr Houghton's arrival in China in September when I at last had an opportunity to discuss the possibilities of the scheme with him. The splendid news of the actual discovery of human remains in the Chou Kou Tien material now lends just the needed additional impetus to review more in detail the whole scheme using the proposed further research on the Chou Kou Tien site as a nucleus around which further to develop the institute plan. This brings me to the question of the building proposals I have suggested to Dr Houghton as desirable should a scheme for the establish-

October 16, 1926.

Dr. Wong Wen Hao,
The Geological Survey of China,
3, Feng Sheng Hutung,
Peking, West City.

Dear Dr. Wong:-

            At the close of our informal meeting in your office last
Saturday you suggested that it would be well to exchange letters setting
forth in general terms the subject of our conversation. Accordingly
I have outlined below the request I have made to Dr. Houghton on the
subject of the Chou Kou Tien research project and further the bearing
of this on the proposal for the establishment of an institute for the
study of human biology. I must again emphasize the fact that the plans
I outline are purely tentative ones which if they are to become realities at all must first alike receive the approval and support both of
the Division of Studies of the Rockefeller Foundation and of the
Geological Survey of China.

            In my opinion the discovery at Chou Kou Tien of late Pliocene
or early Pleistocene human or closely related anthropoid remains is one
of fundamental importance in the field of prehistoric anthropology. It is
now evident that in the late Tertiary or early Quaternary of eastern Asia
man or a very closely related form actually did exist. About this time
also there lived in Java, Pithecanthropus, at Piltdown, Eoanthropus and
at Mauer the man of Heidelberg. All these forms were thus practically
contemporaneous with one another and equally far removed respectively to
the east, to the southeast and to the west from the central Asiatic plateau
which it has been shown most probably coincides with their common dispersal
center. The Chou Kou Tien discovery therefore offers at once both an added
impulse to our projected central Asiatic expedition and a challenge to
undertake a most important additional piece of related research before that
expedition starts.

THE CHOU KOU TIEN RESEARCH PROPOSALS.

            My own time before we leave for central Asia will largely be
taken up with department work together with the preparation of my monograph
on the Kansu and Honan material, while the full services of a qualified
vertebrate palaeontologist from your staff for the Chou Kou Tien research

Part of a letter dated October 16, 1926, serving as a memorandum of a discussion between Weng Wenhao and Davidson Black on the Zhoukoudian research project and the establishment of an Institute for the Study of Human Biology.

are not available. Dr. Andersson has therefore suggested that it would be very **desirable** were it possible to obtain for this work the full time service of one **of the** men who have already become familiar with the Chou Kou Tien fauna in **Dr. Wiman's** laboratory.

In the hope of obtaining such a man I have placed the facts fully **before** Dr. Houghton and have asked him to approach the Division of Studies of **the** Rockefeller Foundation with the request that the sum of Mex. $12,000 a year **over** a two year period be placed at our disposal in order to provide funds to **cover** the salary and field expenses of a vertebrate palaeontologist who would **devote** his whole time to the Chou Kou Tien research. In making this request **the** following points have been emphasized:- (1) That this proposed research **is** to take the form of a cooperative enterprise with the Geological Survey of **China;** and (2) that the material obtained should be prepared for study, the **human** and anthropoid remains remaining in my hands for study and description **in** Palaeontologia Sinica, the other material going to the Geological Survey **for** similar treatment and permanent housing. Further in making this request **it** was definitely understood that while no financial commitment was asked beyond **the** sum mentioned covering a two year period, the Chou Kou Tien project should **have** the added objective of creating a nucleus around which in the future other **cooperative** enterprises would be grouped looking toward the establishment of a **research** institute as outlined below.

PROPOSAL FOR THE ESTABLISHMENT OF AN INSTITUTE FOR THE STUDY OF HUMAN BIOLOGY.

The possibility of the establishment of an institute for the special **study** of all phases of human biology has been tentatively considered by the Division of Studies of the Rockefeller Foundation. It has been suggested that such an institute if founded should devote itself wholly to research work both in the field and laboratory and to the training of qualified individuals in research. The tentative scope of such research may be outlined under three headings:- (1) Human phylogeny (palaeontology); (2) human ontogeny (embryology); and (3) physical anthropology of recent man (morphology and physiology).

It has been considered that such an institute if founded would at the outset be wholly supported by funds received from the Rockefeller Foundation though from the outset also in its programme of **work** it **would** constitute a cooperative enterprise between Chinese and **foreign** investigators. As its work progressed however it would look forward to obtaining support from Chinese sources and eventually to passing wholly into the hands **of** Chinese scientists responsible both for the upkeep and for the continuance of its work.

When the institute idea was first mentioned last spring Mr. Edwin R. Embree, Director of the Division of Studies of the Rockefeller Foundation pointed out that one of the first things on which the Foundation would require assurance before even contemplating any plan would be a knowledge that the proposals to be made would be acceptable to Chinese scientists. Mr. Embree suggested that the Geological Survey of China would be an ideal organization with which to cooperate in developing an institute scheme were it possible to hit upon some method whereby the institute might become the direct means of forwarding the Survey's own plans of development. I pointed out to Mr. Embree that a museum in which adequately to house and display the ancient human remains which the Survey had already placed at my disposal for study

農商部地質調查所
The Geological Survey,
3, Feng - Sheng Hutung,
W. Peking, China.

October 18, 1926.

Dr. Davidson Black,

    Anatomical Laboratory,

        P. U. M. C.,

           Peking.

Dear Dr. Black:-

        I have your letter of 16 inst. setting in general out-
line the scheme of coorperative work we talked of the other day. I
feel much gratified of this scheme of high scientific interest, and
shall appreciate it a great privilage for the Survey to have your co-
orperation. I agree in general with the proposals you outlined in your
letter, there are only a few points which I like to explain a little
more clearly perhaps than I did in our last conversation.

           The Chou Kou Tien Research.

        I agree entirely with the proposals you made for the
Chou Kou Tien research.

        For this research, the Survey will send a Chinese ver-
tebrate palaeontologist who is now in Germany to Sweden to make himself
familiar with the previous material and study so that he can better co-
orperate with the other palaeontologist whom you proposed to engage this
work. The Survey can also provide, when necessary, one or two geologists
for the topographic and geologic survey. The Survey may be able to contribute a small part of the working expenses, but we agreed that we
better may entirely rely on the finds provided by the Division of studies of the Rockefeller Foundation.

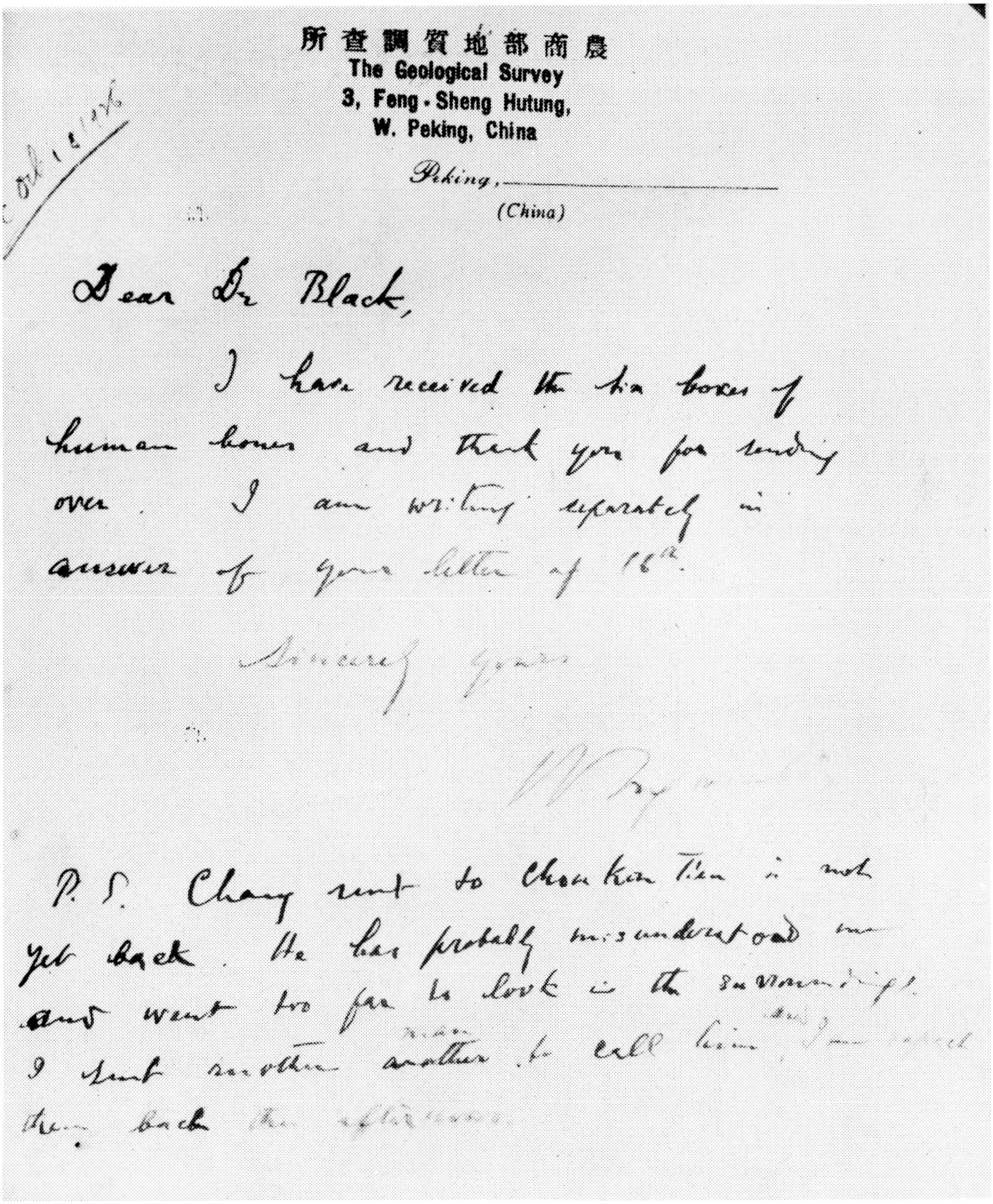

所查調質地部商農
The Geological Survey
3, Feng - Sheng Hutung,
W. Peking, China

Peking,_____

(China)

Dear Dr Black,

I have received the tin boxes of human bones and thank you for sending over. I am writing separately in answer of your letter of 16th.

Sincerely yours

P. S. Chang sent to Chou Kou Tien is not yet back. He has probably misunderstood me and went too far to look in the surroundings. I sent another another to call him, I will send them back this afternoon.

Samples of letters between Weng Wenhao and Davidson Black regarding the research project at Zhoukoudian (*above* and *opposite*).

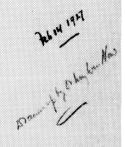

Cooperation between the

National Geological Survey of China

and

The Peking Union Medical College

for research on

Tertiary and Quaternary Deposits in North China

—— oOo ——

I A special fund is constituted for research on Tertiary and Quaternary fossil deposits in North China. A grant of $24,000 (twenty-four thousand dollars) Peking Currency has been made by the Rockefeller Foundation which is to be used for this specific purpose during a period of two years, ending not later than December 31,1929. The Geological Survey will contribute from its research fund an additional sum up to $4,000 (four thousand dollars) for the same purpose and during the same period. All expenditures are to be submitted for approval to the directors of the two cooperating institutions.

The cooperative research chiefly aims at finding and studying remains of early man and contemporary animal life, but has no special interest in cultural studies of a later period, especially things of historic time. Whatever artefacts of historic time may be accidentally found in the course of other work will be handed over to proper Chinese museums.

II Dr. Davidson Black, Head of the Department of Anatomy of the Peking Union Medical College, will take charge of the field work with the assistance of other specialists whom the two institutions will appoint. Two or three palaeontologists will be engaged and attached to the Geological Survey and will specially devote themselves to palaeontological studies in connection with the research. The two institutions in addition will give any necessary assistance with their existing staffs.

III All collections of specimens shall entirely belong to the
Geological Survey, but anthropoid material will be deposited
for study in the Department of Anatomy of the Peking Union
Medical College with the understanding that nothing will be
exported out of China.

IV All results of the research will be published in the **Palaeon**-
tologia Sinica or other series of the Geological Survey (or) in
the publication of the Geological Society of China,

Agreement on co-operation between the National Geological Survey of China and the Peking Union Medical College for research on the Zhoukoudian project. Signed February 14, 1927.

ment of an institute for the study of human biology be developed.

The foregoing presents I think a résumé of the questions we discussed a week ago. I gathered from your comments on that occasion that the development of the plans outlined would meet with your hearty approval and that you even foresaw the possibility that such an institute of human biology might well become in a small way an integral part of the survey itself by carrying on museum and research work in the field of human paleontology.

If on further consideration you still approve the general ideas expressed but would like certain points made more definite or others less definite, please let me know what changes you would suggest for the proposals are still in a fluid state and nothing at all has been settled. Our desire is to frame a proposal that will not merely be acceptable to Chinese scientists but will embody what they themselves wish to see carried out. It will then be our part to see whether we can get the necessary funds.

I should be much obliged if you could let me have your considered opinion on the questions raised at your earliest convenience so that I may transmit this information to Dr Houghton who will in turn submit our suggestions to the consideration of the Division of Studies of the Rockefeller Foundation.

With cordial regards. I remain,

Very sincerely yours,
Davidson Black

October 18, 1926

Dr Davidson Black,
Anatomical Laboratory,
P.U.M.C., Peking

Dear Dr Black:

I have your letter of 16 inst. setting in general outline the scheme of the co-operation work we talked of the other day. I feel much gratified of [sic] this scheme of high scientific interest, and shall consider it a great privilege for the Survey to have your co-operation. I agree in general with the proposals you outlined in your letter. There are only a few points which I would like to explain a little more clearly perhaps than I did in our last conversation.

The Chou Kou Tien Research

I agree entirely with the proposals you made for the Chou Kou Tien research.

For this research the Survey will send a Chinese vertebrate paleontologist who is now in Germany to Sweden to make himself familiar with the previous material and study so that he can better co-operate with the other paleontologist you proposed to engage in this work. The Survey can also provide, when necessary, one or two geologists for the topographic and geologic survey. The Survey may be able to contribute a small part of the working expenses, but we agree that we better now entirely rely on the funds provided by the Division of Studies of the Rockefeller Foundation.

I am well satisfied with the proposed division of the material and the publication of the studies on both the human and other remains in the *Paleontologia Sinica*. It is understood that the skeletal material thus left to you will be always kept in China whether the scheme of the Human Biological Institute will materialize or not.

The immediate object of our investigation is Chou Kou Tien. Yet research may be eventually extended to other hopeful points on which we may later agree.

Establishment of an Institute of Human Biology

This is indeed a splendid scheme, and I much appreciate your concurrence with the idea that such an institute of human biology might become an integral part of the Survey itself by carrying on museum and research work in the field of human paleontology. In this connection we have already talked of the possibility of letting this proposed Institute take care of the rich skeletal material of Honan, Fengtien and Kansu which entirely belong to the Survey from an agreement with Dr Andersson who made the collection. There has been however another scheme of a museum in which the Survey is interested, and before definite engagement I would like to have this question referred to Dr V. K. Ting who will be, as you may be sure, the most enthusiastic supporter of your scheme, but may have perhaps some suggestion to make.

I hope I have made clear our exact standing. While any undertaking of the Survey is to be done with special authorization of the Ministry, in such a scientific matter, however, I think I can speak in the name of the Survey and sincerely hope that our scheme of co-operation will soon become reality.

Yours very sincerely,
Wong Wen Hao

Upon receiving the above letter from Weng Wenhao, Davidson Black wrote to Weng expressing Houghton's and his complete agreement with the points raised in the letter.

On January 3, 1927, Black received a telegram from New York informing him that the Rockefeller Foundation approved the appropriation of $24 000 for the Zhoukoudian project. Black at once telephoned Weng, but it was during the New Year holiday and he failed to reach him. Instead, he wrote a brief letter to Weng the next day in which, apart from announcing the good tidings about the funds, he requested a conference with Weng, Houghton and Andersson for a discussion of the details of the Zhoukoudian excavation. He also notified Weng that he planned to explore the road between Beijing and Zhoukoudian by car and suggested that Weng dispatch one of his assistants to help in the matter.

After much deliberation, an agreement was drafted in early February 1927. A copy

of the document has been kept in the collection of Black's correspondence. The text reads as follows:

Co-operation Between the National Geological Survey of China and the Peking Union Medical College for Research on Tertiary and Quaternary Deposits in North China

Art. I A special fund is constituted for research on Tertiary and Quaternary fossil deposits in North China. A grant of $24 000 (twenty-four thousand dollars) Peking Currency has been made by the Rockefeller Foundation which is to be used for this specific purpose during a period of two years, ending not later than December 31, 1929. The Geological Survey will contribute from its research fund an additional sum up to $4000 (four thousand dollars) for the same purpose and during the same period. All expenditures are to be submitted for approval to the directors of the two co-operating institutions. The co-operative research chiefly aims at finding and studying remains of early man and contemporary animal life, but has no special interest in cultural studies of a later period, especially things of historic time. Whatever artifacts of historic time may be accidentally found in the course of other work will be handed over to proper Chinese museums.

Art. II Dr Davidson Black, Head of the Department of Anatomy of the Peking Union Medical College, will take charge of the field-work with the assistance of other specialists whom the two institutions will appoint. Two or three paleontologists will be engaged and attached to the Geological Survey and will specially devote themselves to paleontological studies in connection with the research. The two institutions in addition will give any necessary assistance with their existing staffs.

Art. III All collections of specimens shall entirely belong to the Geological Survey, but anthropoid material will be deposited for study in the Department of Anatomy of the Peking Union Medical College with the understanding that nothing will be exported out of China.

Art. IV   All results of the research will be published in the *Paleontologia Sinica* or other series of the Geological Survey or in the publication of the Geological Society of China.

On the upper right corner of this two-page mimeographed document, Black marked in pencil, "Drafted by Wong Wen Hao" and in pen, "February 14, 1927". There are some words in pencil added at the end of Art. IV, but they are no longer legible.

A letter to Houghton from the Rockefeller Foundation and signed by the Deputy Director of its Far East Division, Roger S. Greene, is dated March 23, 1927, and reads as follows:

I have been glad to see the copy of the agreement with the Geological Survey of China regarding the terms of co-operation with our department of anatomy for research on Tertiary and Quaternary deposits in North China. I have shown the papers to Dr Pearce who has no criticism to offer. It seems to me that the arrangement made is an admirable one.

(Signed) Roger S. Greene

The Greene letter was a reply to a letter Houghton had written on February 12, which indicates that the agreement had been reached earlier than the date marked in pen by Black on his copy of the document.

6

The First Two Years of Excavation

With the Rockefeller Foundation funds and the concluding of the agreement, the Zhoukoudian project was turned into reality in the spring of 1927. Ding Wenjiang was Honorary Director of the co-operative leadership group, and Black and Weng Wenhao shared the responsibilities of routine work. Four specialists were in charge of fieldwork at the site:

Anders Birger Bohlin, a Swedish paleontologist recommended by Carl Wiman. He was to serve as Field Adviser in charge of planning. He arrived in Beijing with his wife on March 16, 1927.

Li Jie (Li Chi), a geologist of the Survey, now Administrative Director at Zhoukoudian. His duties, apart from collecting geological and geomorphological data, were to deal with local government authorities, landowners, and hired hands.

Liu Delin, a laboratory technician who had worked for the well-known American paleontologist Walter Granger. He had taken part in the fieldwork of the Asiatic Expedition of the American Museum of Natural History. Now he was to be the Assistant on Technical Matters and in charge of laboratory work.

Xie Renfu, a junior assistant to Davidson Black, was to be Assistant to Liu Delin at Zhoukoudian.

One other man, Bohlin's servant, did the cooking, washing and other chores.

The fieldwork began on March 27, 1927, with Li Jie making a 1 : 2000 ratio sketch map of the entire area of the site. He completed the map on April 12 and returned to the city, leaving two hired hands to keep watch at the site.

In 1977, the authors interviewed one of

Swedish paleontologist Professor Birger Bohlin. Born in 1898. He worked at Zhoukoudian in 1927-28 and was a member of the Chinese-Swedish team that explored the northwest area of China. (*Courtesy of Professor Bohlin through Professor Anders Martinsson*)

the hired hands, Qiao Derui, who had worked with Li Jie. This man recalled that he was in his teens at the time and was hired as one of the day labourers. His agility must have attracted the attention of Li Jie, who made him his 'little assistant'; when Li Jie was working on the topographic map, the teenager held the rod for him, a job that required the lad to scamper over the hills all day long. Earlier maps had been limited to the Peking Man site. The areas included in Li Jie's survey reached all the way to the two temples east of the Peking Man site as well as to the county seat of Fangshan.

With the survey over, the actual excavation was to begin on April 16. Black arranged for the transportation of the field workers to the site. Liu Delin and Xie

Top: Geologist Li Jie (C. Lee) (1894–1977);
Bottom: At the Peking Man site in 1972; Bohlin on the left, Black in the middle, Li Jie on the right.

Renfu were to go by train on April 14 and Bohlin and Li Jie by car the following day.

Zhoukoudian village had only the camel caravan inn called Liu Zhen Inn at which the team members could stay. It consisted of only nine tiny adobe rooms, but was desirable because of its proximity to the site—some 200 metres away. The inn has since disappeared, but the memory of this 'headquarters' will always be fresh in the minds of those who worked there.

The Peking Man site was situated south of Laoniukou, appearing in Andersson's notes as 'Locality 53', but renamed 'Cave 1' by Li Jie and Bohlin. In 1929, in a paper co-authored by Teilhard and Yang Zhongjian, it was referred to as 'Locality 1 of Zhoukoudian', the name which has remained attached to it. But the name 'Dragon Bone Hill', the limestone hillock that contained the Peking Man cave, cannot be dated.

The hill was a quarry site owned by a coal company, and the exploration team paid a yearly rent of 90 yuan for the right to excavate there. The rent was doubled the following year. To prevent extortion in the future, the Cenozoic Research Laboratory paid the exorbitant price of 4900 yuan for permanent use of the site, which included the whole of Dragon Bone Hill and half of a hillock to its west.

Davidson Black presented a plan for the work, with Weng Wenhao's modifications, to Bohlin on April 12. It outlined three stages for the year's activities. The first was to make a systematic survey of the site and to clean up the talus strewn about the ground. The second was to blast off the dangerous overhanging limestone breccia and to investigate the deposits brought down by this operation. The third was to start a systematic excavation of what remained *in situ* of the original cave deposit itself.

Black asked Bohlin to provide a weekly briefing in writing, which he could pass on to Weng Wenhao and Houghton. He also instructed that whenever the recovered materials were sufficient to fill a freight car,

The earliest picture taken at the Peking Man site. (*Photo by Birger Bohlin, 1927*)

From: Davidson Black   April 12, 1927.

To: Dr. Bohlin   *Draft copy*   Re: Chou Kou Tien Research.

The following notes will be of assistance to you in carrying on your work in Chou Kou Tien.

1. Mr. Li Chi who is a geologist on the staff of the Survey is in nominal charge of your party and will conduct all negotiations necessary with the local authorities, landowners and laborers. The scientific programme of ~~work~~ *excavation* is your particular charge. Dr. Wong Wen Hao has instructed Mr. Li to this effect and you may count on Mr. Li to offer you every assistance in carrying out this work as you may suggest. *In the unlikely event of a difference of opinion arising between you the matter should of course be referred to Peking.*

2. The work itself will fall naturally into three phases: first the systematic investigation and cleaning up of the talus which now extends from the level of the cave floor to the ground below; second the blasting out of the dangerous overhanging limestone breccia and the clearance and investigation of the deposits brought down by this operation; and lastly the complete and systematic excavation of what remains in situ of the original cave deposit itself. You must use your own discretion in proceeding with this work but do not run any unnecessary risks by carrying on work below the overhanging and unstable cliff face. Mr. Li will engage local quarry men whenever you are ready to remove the dangerous overhanging rock.

3. A personal servant Yea Ch'eng P'ing who will do your cooking, washing and attend to your rooms etc. has been hired as from today's date for you. Mr. Li has already engaged three rooms for you in a private house near the cave deposit. You will provide your own food but this your servant Yea will be able to purchase for you. You will pay this servant his wages ($22.00 per month) and travel expenses to Chou Kou Tien out of your expense account. Yea has agreed to this wage without food allowance.

4. The sum of Mex. $225.00 in small bills and silver will be put at your disposal to pay for various items of field expense. $25.00 of this I shall give to your servant Yea to purchase his *through* railway ticket, cover his travel expenses to Chou Kou Tien *and* to purchase such items as milk, tea, etc. which he should take with him for you. He will account to you for his expenditures. You will let me know if and when you require further funds and will render an account of all expenditures other than personal ones.

5. A field assistant Liu Teh Ling who has worked with Mr. Granger for two seasons will also be provided. He will accompany your servant to Chou Kou Tien the day before you leave Peking. This man will receive Mex. $25.00 per month and a food allowance in the field of $5.00 per month which you will pay from your expense account. He is to devote himself wholly to assisting you in the

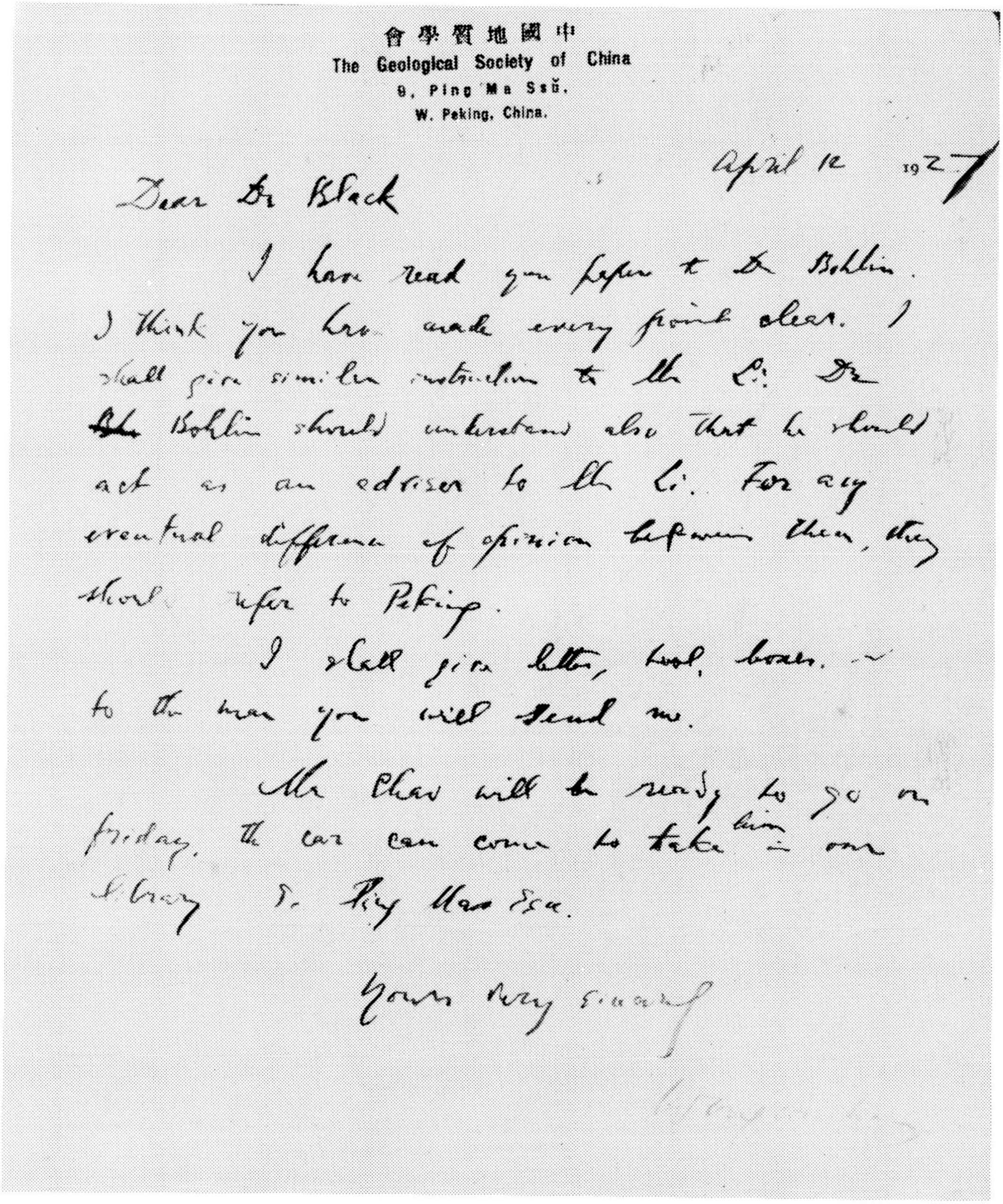

中國地質學會
The Geological Society of China
9, Ping Ma Ssŭ.
W. Peking, China.

April 12 1927

Dear Dr Black

I have read your paper to Dr Bohlin. I think you have made every point clear. I shall give similar instruction to the C. Dr Bohlin should understand also that he should act as an adviser to the Li. For any eventual difference of opinion between them, they should refer to Peking.

I shall give letter, tool, boxes — to the men you will send me.

Mr Chao will be ready to go on friday, the car can come to take him in our library 9, Ping Ma Ssu.

Yours very sincerely

Opposite: Letter from Davidson Black dated April 12, 1927, to Birger Bohlin instructing him on the excavation at Zhoukoudian during the first year.
Above: Weng Wenhao's letter showing his consent to the plans in Black's instructions.

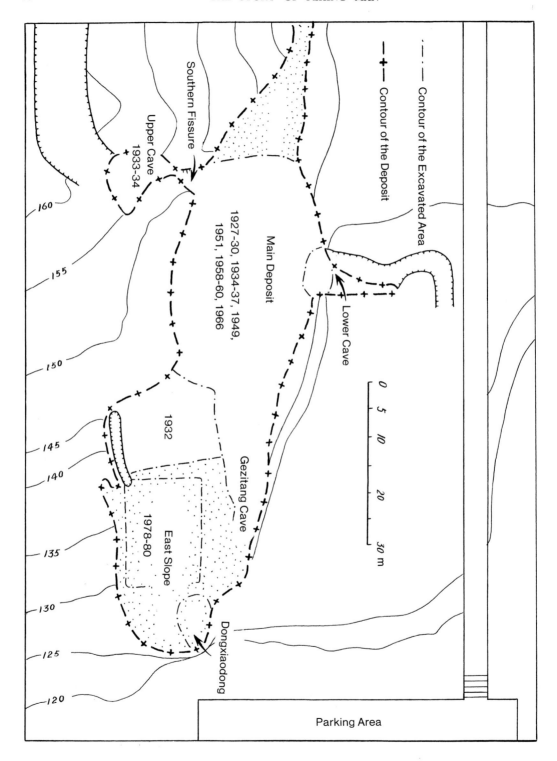

Key diagram illustrating the distribution of the various excavated areas of the Peking Man site.

Top: Systematic excavation at Zhoukoudian in 1927. (*Photo by Birger Bohlin*)
Bottom: The ash layer of the fourth stratum. (*Photo by Birger Bohlin, 1927*)

Li Jie should see to it that they were shipped to the Cenozoic Research Laboratory in Beijing. More will be said about this laboratory in Chapter 7.

Black thought that the whole job at Zhoukoudian could be done in two months, or even six weeks, but he was wrong. The immensity of the fossil-bearing deposits, the great variety of fossils, the complexity of the excavation, and the difficulties of the job were beyond the expectations of all concerned. In fact, even now, after a half century of continual digging, at least half of the deposits remain unexplored. There are just as many problems as ever to be solved and some new ones to tackle too.

Li Jie and Bohlin selected the middle part of the deposits as the place to start digging. Its position lies west of the northern fissure, with a work face 17 metres long and 14 metres wide, narrowing to 16.2 metres in length and 12.3 metres in width at the bottom. After the team reached a depth of 20 metres, they had excavated deposits amounting to 3000 cubic metres. Not until 24 weeks later, on October 18, 1927, did the first digging come to a stop.

It was a triumphant beginning. The fossil specimens came to a staggering 500 crates and included a well-preserved human tooth. Bohlin made the discovery only three days (October 16) before the work was to end. The *in situ* position of this tooth was quite close to the place where Zdansky had found the first human tooth. Black was overjoyed with this suc-

Yang Zhongjian (*left*) and Pei Wenzhong at the office. (*Photo by Bian Meinian, October 1932*)

cess. In a letter (October 29) to Andersson, who was in Stockholm at the time, he related the exciting news:

We have got a beautiful *human* tooth at last!

It is truly glorious news, is it not!

Bohlin is a splendid and enthusiastic worker who refused to permit local discomforts or military crises to interfere with his investigation. Wong telegraphed from Dairen on October 10th urging me to recall Bohlin and Li because of the war but I made careful enquiries here and could see no reason for so doing. So I wrote to Bohlin and explained the situation and told him I didn't want him or Li to run any risks but that as they knew local conditions they must use their own judgement about coming to Peking.

They had 60 men on the job so their daily payroll was relatively large. I couldn't get away myself for I was having daily committee work that demanded my presence here. Hsieh (Xie Renfu) couldn't reach Chou Kou Tien on account of local fighting. That night which was October 19th when I got back to my office at 6:30 from my meeting there I found Bohlin in his field clothes and covered with dust but his face just shining with happiness. He had finished the season's work in spite of the war and on October 16th he had found the tooth; being right on the spot when it was picked out of the matrix! My word, I was excited and elated! Bohlin came here before he had even let his wife know he was in Peking —he certainly is a man after my own heart and I hope you will tell Dr Wiman how much I appreciate his help in securing Bohlin for the work in China.

We have now in Peking some 50 boxes of material which we got in last July when the last military crisis was on but there are 300 more large boxes yet to come from Chou Kou Tien. Mr Li of the Survey is busy trying to get rail cars to bring back this material. It will fill more than two cars! Today I have arranged for storage space for this stuff in the basement at Lockhart Hall where it will be handy for Bohlin working upstairs in the Cenozoic Laboratory.

We have used till now slightly less than half our appropriation and still have about $13 000 for next year.

Digging the eastern half of a deposit left over from the previous year. (*Photo by Birger Bohlin, 1928*)

Landmark erected on Dragon Bone Hill after signing a long-term land lease contract, 1930.

In a paper entitled 'On a Lower Molar from the Chou Kou Tien Deposits',[1] Black described the tooth in detail. He identified it as a left lower molar possessing the same characteristics as the previous find made by Zdansky. Based on this observation and the geographical significance of the tooth, Black suggested a new hominid genus to be named *Sinanthropus pekinensis black and zdansky*. But with the advance of this branch of science, the term has been replaced by *Homo erectus pekinensis*, popularly known as Peking Man, a name coined by A. W. Grabau.

In 1928, Black was away from China most of the year. He went back to Canada at the end of 1927 and visited the United States and Britain later. The work at Zhoukoudian was thus under the direction of Weng Wenhao and A. B. D. Fortuyn of the Peking Union Medical College.

The field team had a considerable change in personnel too. Li Jie left some time during the year; Liu Delin was recruited by the Central Asia Expedition headed by Roy Chapman Andrews and left for Inner Mongolia in April. To fill the vacancies, the team recruited two new members, both graduates of the Geology Department of Beijing University and later to become famous in their field.

One was Yang Zhongjian (C. C. Young), who replaced Li Jie as official representative of the Geological Survey on the

---

[1] *Paleontologia Sinica*, Ser. C, Vol. 7, Fasc. I, December 1927.

Zhoukoudian team. He was the 'Chinese vertebrate paleontologist now in Germany' mentioned in Weng Wenhao's October 18, 1926 letter to Black. After graduating from Beijing University in 1923, Yang went to Germany in 1924 to study vertebrate paleontology at Munich University under Professor Ferdinand Brolli and Professor Max Schlosser. He completed his Ph.D. studies in 1927 and returned to China in the spring of 1928, after a brief stay at Uppsala University in Sweden, where he had familiarized himself with the research on the Zhoukoudian fossils. He was thus well informed about the Peking Man site before he came to work there.

The other specialist was Pei Wenzhong, who had just graduated from Beijing University and was only 24 years old at the time. In the beginning, his main jobs were bookkeeping and dealing with the hired hands while taking some part in the excavation. Bohlin appreciated this young assistant very much.

The work face selected for this year lay to the east of the one selected in 1927, and the digging was started from the top of the hillock. The face was an oblong block 20 metres long and 12 metres wide. No sooner had they begun to work than an internecine war involving troops of Chiang Kaishek, Li Zongren, Feng Yuxiang and Yan Xishan on one side and Zhang Zuolin of Manchuria on the other began to spread into the Zhoukoudian area. The team had scarcely worked for a month since starting in late April. By the end of May Fortuyn had to recall Bohlin and Pei Wenzhong because of the fighting, and work was suspended. When the situation improved, it was already the end of August. To make up for lost time, Bohlin and Pei Wenzhong stuck to their fieldwork until November 25, when a snowstorm struck the site. During the 24 accumulated working weeks of the year, the team completed the excavation of 2800 cubic metres of deposits and amassed 575 boxes of material.

In spite of the three months that were lost because of the war, the team achieved more than they had in the previous year. Besides mammalian fossils, two human mandibles were recovered. One, unearthed in the spring, was the lower right jaw of a young girl. The other, also a lower right jaw, belonged to an adult and had three well-preserved molars attached. It was found only a few days before the fieldwork was suspended for the year. The two specimens brought great excitement to Davidson Black, for they would provide support for the new genus *Sinanthropus pekinensis* that he had established on the strength of a single tooth discovered the previous year.

Black went on home leave to Toronto, Canada, at the end of 1927 and travelled widely in 1928 to fulfil three major tasks. First, he went to New York to discuss the Cenozoic research programme with the Rockefeller Foundation. Their initial donation was to run out in March 1929. Black obtained an additional sum of $4000 for the Zhoukoudian project. Second, he consulted extensively with European and American scholars, such as W. K. Gregory, Milo Hellman, Arthur Keith and Elliot Smith, on the establishment of the new genus *Sinanthropus pekinensis*. In a letter from Toronto to Ding Wenjiang dated March 4, 1928, he expressed his happiness that these scholars seemed to be in agreement with all his major conclusions. Third, he conferred with the British Museum to obtain the services of F. O. Barlow of the Museum, for the reconstruction of the Peking Man molar recovered in 1927. Barlow made two copies, one the original size and the other twice the size of the original.

Thus, although he was not in China, Black did a great deal of work for the Zhoukoudian project in 1928.

7

The Cenozoic Laboratory
Is Founded

The year 1929 has great significance in the annals of Chinese paleontological research, for in that year the Cenozoic Research Laboratory of the Geological Survey of China was formally established. This laboratory was the first institution of its kind in China to specialize in studies of paleogeology and paleontology, with special reference to human paleontology. The founding of this laboratory opened up new avenues for the study of the Cenozoic Era in China. It also led to the discovery of the complete Peking Man skullcap at the end of 1929, a find that shook the academic world.

The Laboratory was the precursor of the Institute of Vertebrate Paleontology and Paleoanthropology of the Chinese Academy of Sciences, which came into being after the founding of New China. The name 'Cenozoic Laboratory' had appeared in a number of records concerning the Zhoukoudian project as early as the spring of 1927, but only two years later did it take form and officially come into being.

The work at Zhoukoudian was faced with the prospect of termination at the end of 1928 because the initial funds from the Rockefeller Foundation would be exhausted by March of the next year, and there was still much to be explored. Furthermore, the site had yielded profusely but had also posed many new questions that were not limited to the Zhou-koudian area—many-sided questions involving geology, paleontology, and geomorphology.

During the winter of 1928, Black, Weng Wenhao, and Ding Wenjiang were in frequent communication in their search for ways and means to face the new situation. Under their consideration was a new and more extensive programme to replace the Zhoukoudian scheme. The new plan covered a period of three and a half years, leaving an extra half year as the transition period to allow for a winding up of jobs carried over from the previous year. Details of the activities were written down for each year from 1929 to 1932, and a total budget of $110 000 was contemplated. The Cenozoic Research Laboratory would, of course, be the body to implement this plan.

The new plan, like the Zhoukoudian one, entailed the co-operation of the Geological Survey and the Union Medical College, and its source of funds was also to be the Rockefeller Foundation. But in order to avert possible complications in the future, the three leading authorities decided to make the Laboratory a truly 'Chinese' institution, a special department subordinated to the Geological Survey.

The thinking behind the new plan may come into better perspective if we view the itemized activities mapped out for 1929-32.

1929-30

D. B. [to] proceed to Java in May to

attend the Pan-Pacific Conference and visit the Trinil (*Pithecanthropus*) site.

Continuation of technical work in laboratory throughout the year preparing specimens collected.

Continuation of Chou Kou Tien excavations where extensive deposits still remain unworked.

Reconnaissance in western Shansi of the probable site from which was derived the hominid tooth described by Schlosser in 1903.

Reconnaissance of Tertiary deposits along the line of the Peking-Hankou railway in collaboration with Dr J. G. Andersson and Pierre Teilhard de Chardin, using freight car as travelling laboratory base.

1930-31

Continuation of technical work in laboratory throughout the year preparing specimens collected.

Continuation of excavation of other known sites at Chou Kou Tien.

Excavation of promising sites discovered in previous year's reconnaissance.

Reconnaissance of cave sites and deposits in Chihli and Shantung.

1931-32

Continuation of technical work in laboratory for 18 months preparing specimens collected.

Reconnaissance of Tertiary deposits in Turkestan via Siberia and Semipalatinsk (12 months) in collaboration with Dr J. G. Andersson.

Continuation of excavation of sites in northeastern China.

Completion of publication of results.

It is evident that the new plan aimed, in essence, at the same goals as the abortive Central Asia Expedition conceived by Davidson Black and J. G. Andersson a few years earlier, the plan that was replaced by the Zhoukoudian project. The many consultations yielded, on February 8, 1929, two documents drafted by Black and Weng Wenhao. The full texts follow.

Peking, February 8, 1929

Constitution of the Cenozoic Research Laboratory of the Geological Survey of China

1. The aim of this Laboratory is to carry on an extensive plan of human paleontological research; that is, the Laboratory aims to collect, study and describe fossils of Tertiary and Quaternary age in China with special reference to the problems of human paleontology.

2. The administration of the Laboratory is under the control of the Director of the Geological Survey with the assistance of the following persons:

Dr V. K. Ting: As Honorary Director of the Cenozoic Research;

Dr Davidson Black: As Honorary Director of the Laboratory;

Dr C. C. Young (or another Chinese paleontologist): As Assistant Director who will especially work on the paleontological part other than anthropological.

Other specialists may be appointed or asked by the Director of the Survey to collaborate in the work of the Laboratory.

3. A special fund will be granted by the Rockefeller Foundation to be dispersed through the Peking Union Medical College for the expenses of the Cenozoic Research.

4. All material collected shall entirely belong to the Geological Survey of China, including the anthropological specimens which will temporarily be deposited in the Peking Union Medical College for study and when kept by the Survey shall be always accessible for study by the scientists of the former institution. Nothing shall be exported out of China.

The Cenozoic Research has no special interest in cultural studies and will not collect archaeological artifacts. Whenever artifacts of historic periods may be accidentally found, they shall be handed over to the proper Chinese museum.

Detailed Understanding with the P.U.M.C. and Dr Davidson Black

1. All geological and paleontological pa-

Peking, February 5, 1929.

CONSTITUTION

of the

Cenozoic Research Laboratory of the Geological Survey of China.

1. The aim of this laboratory is to carry on an extended plan of human
    palaeontological research; that is the laboratory aims to collect,
    study and describe fossils of Tertiary and Quaternary age in China
    with special reference to the problems of human palaeontology.

2. The Administration of the Laboratory is under the control of the Director
    of the Geological Survey with the assistance of the following persons:

    Dr. V. K. Ting: As Honorary Director of the Cenozoic Research.

    Dr. Davidson Black: As Honorary Director of the Laboratory.

    Dr. C. C. Yang (or another Chinese palaeontologist) as Assistant Director
    who will especially work on the palaeontological part other than
    anthropological.

    Other specialists may be appointed or asked by the Director of the
    Survey to collaborate in the work of the Laboratory.

3. A special fund will be granted by the Rockefeller Foundation to be
    dispersed through the Peking Union Medical College for the expenses
    of the Cenozoic Research.

4. All material collected shall entirely belong to the Geological Survey
    of China including the anthropological specimens which will temporarily
    be deposited in the Peking Union Medical College for study and when
    kept by the Survey shall be always accessible for study by the
    scientists of the former institution. Nothing shall be exported
    out of China.

    The Cenozoic Research has no special interest in cultural studies and
    will not collect archaeological artifacts. Whenever artifacts of
    historic periods may be accidentally found, they shall be handed over
    to proper Chinese Museum.

Detailed understanding with the P.U.M.C. and Dr. Davidson Black.

1. All geological and palaeontological papers shall be published in the
    series of the Geological Survey or Geological Society of China. Dr.
    Black may however publish part of his anthropological studies else-
    where with the consent of the Director of the Geological Survey
    and if possible the same paper so published should appear at the
    same date in the Palaeontologia Sinica.

2. Dr. C. C. Yang will be paid from the special Fund $200 per month the
    first year, $220 per month the second year and $250 per month the
    third year, and Mr. Pei $60 per month the first 6 months, $80 per
    month the second 6 months, $90 per month the second year, and $100
    per month the third year.

3. The P. U. M. C. will allow the continued use of the rooms of Lockhart
    Hall for the C. R. Laboratory. But the Survey is free to remove part
    or all of the material therein stored to its own compounds in West
    City when judged desirable.

4. It is understood that the Director of the Laboratory will also
    supervise the field work and make annual report.

Constitution of the Cenozoic Research Laboratory of the Geological Survey of China (*opposite*) and the 'Detailed Understanding' memo (*above*), both dated February 8, 1929. They were drafted by Weng Wenhao and Davidson Black.

At the office of the Zhoukoudian project. *Left to right*: Pei Wenzhong, Li Siguang, Teilhard de Chardin, Bian Meinian, Yang Zhongjian, G. B. Barbour. (*Photo by Jia Lanpo, May 9, 1934*)

Opposite: Pioneers of geological research in China.
Top: *Front row from left to right*: Zhang Hongzhao, Ding Wenjiang, A. W. Grabau, Weng Wenhao, Teilhard de Chardin. *Middle row from left to right*: Yang Zhongjian, Zhou Zanheng, Xie Jiayong, Xu Guangxi, Sun Yunzhu, Tan Xichou, Wang Shaowen, Yin Zhanxun, Yuan Fuli. *Back row from left to right*: He Zuoling, Wang Hengsheng, Wang Zhuquan, Wang Yuelun, Zhu Huanwen, Ji Yunsen, Sun Jianchu. The picture was taken at the residence of Grabau in Beijing in the summer of 1933.
Bottom: Scientists in front of a camel caravan inn where they stayed as a study group on Zhoukoudian.
Left to right: Pei Wenzhong, Wang Hengsheng, Wang Gongmu, Yang Zhongjian, Birger Bohlin, Davidson Black, Teilhard de Chardin, G. B. Barbour. The picture was taken in 1928.

pers shall be published in the series of the Geological Survey or Geological Society of China. Dr Black may however publish part of his anthropological studies elsewhere with the consent of the Director of the Geological Survey and if possible the same paper so published should appear at the same date in the *Paleontologia Sinica*.

2. Dr C. C. Young will be paid from the special fund $200 per month the first year, $220 per month the second year and $250 per month the third year, and Mr Pei $60 per month the first six months, $80 per month the second six months, $90 per month the second year, and $100 per month the third year.

3. The P.U.M.C. will allow the continued use of the rooms of Lockhart Hall for the C. R. Laboratory. But the Survey is free to remove part or all of the material therein stored to its own compounds in West City when judged desirable.

4. It is understood that the Director of the Laboratory will also supervise the field-work and make an annual report.

These two documents had as their blue-print the official agreement concluded on February 14, 1927 (see Chapter 5), the only

change being Article IV concerning the publication of papers. The stipulation in the 1927 agreement had been: "All results of the research will be published in the *Paleontologia Sinica* or other series of the Geological Survey or in the publication of the Geological Society of China." The new document made a saving clause for Dr Black upon his own request.

The Chinese government authorities ratified this constitution on April 19, 1929, and in the ensuing months the activities of the Laboratory centred on soliciting funds from the Rockefeller Foundation and staffing the organization. Not until December 2 did Black feel relaxed enough to write to Andersson: "I have at last got the affairs of the newly organized Cenozoic Research Laboratory on a fairly routine basis and my budget has been accepted as presented."

However, the research workers of the Laboratory had lost no time. P. Teilhard de Chardin and Professor G. B. Barbour (Yanjing University, a geologist and geomorphologist) had made a reconnaissance trip in February and March of 1929 to central Shanxi Province for the purpose of study-

A sketch of the Zhoukoudian site (Locality 1) by G. B. Barbour.

Figure 3. The Choukoutien Locality 1 (*Sinanthropus* deposits) from a field sketch by Professor G. B. Barbour in 1929.

ing the Cenozoic deposits in that area. At the same time, Li Jie and Pei Wenzhong explored the sites in Henan Province. That summer, Teilhard and Yang Zhongjian made a three-month reconnaissance trip in Shanxi and Shaanxi Provinces and in the southern part of the Ordos Plateau, ending their studies in mid-September. The trip was quite fruitful, and Davidson Black suggested that in the next fieldwork season they should extend their surveys further west to get an overall view of the northern China Cenozoic environment from the eastern seaboard to Gansu Province.

Also, in the latter part of April, Black took part in the Fourth Pacific Science Congress Meeting held in Java, at which he displayed the reconstructed Peking Man fossils. His work in this respect and the new genus he had established won praise from his colleagues at the meeting.

Of all the work during the first year of the existence of the Cenozoic Laboratory, the Zhoukoudian project was of the most importance, and its achievements turned out to be the most impressive. Teilhard de Chardin and Yang Zhongjian completed a preliminary report on the geology and paleontology of the area. Then, towards the end of the fieldwork season, Pei Wenzhong found the first complete skullcap of Peking Man, to be described in detail below.

The report by Teilhard and Yang summed up the work at Zhoukoudian over the three years from 1927. Entitled 'Preliminary Report on the Chou Kou Tien Fossiliferous Deposits',[1] the paper gave a brief account of how the site was discovered, the geological and geomorphological characteristics of the area, the excavations undertaken in the three years, the division of the fossil-bearing deposits into layers, the dating of the deposits, and the age

_____
[1] *Bulletin of the Geological Society of China*, Vol. 8, No. 3, 1929.

sequence of the various sites in the area. It was in this paper that the fossiliferous deposits at the Peking Man site were divided from the top into ten layers, based on the characteristics of the fauna, which the authors concluded was "evidently of Pleistocene age" and "undoubtedly older than and almost entirely distinct from the loessic fauna," but "clearly younger than the Nihewan Sanmenian fauna." Thus the authors laid solid groundwork for later studies on the Zhoukoudian finds, as well as on the Quaternary geology in North China.

As the digging went deeper, in the 1950s, Jia Lanpo added three more layers to the original ten and defined the structure further down as a 'basic gravel layer' In recent years, as more evidence has come to light, this layer has been redefined as the fourteenth layer, with three more layers (15 to 17) added to it.

The entire mass of fossiliferous deposits, from the thirteenth layer up, is of middle Pleistocene age, the intervening period between the Sanmenian and Loessic ages as determined by Teilhard and Yang in their paper and commonly referred to as the 'Zhoukoudian age'. This dating, determined a half-century ago, still holds good.

*   *   *

Yang Zhongjian

Yang Zhongjian is remembered to this day for his honesty and his indomitable spirit. During the extremely adverse circumstances of the 'cultural revolution', he wrote over thirty papers. He was also a gifted teacher as the following story, told by Jia Lanpo, indicates.

One winter day in 1932, Yang Zhongjian took out two boxes of specimens containing animal teeth and asked Jia to classify them. With two years of experience behind him, Jia Lanpo thought he would have no difficulty with the task, so he agreed right away and finished the classification very quickly. He clearly identified each tooth —hyena, wild boar and so on. But Yang Zhongjian was not satisfied. "I don't want this," he said, "I want you to identify the genus and species and write them in Latin." At that time Jia Lanpo's ability was not equal to the task.

He went back to his office and started over. All the specimens now confused him. He began asking questions of other people and consulting books. Making careful observations of this tooth, measuring that one, he worked for several days to finish the job. When he handed in his work to Yang Zhongjian, Yang examined the labels carefully, checked the specimens, and asked Jia to explain the basis for his identifications of genus and species. This time Yang was pleased. Saying with a smile, "So you'll never forget them!" He gave all the specimens and labels to Jia Lanpo to keep.

Yang's examination had been strict, but it taught Jia how to work and laid a good foundation for his later research. He kept the two specimen boxes and used them as textbooks until the Peking Union Medical College was occupied by the Japanese army, when they disappeared.

8

The News That Shook
the Academic World

In 1929, both Birger Bohlin and Yang Zhongjian were absent from Zhoukoudian. Bohlin had joined an expedition, and Yang had joined Teilhard de Chardin in exploring the Cenozoic geological structures in Shanxi and Shaanxi. After conferring with Davidson Black, the head of the Geological Survey of China, Weng Wenhao put Pei Wenzhong in charge of the Zhoukoudian project.

On a glorious April day that year, Pei, Black, Teilhard and Yang arrived at the site for a conference on further excavation plans. It was decided then that the target was to be the middle section of the areas which had been dug in 1927 and 1928, from the fifth layer on down to the very bottom of the fossiliferous deposits. This fifth layer had been erroneously identified as the bottom because it was a hard calcarinated ash layer containing fossils.

Apart from the technicians, the staff at Zhoukoudian had only two persons, or sometimes just one, in charge of scientific as well as administrative affairs. In 1927 the tasks were shared by Li Jie and Bohlin, and in 1928 by

Yang Zhongjian and Bohlin. But in 1929 Pei alone had to deal with everything. Pei recalled that he was seized by melancholy after the departure of Black, Teilhard and

The excavation in 1929 started at this point. (*Photo by Pei Wenzhong*)

Yang. Living alone in the mountains and confronted with the extraordinarily hard fifth layer, which would not yield even to explosives, the job had turned into something tasteless. Yet this apparently blind alley soon became a broad thoroughfare in the latter half of the year.

This fifth layer, though hard, was not thick; and the target area, being small, was removed not long after the work was started. At the sixth layer, more fossils were found as the digging proceeded. And in the seventh layer, they were profuse. As Pei relates in his book on the excavation:

> One day we obtained 145 jaw bones of thick-jawed deer. The fos-

sils of this layer not only occur in quantities, they are in good order as well. The complete pig and buffalo skulls and deer antlers were recovered at this layer. The fine sand deposit that yielded these was not

Top: Digging in progress (1929) at the place where the main cave and the north fissure coalesce. (*Photo by Pei Wenzhong*)
Left: The Peking Man skullcap was found underneath this spot. (*Photo by Pei Wenzhong, October 2, 1929*)

calcified, which rendered the digging easy. It is a pity that the work area was restricted as both the southern and eastern parts were threatened by overhanging rocks if extended further.

The digging for that season stopped between the eighth and ninth layers, where a few Peking Man teeth were found, and the site was designated 'Ape-Man Locus C'.

On September 26, work resumed. As the deposits became more scarce, the excavated area narrowed down until the space was big enough for only a few men to work in. Pei thought that they had reached bottom, but then he sighted a crack in the southern side, estimated to be some 40 metres from the surface. This was afterward named the Ape-Man Cave.

Pei and another worker were lowered into the crack, ropes fastened at their waists. They were delighted to find a profusion of fossils within it. It was now the end of November and fieldwork was supposed to be suspended for the season, but the many fossils in the 'cave' impelled them to go on working for another few days.

No one expected that on Monday, December 2, a complete Peking Man skull would be retrieved a little after 4 p.m. Wang Cunyi, a technical adviser at present of the Institute of Paleontology and an eye witness, was twice interviewed in 1980 by the writers of this book.

He stated that:

In the afternoon after four o'clock, it was

Top and *bottom*: A road was cut along the north fissure for transport purposes. (*Photo by Pei Wenzhong, 1929*)

near sunset and the winter wind brought freezing temperatures to the site. Everybody felt the cold, but all were working hard at finding more fossils.

There were four people down in the pit, but I can recall the names of only three —Qiao Derui, Song Guorui and Liu Yishan, now all deceased. I was working elsewhere at the site when the Peking Man skull was found. However, I had seen the place, as all of us had. The large number of fossils attracted everyone of us and we all went down to take a look, so I know what it was like down there in the crack.

We generally used gas light, for it was brighter. But the pit was so small that anyone working there had to hold a candle in one hand and work with the other.

The episode so attracted the newcomer,

Jia Lanpo, that he kept a detailed account of it, which is the basis for the following.

Maybe because of the cold weather, or the hour of the day, the stillness of the air was punctuated only by occasional rhythmic hammer sounds that indicated the presence of men down in the pit. "What's that?" Pei suddenly cried out. "A human skull!" In the tranquility, everybody heard him.

Pei had gone down often after the sighting of the fossils, and now, when he was told there was a round-shaped object there, he had stayed there and worked with the technicians. As more of the object became exposed, he had cried out. Everybody around him was excited and gratified at the long-awaited find.

Digging a pit. (*Photo by Pei Wenzhong, 1929*)

Candles provided light in the pit. The first complete Peking Man skullcap was found with the help of candle light. (*Photo by Pei Wenzhong, December 1929*)

Some suggested that they take it out at once, while others objected for fear that, working rashly in the late hours, they might damage the object. "It has been there for so many thousands of years, what harm would it do lying there for one more night?" they argued. But a long night of suspense was too much to bear. Pei Wenzhong thought hard and at last decided to get it out then, instead of waiting for the morning.

Half of the skull was embedded in hard clay. When Pei finally freed it from the clay, he was sorry to see that there was a crack caused by concussion in digging. The crack proved insignificant and had no effect on later research. When glued together, the skullcap appeared to be perfect.

"I was too excited to enjoy supper," Pei has recounted. "I was thinking [about] how to let the Peking office know. I wrote a letter to Weng Wenhao and dispatched a man to deliver it the next morning. After the messenger had gone, I felt uneasy again for the letter would reach him only late that night when everybody was in bed and Weng would have no time to let the people concerned know about the big event. So thinking, I sent a telegram to Black saying: 'Found skullcap—perfect —look[s] like man's.' "

It is interesting that the letter and telegram were scarcely believed. The sceptics either doubted Pei's ability to correctly identify the specimen or simply refused to believe in such good luck. For example, in a letter to Andersson, dated December 5, Black wrote: "I had a telegram from Pei from

Chou Kou Tien yesterday saying he would be in Peking tomorrow bringing with him what he thinks is a complete *Sinanthropus* skull!! I hope it turns out to be true."

Pei personally delivered the skullcap to Beijing on December 6. When first unearthed, the fossil was rather wet and soft and easily damaged. It had to be dried before delivery to Beijing. As Wang Cunyi has related, Pei, Qiao and he stayed day and night at a fireside to dry the specimen. After that was done, a few layers of gauze were glued to it. Then it was covered with plaster and dried again, after which Pei wrapped it in two thick cotton quilts and

two blankets and tied it with rope like ordinary luggage.

Pei later wrote an account of his trip to Beijing:

Then we travelled by bus between Fangshan and Peking. There was a check-point at the Xibianmen Gate in Peking where luggage would be examined as a matter of routine. I made preparations for that with a few fossils to show to the officer, intending to tell him it was the same kind of thing inside the wrapped luggage and to ask him not to open it. If he insisted on opening the bundle, the plaster and gauze would have to be kept intact. If he still insisted on taking a look at what was inside, I would

The first Peking Man skullcap sees the light of day. (*Photo by Pei Wenzhong, December 2, 1929*)

Opposite:
Top: The skullcap broke into fragments, but was restored successfully. (*Photo by Pei Wenzhong, December 2, 1929*)
Bottom: The first reinforced Peking Man skullcap.

ask him to arrest me first. The man was polite. I only had to open the bundle to let him see.

So the skullcap arrived safely in Beijing. As soon as Black had it, he began working on its reconstruction. Using a needle, Black removed every bit of remaining clay so that the skullcap appeared in its original form. His excitement was beyond description. Losing no time, he wrote letters to J. G. Andersson, G. Elliot Smith, W. D. Matthew and H. F. Osborn, reporting the glad tidings and praising the scientists doing the fieldwork at Zhoukoudian. The following is extracted from his letter to Elliot Smith:

Again the year's work at Chou Kou Tien closes with a grand climax, for on December 2nd W. C. Pei in charge of fieldwork there discovered the greater part of an un-

crushed adult *Sinanthropus* skull! (Later F. Weidenreich reidentified it as a juvenile skull—the authors.) He recognized it *in situ* and excavated it with care himself bringing it to me on December 6th with the field wrappings still wet. The whole mass included a great block of travertine in which the skull is half embedded. I intend to send Christmas cables to you and Professor Keith announcing the good news which will be officially announced at a meeting of the Geological Society of China to be held on December 28th. As I cannot say much in a cable I am sending this note to supplement the latter and I would be glad if you would pass on the news to Dr Smith Woodward, Gregory, Watson *et al.*

Mr W. C. Pei is a corking field man and C. C. Young a first class lab man and good in the field too while Teilhard de Chardin is a host in himself.

Reconstruction of the unearthed skullcap was done overnight. Pei Wenzhong and Wang Cunyi spent the whole night drying the fossil and wrapping it with gauze paper to prepare it for delivery to the Beijing office. (*Photo by Pei Wenzhong, December 3, 1929*)

At 2 p.m., December 28, a special conference of the Geological Survey of China was held at its office. Weng Wenhao presided over the conference. Pei Wenzhong, Davidson Black, Yang Zhongjian and Teilhard de Chardin spoke about the excavation at Zhoukoudian, the newly discovered Peking Man skullcap, the mammalian remains associated with the Peking Man fossils and the deposits at the Zhoukoudian site. The audience included scientists and journalists, and all were excited. News of the extraordinary find flashed around the world after the gathering, and for a time it was the topic of the day throughout the world as well as in Beijing.

Yet there was another find of the same kind that was not publicized, according to a paper written by Pei in 1934. In this he said:

> I should mention here my deep apology for my negligence of another skullcap unearthed at Locus D of the Zhoukoudian site. I was told by a technician who came back to the site from Beijing that in the spring of 1930, a lab worker found a similar skullcap among the specimens collected at Zhoukoudian the previous year. Its *in situ* position was said to be in the lower part of Layers 8 and 9, approximately three metres above Locus E where the complete skullcap was found in 1929. This unidentified fossil was fragmented and had missing parts. But when glued together, it was a nearly perfect skullcap. My indulgent friends often said that it was so thickly covered with clay that the object was not recognized in the field. I knew they were covering up for my negligence, which I have to admit.

Pei Wenzhong

Pei Wenzhong

Pei Wenzhong was a hard worker, whose easy-going approach and cheerful disposition endeared him to his colleagues. He often told other people that when he faced his first pile of fossils at Zhoukoudian, he couldn't distinguish pig, horse, cow, or sheep. Through practical experience and diligent study, he eventually in-

Pei Wenzhong holding his new find, the Peking Man skullcap, encased in plaster. (*Photo by Wang Cunyi, at the camel caravan inn, December 3, 1929*)

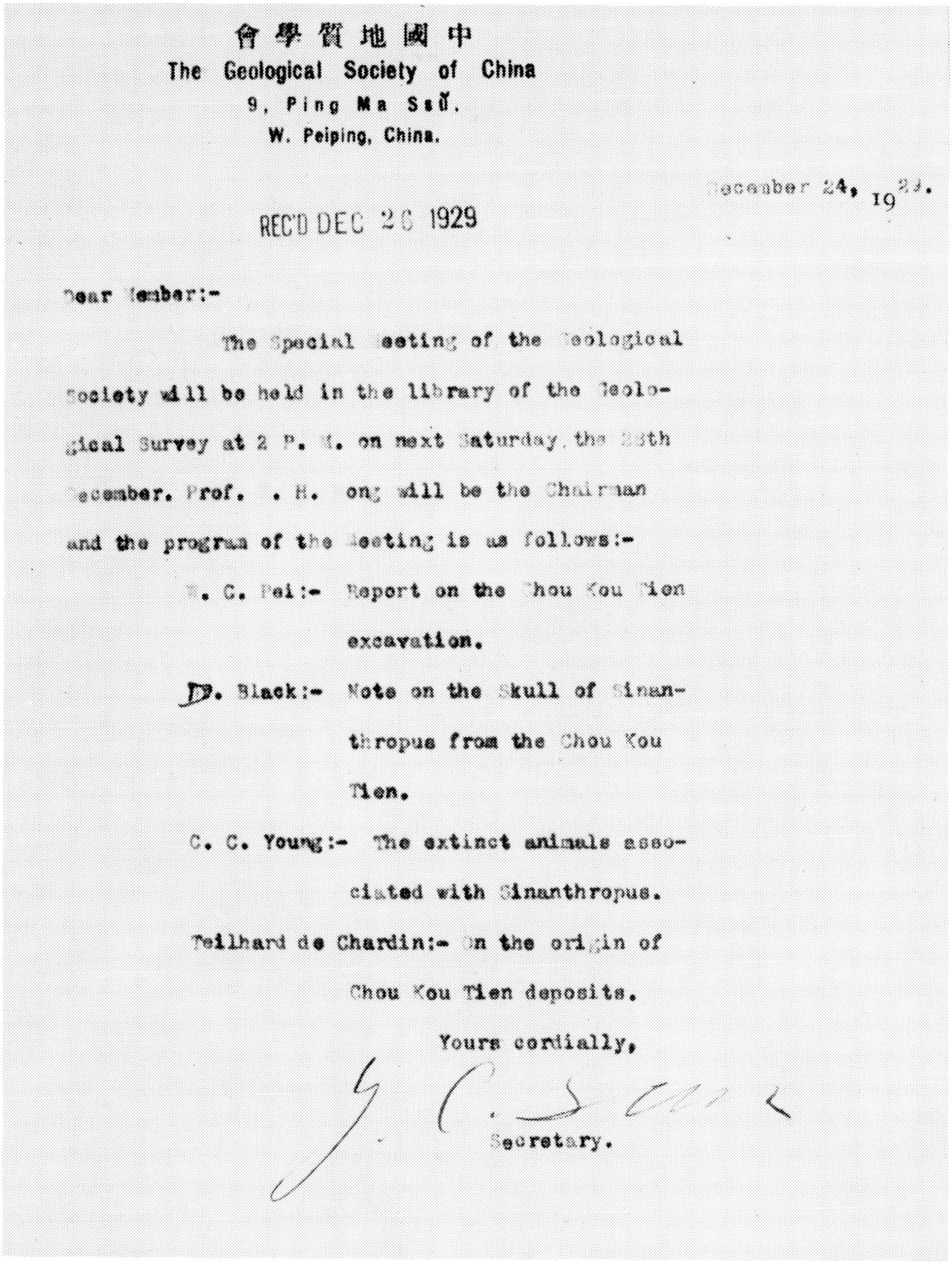

中國地質學會
The Geological Society of China
9, Ping Ma Ssŭ.
W. Peiping, China.

REC'D DEC 26 1929

December 24, 19 .

Dear Member:-

The Special Meeting of the Geological Society will be held in the library of the Geological Survey at 2 P. M. on next Saturday, the 28th December. Prof. W. H. Wong will be the Chairman and the program of the Meeting is as follows:-

W. C. Pei:- Report on the Chou Kou Tien excavation.

D. Black:- Note on the Skull of Sinanthropus from the Chou Kou Tien.

C. C. Young:- The extinct animals associated with Sinanthropus.

Teilhard de Chardin:- On the origin of Chou Kou Tien deposits.

Yours cordially,

Secretary.

The invitation letter from the Geological Society of China for a special conference on the finding of the first Peking Man skullcap. It was held on Saturday, December 28, 1929, with Weng Wenhao presiding and Pei Wenzhong, Davidson Black, Yang Zhongjian and Teilhard de Chardin briefing the audience.

Top: Pei Wenzhong (*left*) and Wang Cunyi (*right*) often took part in the digging and restoration of specimens. The picture shows the two sectioning a rabbit specimen for comparison with a human's (1929).
Bottom: Crating the specimens for shipment to the Beijing headquarters, 1929.

troduced the high standards for which the excavation work at Zhoukoudian is known.

Pei was a great researcher in the areas of Quaternary geology, vertebrate paleontology, paleoanthropology and archaeology, as well as an expert in field excavation work. He knew how to handle the most delicate fossils. We still remember the day in the early 1930s when we were excavating Locality 13 at Zhoukoudian and found a badly damaged rhinoceros skeleton lying on its side. The technicians who discovered it were afraid to try to get it out. Later Pei dug it out himself calmly, unhurriedly, and carefully extricating every bone from the hard layer. Then he put them together to form a complete skeleton and stored it in the exhibition hall of the Geological Survey of China.

9

Stone and Bone Artifacts and the Use of Fire

The quartz fragments found at the Peking Man site attracted the attention of Dr Andersson from the outset. From the first he thought they might be artifacts fashioned by human beings. His observation has now been fully corroborated.

But in 1927, when large-scale excavation started at the Peking Man site, the common occurrence of such fragments did not attract much attention. In a paper written in 1929, Black stated that the site had not yielded 'any artifacts of any nature,' nor was there 'any trace of the usage of fire.' The discovery of the first complete Peking Man skullcap in 1929 resulted in a re-evaluation of this position. Pei Wenzhong reported the recovery of one piece of quartz at the site that showed marks of a 'blow'. This piece, however, was picked up from the ground and had not necessarily occurred in association with the skullcap.

In preparing the ground for the fieldwork in 1931, a layer of loose deposits was found to be rich in quartz fragments. In July of the same year, another layer of quartz fragments was sighted in the 'Pigeon Hall' area. Both layers not only abounded in fossils and quartz fragments, but were easy to work on as well.

Jia Lanpo began his apprenticeship by digging for stone artifacts at the Pigeon Hall site. That was in 1931 when he first came to Zhoukoudian with Bian Meinian. There were then eight technicians digging

at the site and a number of hired hands carrying the earth away. Jia Lanpo took note of a layer containing a loose black substance (later it was determined to be ash) and a lot of quartz fragments, and he was at once interested in it. The technicians were by now proficient fossil hunters, who could tell by sound whether the objects they struck with their spades were quartz or not. This skill won great admiration from Jia Lanpo. He made up his mind to learn from them, and he too could soon tell the sound of struck quartz.

Each day during the operation in 1931, large basketfuls of stone artifacts were delivered twice daily to Jia Lanpo at the site headquarters. He gave a name to the ash layer that yielded these artifacts—'Quartz Horizon 2'—and later extended its use to the serial numbers given to all recovered material that bore signs of being used or worked upon by humans. He started from Q2 : 0001 and ended in the Q2 : 8000s.

It was by no means easy to identify these early human tools. After all, it took ten years before Andersson's observation that their occurrence "might be due to the agency of some ancient type of humanity" was finally corroborated. There are nowadays people who pride themselves on being able to tell the difference between an

Opposite:
Top: Ash deposits in Layer 11. The town in view is Zhoukoudian. (*Photo by Jia Lanpo, April 29, 1935*)
Bottom: Ash deposits in Layer 12. (*Photo by Jia Lanpo, May 6, 1935*)

artifact and a common stone, and some of these people try to devalue work done in the past so as to enhance their own reputations. But it was a long and arduous journey from incognizance to recognition. We are able to see further today only because we are standing on the shoulders of our predecessors, and later comers will in turn see still further and more clearly by standing on our shoulders.

Flakes are the mainstay of the Peking Man artifacts; cores are few in number. They are all small in size. Many are well-trimmed pieces weighing less than five grammes. The raw material was pebbles from the river bank and pieces of vein quartz, sandstone, quartzite and chert. Some of the tools that have been found are of rock quartz from a granite hillside two kilometres away. Using pebbles as hammers, Peking Man was able, by different methods, to produce flakes. Stone hammers were used in trimming the flakes, but some seem to have been struck by hammers of wood or bone. In most cases, the trimming is found on one side only, and the blows were struck from the obverse to the reverse surface.

Among the types of tools found are choppers or chopping tools made of round, flat sandstone or quartz pebbles by trimming one or both sides. These were probably used to fell trees or to make hunting sticks. Scrapers made of flakes of various sizes are common. They are found in many shapes—disc, linear, convex, concave and complex. One big concave scraper is obviously suited for shaping hunting sticks, as its blade is as large as a tree trunk the size of the human arm. A small scraper might have been used as a knife for general purposes. Its point is the

Ash deposits in Layer 4. The deposits were six metres deep and covered with vegetation. (*Photo by Wang Zhefu, summer 1978*)

Top: Charred bones unearthed at the Zhoukoudian site.
Middle: Deer skulls with antlers cut off by Peking Man.
Bottom: Charred pebbles unearthed at the Zhoukoudian site.

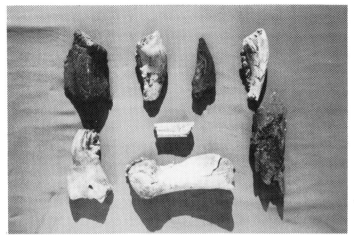

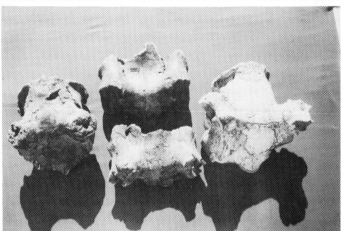

most refined among all the Peking Man tools so far found. The size of a human finger and fashioned with great care, this tool represents a high degree of sophistication in technique.

One stone point that looks like an awl was designed with two shoulders. Its quality of workmanship is so impressive that if placed among other paleoliths, it would have been highly valued. Because of the sophistication of technique shown in this tool, we have made the bold statement that no contemporary site ever yielded a stone artifact that can compare with this one in workmanship. And in 1957 Jia Lanpo and Wang Jian, Deputy Director of the Institute

of Archaeology of Shanxi Province, made the statement that "Peking Man artifacts are not the earliest manmade tools," which "can only be found in the Nihewan bed of the early Pleistocene."

Guesses as to the uses to which the points were put include that of skinning animals, digging out worms from under the bark of a tree for food, and separating sinews from animal bones. The hammer stone and anvil were obviously tools for the production of other tools. Marks on the hammer stone testify to the fact that Peking Man had considerable manual dexterity. Apart from these, there are some flakes that bear no signs of secondary

At the invitation of the Cenozoic Research Laboratory, archaeologist abbé Henri Breuil of France visited China in April 1931. He made studies of the stone artifacts from Zhoukoudian and paid a visit to the site before he gave confirmation to Pei Wenzhong's finds. The picture shows the French visitor with Weng Wenhao (*middle*) and Pei Wenzhong (*left*) at the field office at Zhoukoudian.

work but do seem to have been used.

At a conference of the Geological Society of China, held on November 3, 1931, Professor H. Breuil, a French Catholic Father, reported on his findings after examination of the bone fragments at the Peking Man site. He asserted that these are evidence of a Peking Man culture. His observation attracted wide attention. He later published a paper on these bone and antler implements.

The bulk of these bone fossils are shattered pieces, once referred to as 'junk' and ignored. But how did these bones reach such a state? Competing explanations include the following: frequent cave roof collapse; cracking of bones by humans to get at the edible bone marrow; and toolmaking. All these suggestions are reasonable. The complete Peking Man mandible retrieved in 1936 was reconstructed from fragments evidently caused by fallen rocks. The practice of marrow eating is known to have been adopted by much earlier people in Africa, and it must have been a practice at Zhoukoudian, too. Yet no single hypothesis can explain all the cases, though toolmaking has been found to be valid in more cases than have the other two suggestions.

The cultural evidence includes the use of fire as well as the use of bone and antler artifacts.

The use of fire is a landmark in man's history. The Peking Man site provided such strong evidence of fire use that no one now doubts the fact. At the beginning of excavation, however, the black substance that was clearly present did not re-

sult in this conclusion. No one declared it to be evidence of the use of fire until the winter of 1930, when Teilhard de Chardin brought a cinder with him to Europe and compared it with finds from prehistoric sites on the European continent. Dr Gaubert of the Laboratory of Mineralogy at the Paris Museum made the analysis. The following, in summarized form, is a report of his results:

1. Boiled in hydrochloric and nitric acid, the phosphates and carbonates of lime were dissolved leaving a black residue. This demonstrates that their black colour can not be due to any oxide of iron or manganese. The black residue thus remaining is

Bian Meinian and Jia Lanpo drill a hole to place explosives. (*Photo by Pei Wenzhong, 1931*)

entirely consumed when heated in a bunsen flame. It is therefore to be concluded that the black residue is carbon.

2. The black residue remaining after boiling with hydrochloric acid is redissolved when reboiled in sulphuric acid containing potassium bichromate. This action is also indicative of its origin from carbon.

In April 1941 another black substance sample, together with a charred bone, was taken from Quartz Horizon 1 and delivered to the laboratory of Professor B. E. Read of the Department of Pharmacology at the Peking Union Medical College. The results obtained by his analysis were as follows:

1. Boiled in a large excess of hydrochloric acid, only a fraction (about one-third) was dissolved. The black residue, when fused with nitre and caustic soda, was entirely decolourized, indicating the absence of heavy metals in the insoluble fraction.

2. Heated with copper oxide, the gases that evolved were passed into lime water. A heavy precipitate resulted, which dissolved when excess carbon dioxide gas was added.

The evidence of the use of fire by Peking Man includes ash, cinders and charred bones and stones. The ash is represented by purple, yellow, grey, white, or black

Collaborators at the field office. *From left to right*: Pierre Teilhard de Chardin, Bian Meinian, Yang Zhongjian and Pei Wenzhong. (*Photo by Jia Lanpo*)

substances. It is so friable that it can be crumbled by hand, revealing its damp interior. When dry, it is very light. The ash is often found in layers and occurs at the bottom of Layer 3, in Layer 4, between Layers 8 and 9 and in Layer 10. These ash layers vary in thickness as well as in colour. Grains of charcoal are often seen in the layers that contain a black substance. There is as yet no satisfactory explanation for the differences in colour between substances that are materially the same. And in spite of their bright colours, the bones and stones found in these substances are all burnt.

The scorched bones are cracked or even twisted, appearing in blue, green, grey, brown, or black hues. The burnt stones are also cracked, and limestone found in the ash deposits has all turned into lime. This was clearly shown in 1951 when limestone was found in an ash deposit. On being squeezed by hand, it was found to be a damp clot. When later dried, it turned into a white solid.

Peking Man certainly used fire, but was not the earliest human to do so. By then, the use of fire had already undergone tremendous development. The fact that some ash substances are found in piles shows that Peking Man knew how to control fire. Evidence of the use of fire has also been found at sites of much earlier date than that of Peking Man. These other sites are Zhoukoudian Locality 13; Kehe culture site in Ruicheng County, Shanxi Province; and the Lantian Man site at Gongwangling in Lantian County, Shaanxi Province. The last one dates to 0.8-1.0 million years B.P.

Black substances found at all these sites have proved to be carbon under laboratory analysis. Large grains of charcoal have been found in the ash deposits. In a paper on the excavation at the Gongwangling site, the archaeologists Dai Erjian and Xu Chunhua wrote: "Apart from stone arti-

facts, the site yielded charcoal, which is, as mentioned above, quite possibly a result of the use of fire by the Lantian *hominidae*. If so, the important cultural factor of the use of fire should be another element of the Lantian hominid culture."

But even these sites are not the earliest ones in China where evidence of fire use has been found. At the 1.7-million-year-old Yuanmou Man site near Upper Nabang Village in Yuanmou County, Yunnan Province, large quantities of charcoal grains, ranging from sesame-seed to bean-size, have been found. The three layers of deposits are cumulatively three metres thick.

At the Xihoudu (Hsihotu) culture site, of 1.8 million years' antiquity, in Shanxi Province, charred bones similar to those found at the Peking Man site have been excavated. They appear in black, grey, or grey-green deposits, and the bulk of the assemblage of bones consists of mammalian ribs, deer skulls and horse teeth. Laboratory tests show that their colours are not a result of mineral presence. A report made by the fossil-dating specialist Li Xingguo of the Chinese Academy of Sciences reveals the results given in Table 9-1.

**Table 9-1.
Samples from the Xihoudu Site**

	Dark grey bones, presumably burnt	Unburnt yellowish bones
Weight of sample, grammes	15.0	20.0
Weight lost after being treated with flame, %	11.3	9.5
Strontium carbonate content, grammes	0.2	3.4
Carbon content, %	0.1	1.4

Note: Samples collected by Jia Lanpo and Wang Jian, researchers of the Chinese Academy of Sciences.

The figures show that the burnt bones lost more weight and contained less strontium carbonate and carbon than did the unburnt ones. This was due to organic matter in these bones that during burning first turned into carbon, large amounts of which were then transformed into carbon dioxide and disappeared.

This is an important discovery. It shows that as far as is known to us the earliest traces of the use of fire have been found in China. The Xihoudu data have pushed the date for the first use of fire by humans back more than a million years. The idea that the above evidence might have resulted from the natural occurrence of fire is not convincing because the burnt bones were found in association with other traces left at sites by early humans. Furthermore, combustion by natural causes does not take place easily.

10

Improvement in Methods of Excavation

Excavations at Zhoukoudian were now conducted on a large scale. There were some one or two hundred people at work in an area of two square kilometres all the time, and often they were digging at two or three sites simultaneously. Due to the massiveness of the scale, the number of sites, and differences in the deposits at these sites, there was no overall plan for the work in progress. Everything was decided on the spot by the leader in charge. It was a process of trial and error.

In the earliest days at the Peking Man site, from 1927 to 1931, the *in situ* locations of the finds were not neglected, but rules were not always strictly followed. Thus records were often too rough to be of help to the researcher. This was especially true of the mammalian fossils, which were lumped together regardless of where they were found in the layers of a deposit. The faulty approach led to varying conclusions about the climatic environment at Zhoukoudian in Peking Man's time, even though sporopollen analysis was done on all the fauna. We now know, of course, that if a sample, whether fauna or flora, is not representative, the conclusion will be irrelevant. Since Peking Man lived at the site for as long as 500 000 years, the fauna and flora could not have remained the same over such a long period of time because climatic changes were bound to occur. (This length of time was determined by recent archaeomagnetic, fission-track

and thermoluminescence dating, which reveals the age of the specimens obtained at the site to be 700 000 to 200 000 years B.P.

When Jia Lanpo began to work at Zhoukoudian in 1931, the heads of the Cenozoic Research Laboratory of the Geological Survey of China were Davidson Black, Honorary Director; Pierre Teilhard de Chardin, Adviser; and Yang Zhongjian, Deputy Director. They were the ones who decided on the plans. But it was Pei Wenzhong who implemented these plans and directed the fieldwork. Indeed, Pei Wenzhong retrieved many of the significant finds with his own hands.

Every year prior to the start of the fieldwork, the locality and extent of the digging were mapped out, and that was the 'plan' that guided the work. In Pei Wenzhong's book *Choukoutien Excavations*[1] he relates:

> I can remember that our technicians had no fixed place to work, just like the hired hands at the site, who dug at random. When a fossil was sighted, a technician, or someone else assigned by me, would try to free it. In the designated zone, workers were everywhere. They blasted hard rocks away or dug with a shovel when the ground allowed. The fossils thus uncovered were sometimes so desultorily [*sic*] handled that no one knew exactly where they were dug up. Worst of all, the workers avoided excavating areas that were hard to work,

[1] *Geological Memoirs*, Ser. B, No. 7, 1934.

Digging at the Pigeon Hall area of the Peking Man site in 1931. (*Photo by Pei Wenzhong*)

Bian Meinian (*right*) and Jia Lanpo at the entrance of the cave at Pigeon Hall. The cave is not a natural one, but was cut by the kiln workers. (*Photo by Pei Wenzhong, May 14, 1933*)

and later when softer places had been worked to great depths, these areas would stand out in proud eminence. The serial numbers marked on the specimens were completely invalidated because their *in situ* positions were unknown.

Reforms follow after imperfections are found. The fieldwork at Zhoukoudian underwent a revolution in the spring of 1932. The new method then adopted was considered quite precise at the time. It was called 'trenching', and it replaced random digging. Under this new method, once a section of ground was selected for exploration, a trench 1.5 metres wide and 5 metres deep, with four or five divisions each 3 metres long, was dug. With the stratigraphic information obtained from the exposed earth, excavation could then be conducted block by block, each 1 square metre in size.

Because some sections had chunks of hard rock that were larger than 1 square metre in size, the standard was readjusted to 3 metres in length and breadth and 5 metres in depth. When each block was excavated to this depth, a new trench would be dug. A technician and a skilled hired hand were in charge of the digging for each block, and several workers helped in sifting fossils from the earth and rocks that were taken from each specific block.

This practice proved invaluable to continued research. Though first used merely as an experiment on the east slope, the records were quite reliable for future reference. The *in situ* position of each specimen could be clearly identified. The method was im-

proved and elaborated upon in 1933 when the Upper Cave site was explored. The deposits at this site were free of big rocks, so that the size of the block could be reduced to 1 metre in length and breadth, and half a metre in depth. As the area of deposits in the cave was not large, trench-

The trench dug at the east slope. The temple in the woods was built during the Ming Dynasty. (*Photo by Bian Meinian, June 21, 1932*)

Layer 3 at the east slope consisted of nothing but huge lime rocks, indicating that the roof had collapsed while the layer was being formed. (*Top: By Bian Meinian, May 26, 1932. Bottom: By Bian Meinian, June 2, 1932*)

ing here was not needed. Four blocks were assigned to each technician, with one block to be dug first to expose the earth structure for information that could be utilized in working on the other blocks.

Then, flat-surface and cross-section sketch maps were drawn. Prior to excavation, a flat-surface sketch map of 1 : 50 in scale was made. Later, every half metre was

regarded as a separate surface, and a map of the same scale was made. Every two metres, cross-section maps of north-south as well as east-west direction were drawn, in which stratigraphic information was delineated. Drawings were made of significant finds on both the flat-surface and the cross-section maps.

Apart from the maps, 'record pictures'

Top: Workers clean the loose deposits at the east slope. (*Photo by Pei Wenzhong, April 12, 1932*)

Bottom: Digging at the east slope, seen from a distance. A trench was cut the day before the picture was taken. (*Photo by Pei Wenzhong, June 2, 1932*)

were taken three times a day from fixed angles to the south, east and west. These photographs recorded work-in-progress scenes for future reference. In addition, there were 'routine pictures' taken twice a week, also from fixed points on the ground and at fixed angles—east, north and west. These routine pictures covered the whole hill area instead of single sites, so that the gradual change at Dragon Bone Hill be-

cause of the excavations might be observed from the photographs.

Geologist Bian Meinian began working at Zhoukoudian at the same time as Jia Lanpo, in 1931. A graduate of Yanjing University, he was trained not only in geology but in biology as well, and his proficiency in both fields lent itself readily to the excavation at the site. An honest young scholar, he helped Jia Lanpo acquire much

Left to right: Pei Wenzhong, Ge Dingbang, Shou Zhenhuang and Bian Meinian at Zhoukoudian. (*Photo by Jia Lanpo, December 13, 1934*)

knowledge that served as a solid foundation for Jia's later work at the site, when he
was in full charge of the excavation.

From 1934 on, the focus of work turned
to the Peking Man site, leaving only a small
part of the work force to continue digging
at the lower-level deposits of the Upper
Cave. In the spring of the year, Pei Wenzhong, Bian Meinian and Jia Lanpo arrived in Zhoukoudian. Together with a
few technicians, they surveyed up and
down the site, taking measurements at its
middle part, which was selected as the
target area for the year. They prepared a
general plan for the area that was, according to the sketch map, approximately 50
metres long from east to west between the
lower level of the Upper Cave and the
'Pigeon Hall' and 25 metres wide from

south to north between two fissures. The
digging was to begin at the top and go to
the base of the deposits.

They cleared the ground of weeds, dirt,
rocks and tree branches until the deposits
could be seen, then levelled them for division into blocks and the making of a
flat-surface sketch map. By now Jia Lanpo
was experienced enough to work on his
own. He first determined the two middle lines, west-east and north-south. Using these lines, he marked the blocks, each
2 square metres in area and 1 metre in
depth. This was twice the size originally
conceived, due to the stony earth structure.
Then each block was given two serial symbols, A, B, C, D, E . . . representing its
west-east parallels and 1, 2, 3, 4, 5 . . . its
north-south meridian lines. A specimen

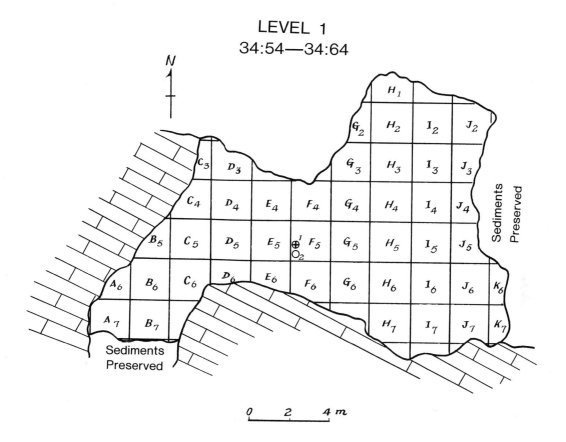

LEVEL 1
34:54—34:64

The flat-surface sketch map showing the grid for Level 1.

Digging at the roof of the middle part of the deposits at the Peking Man site. (*Photo by Jia Lanpo, May 29, 1934*)

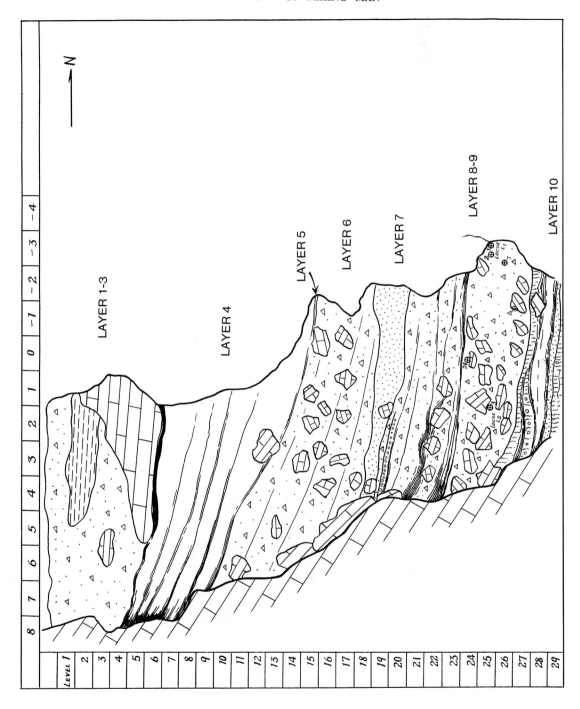

The vertical cross-section sketch map showing the levels for the grid section I–J.

Top: Digging at the lower part of Layers 1-2. (*Photo by Jia Lanpo, June 17, 1934*)
Bottom: A simple mechanical device had greatly facilitated the fieldwork. (*Photo by Jia Lanpo, 1933*)

would always bear a serial number, such as A1 or D5, indicating its *in situ* position.

Other reforms included the transportation of soil and rocks downhill. In the autumn of 1933, Pei Wenzhong coined the slogan: 'Mechanize the Digging'. Before that the soil and rocks that were removed were transported downhill in baskets with shoulder poles, for a distance of 400 metres or more each round trip. This was a waste of manpower and funds. In the spring of 1932, when the east slope was excavated, it had cost 400 yuan to transport the huge pile of shifted soil, an amount equivalent to the expenses of 1000 worker-days according to the prevailing wage rates.

In 1933, a simple device was introduced

which worked with an efficiency 34 times that of the basket and shoulder-pole method. It involved a few pulleys; two steel tube towers, one each at the end of the transport line; and a half- inch-thick cable. Gravity pulled the loaded baskets down, and their momentum pulled the empty

Fossils of small mammalian species such as bats and rodents occurred in quantity in the ash layer of Layer 4, and most were charred. (*Photo by Jia Lanpo, October 17, 1934*)

Work in progress at Layer 4, which consisted of soft deposits in bright colours. The trench walls were kept for drawing a cross-section sketch. (*Photo by Jia Lanpo, April 19, 1935*)

Preparing to dig at Level 15 (Layer 6). Each technician and his assistant were assigned a block. (*Photo by Jia Lanpo, September 30, 1935*)

basketfuls up. The rate was 180 basketfuls per hour, a phenomenal achievement in increased productivity.

*   *   *

Bian Meinian

Bian Meinian, a good friend of Jia Lanpo's, worked closely with him at Zhoukoudian. After Bian went to the United States they lost contact with each other until October 1982.

Bian's father was a banker, his mother the granddaughter of Li Hongzhang, Governor-General of Zhili and Commissioner for Northern Affairs. Bian did not behave like the 'pampered son' of a wealthy or influential family, but was a kind and honest person who was respected by his colleagues. People usually called him Mr Bian, but because he was tall, he was sometimes called 'big Bian'.

Although Bian had a drinking problem, he was conscientious and meticulous in his work. People often remarked on the hours he spent diligently digging, first with his back arched, then in a kneeling position. No job at Zhoukoudian was beneath his dignity, or escaped his sense of humour. Even now, some of the old people who used to work with him recall his gift for telling jokes and making his colleagues laugh.

11

Have We Dug at Our Ancestral Shrine?

Among the human fossils unearthed at the Upper Cave site, there were complete and fragmented skullcaps, upper and lower jawbones and skeletal pieces of seven or eight individuals of various ages and both sexes. Judging from the skullcaps and teeth, there were four adults, one adolescent and two children, one 5 years old and the other possibly newborn or a foetus because of the thinness of the skull fragment. Of the four adults, two were male and two female. Found at the burial ground were a man over 60 years old and two younger women.

The roofless entrance of the Upper Cave site. The roof was so badly eroded that it had to be cleared before digging could begin. (*Photo by Pei Wenzhong, 1930*)

These three individuals were represented by complete skulls, while the adolescent, whose sex could not be determined, was represented by only a skullcap. They were all retrieved from the lower chamber; the rest of the assemblage was found in the upper chamber.

The skull of the old man, perfectly preserved and complete with all teeth, was recovered from the lower chamber on November 9, 1933. When first sighted, the cap was positioned upward, slightly turning to the left. Behind the skull was a fragmented pelvis and a pair of thigh-bones. The right thighbone was broken at its two ends, the left one better preserved. There was also a fragmented shoulder blade nearby. Found in association with the bones were perforated marine shells and fox canines, and a piece of hematite, that had been placed on the remains. The soil in which the pelvis and thighbones were embedded appeared red, no doubt a result of hematite colouring. The occurrence of hematite, which is common in graves of the late paleolithic age in Europe as well as in some of the neolithic graves found in Gansu Province, China, is a sign

Trial digging at the Upper Cave site. Rabbit fossils occurred in quantity. (*Photo by Jia Lanpo, 1930*)

Fossil-bearing deposits were exposed after the entrance and part of the roof of the Upper Cave site were cleared for digging. (*Photo by Pei Wenzhong, May 20, 1933*)

Digging at the Upper Cave site in full swing. (*Photo by Pei Wenzhong, June 10, 1933*)

Top: Roof at the western part of the cave is exposed. (*Photo by Jia Lanpo, July 4, 1933*) *Bottom*: Digging at the southern part of the Upper Cave site. (*Photo by Jia Lanpo, July 17, 1933*)

that interment had taken place.

The human remains were so scattered that the grave must have been disturbed some time after burial. The remains of the old man were the least disturbed, yet only an upper part of his lower limb was found. Few of the bones (seven thighbones, two pelvises, two shinbones, and fragmented radius and kneecaps) were found in their normal position. Even where the position was in order, they were often not at the same level as the rest of the remains of a single individual. Some were found off their normal position by several metres.

Conjectures about the cause of the scattering have been many. Professor Franz Weidenreich speculated that the remains might have been disturbed by predatory animals, by subsequent humans, or by an earthquake.

Hyena remains abounded in the cave. These nocturnal animals have claws strong enough to dig into the ground to find the remains of animals, or human burials. Badger fossils were also abundant; their front claws and snouts are also good for digging. A badger will prey on rodents, rabbits and frogs, and it will feed on plant food and carrion too. Yet any beast that attempted to go into the lower chamber to get at the carrion would have to pass through the upper chamber which was the human habitat. At the middle of this upper chamber was a huge heap of ash that

Top: Digging at the western part of the Upper Cave site on November 9, 1933, when the tomb of an early human was unearthed.
Bottom: The skullcap of an old man was found at the tomb.

Opposite:
Top: Work in progress at the eastern part of the Upper Cave site. (*Photo by Jia Lanpo, June 9, 1933*)
Bottom: Deposits at the site are greyish earth with limestone rock fragments. The nearer to the southern wall, the more these rocks occurred. (*Photo by Jia Lanpo, June 13, 1933*)

would have barred the way. It is thus unlikely that such animals ever reached the lower chamber.

Weidenreich asserted that the owners of the three skulls and one skullcap were murdered, because these fossils had cavities, cracks, or perforations that resulted from hard blows by heavy objects when flesh and skin were still attached. Pei Wenzhong, however, disputed this in his book *A Study on Pre-Historic China.*[1] He stated: "By observing these materials, Weidenreich's hypothesis seems reasonable. But let us not forget the loose structure of the roof of the cave from which rocks would often fall. It is rather hard to tell the difference between injuries of the newly buried through the agency of man or from such natural causes."

We believe that of the two hypotheses,

[1] The Commercial Press Limited, Shanghai, 1948.

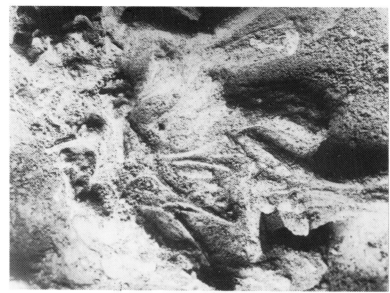

Top: The fossilized skeleton of a deer. (*Photo by Jia Lanpo, July 18, 1933*)
Bottom: Stalagmites seen in the eastern part of the Upper Cave site, where a big pile of ash deposits occurred, indicating that the place was once a habitat of early humans. (*Photo by Jia Lanpo, July 22, 1933*)

the first is more convincing. The deposits in the cave had only small rocks that appeared to be more numerous towards the southern side. Rocks were especially few and small in the lower chamber where the burials took place. The cavity on the front lower left side of the skull of the old man was 15.0 by 12.4 millimetres and 3.0 millimetres deep, with cracks clearly appearing inside the cavity but not so obvious on the periphery. A cavity of such a size is unlikely to have been caused by a falling rock, unless it was a big rock that could damage the hard skull.

Weidenreich concluded that the fossils represented seven individuals—one old man, one younger man, two younger women, one adolescent whose sex could not be identified and two infants. Actually there were more. Individual human teeth

Top: The work face was extending to the western section of the site. (*Photo by Pei Wenzhong, October 15, 1933*)
Bottom: Three perforated teeth were unearthed here. (*Photo by Jia Lanpo, October 25, 1933*)

had also been found in the upper part of the cave deposits. A lower jawbone, identified as belonging to the individual represented by the No. 102 female skull, was actually of a different person, as their ages prove. Also the *Daily Journal*, a sort of logbook kept at the time, has no entry to indicate that the mandible was found in association with the skull, as there were in the cases of the Nos 101 and 103 skulls and mandibles.

Weidenreich, after more elaborate study on the three complete skulls, arrived at the conclusion that each possesses different racial characteristics, one resembling the primitive Mongolian type, one the Melanesian type and one the Eskimo type. How is it that remains of such a heterogeneous group were found at one site? The injuries in these skulls led Weidenreich to conclude that heterogeneity might have been the result of a tribal war in which the three killed were buried together. In an article published in 1962, the historian Shang Yue accepted, in the main, Weidenreich's view. He held that "disputes over fish or animal prey or a territory, or intrusion of a hunting band, might all have been possible causes of conflict among these groups." And, "since the possibility of group conflict existed, the injuries in the three skulls are evidently a result of external group conflict, not internal causes within a commune."

An earlier study made by the anthropologist Wu Xinzhi on the reconstructed skulls resulted in a slightly different view. In a paper entitled 'Racial Identity of Upper Cave Man' (1960), he asserted that "in spite of the complexity of the characteristics of the three skulls, they do share one thing in common, namely, they all show in varying degrees distinct Mongolian morphological features. In terms of measurements, they all share the primitive features of many *Homo sapiens* remains found in the world and in China. This apart, their other features in general bear a close resemblance to the modern Mongoloids in various geographical regions (especially the Chinese, Eskimo and natives of the Americas). Thus we have every reason to believe that Upper Cave Man is ethnically a primitive Mongoloid. Probably the three branches of Mongoloids mentioned above evolved from Upper Cave Man or some earlier human with similar physical features."

Though the ethnic identity of the Upper Cave Man has since been better clarified, other problems such as the cause of his death and details of his burial remain obscure and will be so forever, as there are no more fossil-bearing deposits in the cave to provide further evidence.

Many assertions are mere conjectures. On the disorderly condition of the human

Lower down, the fossilized corpse of an old man was unearthed. (*November 5, 1933*)

Top: The skullcap of a female was unearthed. It was given the serial number Pa. 102. (*Photo by Jia Lanpo, November 3, 1933*)

Bottom: The burial ground of Upper Cave Man. (*Photo by Jia Lanpo, November 3, 1933*)

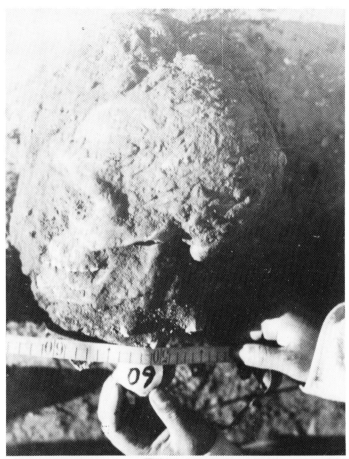

The complete skullcap (*top*) and part of the lower limbs (*bottom*) of a male were unearthed. (*Photos by Jia Lanpo, November 9, 1933*)

A perforated tooth was retrieved soon after the work started on November 15, 1933. (*Photo by Pei Wenzhong*)

skeletons in the cave, Jia Lanpo, in his book *Early Man in China*,[1] says: "A second burial seems more creditable." The truth is, the few simple statements recorded in the *Daily Journal* at the time of excavation were not of much help to later researchers. No one at the site then anticipated the discovery of a burial ground. They were glad to have seen the fossils and paid due attention in digging, but not to the same degree as at the Peking Man site.

As Jia Lanpo recalled, it was a technician by the name of Tang Liang who dug out the first skull. He put it in a wicker basket with soil at the bottom. It was delivered to the headquarters by Bian Meinian and Jia Lanpo who identified the reddish soil as containing hematite. Only at that point did it occur to the Director, Pei Wenzhong, that there might be a burial ground. He at once hurried to the site to organize the work anew, but a considerable part of the deposits had already been disturbed.

The 860 cubic metres of deposits to a depth of 20 metres yielded only 25 identifiable stone artifacts and some pebbles and quartz that bore no signs of having been worked upon, even though they were materials for tool-making. Among the artifacts

were a flint concave side-scraper, flint end-scrapers, sandstone pebble implements, quartz side-scrapers, quartz nuclei or small choppers, and a few 'bipolar flakes'. The bone implements were equally scanty. Apart from one bone needle, one polished red deer antler, and one polished sika deer mandible, there were only a few limb bones that showed signs of having been struck by a human being. The workmanship on these tools, stone or bone, was very primitive, and only the bone needle and the polished antler may represent the time of the Upper Cave Man. To one not familiar with ancient artifacts, it is impossible to distinguish them from Peking Man tools. But some of them show much more primitive features.

Two explanations have been offered by Pei Wenzhong on how these artifacts were deposited at this site. One is that the Upper Cave dwellers, whose habitat lay directly over that of Peking Man and who, in entering or leaving their own cave home, had to pass the ground where Peking Man had lived, must have picked up artifacts left by their precursor. Another is that because quartz is good for making bipolar flakes, both Peking Man and Upper Cave Man produced such tools with that material. But Shang Yue, in the paper quoted above,

---

[1] Foreign Languages Press, Beijing, 1980, p. 51.

The dig was reaching the lower recess of the site. (*Photos by Jia Lanpo, November 28* (*top*), *December 9* (*bottom*), *1933*)

struck an entirely different note. "Having been defeated in the conflict," he wrote, "the Upper Cave dwellers took along their better tools and abandoned the sick and wounded and expecting mothers in their hurried escape. Then the many valuable burial objects found in the lower chamber were perhaps left untouched by both groups because of a taboo."

Views also varied on the nature of the polished red deer antler. At first, the piece was taken to be a common antler remnant. Then it was, in the laboratory, identified as an implement. Bearing the serial number UC:33:111:J6, it was recorded in the *Daily Journal* as having been found on November 19, 1933, at a place near the east limestone wall of the lower chamber, close to the position of the No. 101 skull of the old man.

What was it? A red deer antler is naturally four-tined. In this specimen, the up-

Top: Deposits at the lower chamber of the site coalesced with the deposits of the Peking Man site. (*Photo by Jia Lanpo, December 12, 1933*)
Bottom: Animal skeletons jumbled up in the lower chamber of the Upper Cave site. (*Photo by Jia Lanpo, May 20, 1934*)

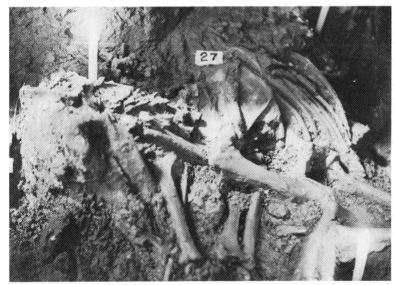

per two tines were missing, clearly cut off by some human, leaving polished surfaces. One of the lower tines had only a stump left, and on its surface were fine grooves indicating its being not only polished but scraped by a sharp blade as well.

Pei Wenzhong, who first studied it, offered no explanation for its usage. But he did say: "Many such objects have occurred at late paleolithic cave sites in Europe and have been referred to as *batons de commandement*." The historian Jian Bozan, in his *An Outline of Chinese History* (vol. 1), says: "I hold this sika antler to be a *baton de commandement* . . . I think it is perhaps an object left by an earlier man but made use of by the creators of the Upper Cave culture."

In the 1950s, when Jia Lanpo was writing the book *Upper Cave Man*,[1] he placed a replica of the specimen on his desk for observation, and his impression was that it was an abandoned spearhead. The stump could have been fastened to a wooden shaft to make the hard and stubborn antler a formidable weapon. Jia Lanpo, in fact, demonstrated this with the model.

In any case, the lower chamber of the cave was a burial ground, and Upper Cave Man may be regarded as the ancestor of the Mongoloid. In this sense, the Chinese scientists may have done something that Shakespeare forbade through the inscription on his gravestone: "Blest be the man that speares these stones,/And curst be he that moves my bones."

---

[1] Published by the Longmen United Press in 1951.

12

Why the Ornament?

A collection of perforated animal teeth, marine shells, stone beads, small pebbles, fish bones, and grooved bone tubes was found at the site. These were no doubt ornaments. Some were found in the burial chamber, and so it is certain that they were objects buried with the dead.

The most numerous among this assemblage were animal teeth—120 all told. Holes had been pierced in them with sharp tools from two sides of the root. Some of these holes were smoothed and enlarged, evidently through long wear. The holes in the three marine shells were apparently made by grinding their thin parts against a rock. As a result, the greater part of the cuspidate edge was missing.

The perforated stone beads were the smallest and most refined of the objects, with the longest diameter being only 6.5 millimetres. They are of white limestone. The process by which they were manufactured must have been first to hammer a piece of stone carefully into a rectangular or angular flat piece, and then to pierce the two faces from opposite directions until a hole was completed through the object. Only one small perforated oval pebble was found. It is of greenish igneous rock, with a length of 39.6 millimetres. It was smoothed on one side by hand and on the other by natural forces. The hole was pierced from two sides, with a precision possible only after human intelligence had reached a relatively high level.

A particularly rare find was a very small hole on the supraorbital bone of a fish of the *Ctenopharyngodon* species. It could only have been made by a rather sophisticated tool. There were three abdominal vertebrae of large fish, probably carp, and six caudal vertebrae of medium-sized fish. Though not perforated, their transverse process and spines had been cut off to be made into ornaments.

The grooved tube bones were four in number, ranging from 20 to 38 millimetres in length with a width of 14 millimetres. The very large medullary cavity in these bones and the absence of sponge tissue in the cavity may be taken as proof that they were the leg bones of birds. Each had become smoothed through long use. One to three furrows were carved transversely on the surface of each of these bones for the purpose of fastening.

There are other paleolithic sites in China of both earlier and later age than that of the Upper Cave site that have yielded ornaments. But none have matched the Upper Cave in the number and variety of objects found. At the Shiyu site of Shuoxian County, Shanxi Province (28 000 years in antiquity), only one such object was found. It was made of graphite, flat and oval in shape, rubbed smooth, and pierced at the centre. Also the Shuidonggou site in Lingwu County, Ningxia Hui Autonomous Region, has produced flakes of perforated ostrich egg shells. Neolithic sites in China

Top and *bottom*: Ornaments of Upper Cave Man.

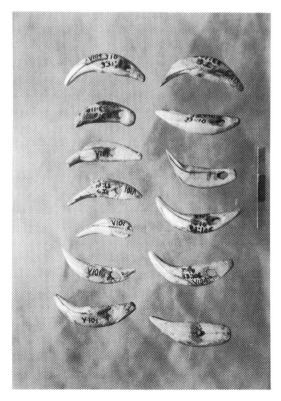

have, of course, yielded more refined ornaments in greater numbers.

Such paleolithic objects have also been found in great numbers at many sites in Europe. Perforated animal teeth have been found at sites of both the Aurignacian and the Magdalenian ages. These rank in time with the Shiyu site and the Upper Cave site, respectively. Especially numerous were ornaments of the Magdalenian age. The following list partially indicates such finds:

A string of perforated and carved lion and bear teeth, in Sorde, southwestern France.

Perforated ivory flakes and cave bear teeth, in graves of the Aurignacian age, Paviland, Wales, Britain.

Perforated deer teeth, at mesolithic sites in Ofnet in the Danube valley, southern France. Similar objects have been found at Mas d'Azil in the Pyrenées region of France.

Perforated sea shells, in Combe Capelle, France. The site also yielded stone artifacts of fine workmanship of the Aurignacian period. Found in association with an undisturbed skeleton was a neck ornament made of perforated clam shells. A similar neck ornament made from Mediterranean shells has been found together with stone artifacts of the Magdalenian period in Laugerie Basse, France.

Neck ornaments, mostly made of periwinkle shells, in great number at the Cro-Magnon cave site in France.

Perforated shells and deer teeth, found

around a human skull in a cave site in Baousso da Torre, Spain. The deer teeth and 167 shells composed a necklace.

Incomplete perforated small white pebbles, at a site in Font Robert, France, of the Aurignacian-Solutrean transitional period. Ornaments of this kind became more common in the Solutrean and Magdalenian ages. Perforated limestone pebbles were found at sites in Moravia, Czechoslovakia, also.

Ornaments made of fish spinal columns, found at many sites (although perforated supraorbital bones of fish remain unreported).

At the Barma Grande cave site in Italy, human remains of six individuals were found, all in association with burial objects, including shells, animal teeth and fish spinal columns. Bone pendants made of big bird bones with transverse furrows for ornament purposes were common in the late paleolithic era, represented by the Magdalenian age. They have been found at sites such as Laugerie Basse and La Grotte Espelugue.

It is well known that ornaments were more popular among primitive tribal people than among more advanced groups. Eskimos have had to cover their bodies because of the freezing weather, but some tribal peoples have worn nothing except ornaments. Such ornaments may be divided into two kinds. One type is permanent: pattern scars on the skin, tattoos, and rings worn in earlobes, nostrils and lips. The other is not fixed: hair-dos, headgear, necklaces and waist and limb ornaments.

Some of the ornaments unearthed at the Upper Cave site were dyed red. The dye was especially obvious around the holes that had been drilled in them. Among the 120 perforated teeth, 25 were distinctly dyed red, and some of the rest also had traces of red colour, although faded. The perforated beads and small pebbles had all been dyed; the red colour was preserved in the holes of the latter. One can surmise that these early humans dyed their ligatures of animal hide, deer tendon, or fibre red, as is done at the present time by the Aborigines in Australia. The Aborigines coat their headbands of animal hide, kangaroo tendon, or plant fibre with red or white mud.

What is the psychology behind the wearing of ornaments? According to earlier assertions, the wristlet was derived from the handcuffs of slave societies, and earrings have been handed down from feudal societies in which women wore them so that they would not be able to look sideways. Such conjectures are baseless. The advent of wristlets and earrings occurred much earlier in the primitive age.

It is claimed that personal adornment is an indication of a people's love of beauty. This may be so, but aesthetic standards differ from nation to nation and even from tribe to tribe. In our time, ornaments are valued most if they are made of scarce, shiny and expensive materials. They probably have an entirely different meaning today from that which they had in the primitive age. It has been shown that in our own time many tribal people use ornaments chiefly as a means of attracting the opposite sex. This is tenable, for in many such tribes, women are outnumbered by men. To win himself a spouse, a man has to employ many devices and stratagems. When an Australian Aborigine was asked why he wore ornaments, his answer was straightforward: "To attract the attention of women."

With Upper Cave Man, personal adornment was, we conjecture, chiefly a demonstration of bravery and wisdom, although sex appeal may also have played a part. A tooth may have been saved each time a beast was killed and later made into an ornament to show the prowess of the hunter. Table 12-1 is an incomplete tally of the perforated teeth found at the Upper Cave site. The kinds of teeth are also significant, as shown in Table 12-2.

Table 12-1
Perforated Teeth Found
at the Upper Cave Site

Animal	Number of Teeth	Percentage
Badger	60	50.8
Wolf	37	31.4
Deer	17	14.4
Weasel	2	1.7
Tiger	1	0.85
Wild Cat	1	0.85

Note: Two canines of an unidentified carnivorous animal in this assemblage were not counted.

Table 12-2
Kinds of Teeth Found
at the Upper Cave Site

Kinds of Teeth	Number	Percentage
Incisors, tiger	1	0.85
Incisors, deer	3	2.56
Upper canines	38	32.20
Lower canines	76	64.40

Why were canines so favoured as material for ornaments? Two reasons may be suggested. One is that canines are more attractive, and they have the longest roots and a large cavity, which made them easy to pierce from both sides. Another more significant reason is that canines are the least numerous of the teeth and, for a carnivorous animal, the sharpest. A badger, for instance, has thirty-four teeth, but only four canines. A small number would be easier to remember, and the sharpness of the canines might symbolize bravery. The perforated pebbles and stones were perhaps symbols of wisdom.

What accounts for the presence of marine shells at the site? It was once believed that the nearest distance from Zhoukou-dian to a seashore was 165 kilometres. Geological evidence, however, shows that the distance at that time may not have been as great as this. The hematite that was also found was thought to have occurred in Xuanhua to the north of Beijing. The source has since been found to have been in the glacial boulder clay in the nearby foothills of the Taiping Mountains.

A fresh-water shell, large in size and fragmented, was found at the site. It has a round hole in the middle, but the hole does not look like one that was intentionally pierced—it may have been made accidentally during excavation. This shell was previously believed to have come from south of the Huanghe (Yellow River). The latest archaeological evidence, however, shows that two kinds of clam (*Lamprotula* and *Unio*), dating back 3600 years, once lived in the sand gravel bed of a reservoir on the bank of the Sanggan River in Yangyuan County, Hebei Province.

The finding of fish-bone ornaments indirectly reveals several interesting points: (1) Upper Cave Man not only gathered and hunted, but fished as well. This was a tremendous advance in the economic life of early human beings. (2) These fish bones belong to a species living today in North China. The largest of these Upper Cave Man artifacts, the perforated supraorbital bone, indicates that the size of the fish could be 80 centimetres. There must have been a big river or lake nearby at that time, one in which such a large fish might survive. (3) Though no fishing gear has been found at the site, a fish of such size had to have been caught by some implement. Since the use of a hook cannot have developed that early, spearfishing seems likely. Fishing spears are commonly found at European sites of the Magdalenian age. Most of their points were made of bone or antler.

13

The Earliest Inhabitants at Zhoukoudian

Locality 13 in the Zhoukoudian fossil-bearing sites is of greater antiquity than Locality 1, where the Peking Man remains were found. At the latter site, the tenth layer yielded a Peking Man lower mandible dating back 462 000 ± 45 000 years, as fission-track testing has revealed. But Locality 13 is even older than this. Standing on the south slope of a limestone foothill, Locality 13 is approximately 1 kilometre south of the Peking Man site.

It is a fissure deposit site. The reddish clay deposits are 15 metres long, 6 metres wide, and 5 metres high and stand like a wall because the limestone that once surrounded them has been removed by kiln workers.

Digging at this site began on November 17, 1933. As a trial operation, only one technician worked at the site. But four days later, several labourers were assigned to help clear the ground. The quantity of the fossils found here gave significance to the site, and the serial number 'Locality 13' was assigned to it.

On December 19, work at the site was suspended. It was resumed on April 24, 1934, and terminated on July 1. Thus the site was excavated for 102 workdays before all attention turned to Locality 1. During this time 400 cubic metres of deposits were sifted and 161 boxes of fossils recovered.

Teilhard de Chardin and Pei Wenzhong did the research on the finds at Locality 13, and the results were published under the title 'The Fossil Mammals from Locality 13 of Choukoutien'.[1] The main points of this report were as follows:

The deposits at this site may be divided into two layers. The upper layer is four metres thick, composed of a reddish clayey granular material. Huge limestone rocks are present in the southeastern section. Probably due to weathering, the surface soil has turned dark. In the lower layer, the deposits contain an increasing number of limestone rock fragments as one goes deeper, and lime has leached into the soil. But further down towards the base, rock fragments are predominant, occasionally mixed with large stalagmites.

The mammalian fossils found at the site included those of hedgehog (*Erinaceus olgai*), transformed wolf (*Canis variabilis*), Chinese raccoon dog (*Nyctereutes sinensis*), jackal (*Cuon alpinus*), brown bear (*Ursus* cf. *arctos*), badger (*Meles* cf. *leucurus*), sable (*Martes* sp.), alpine polecat (*Mustela* cf. *altaica*), short-snouted polecat (*Mustela constricta*), Chinese hyena (*Hyaena sinensis*), last sabre-toothed tiger (*Epimachirodus ultima*), leopard (*Panthera* cf. *pardus*), pika (*Ochotona* cf. *daurica*), bobak marmot (*Marmota bobak*), mole-rat (*Myospalax epitingi*), porcupine (*Hystrix lagrelii*), Merck's rhinoceros (*Dicerorhinus kirchbergensis* or *Rhinoceros mercki*), woolly rhinoceros (*Coelodonta antiquitatis*), Sanmen one-toed

---

[1] *Paleontologia Sinica*, New Ser. C, No. 11, 1941.

horse (*Equus sanmeniensis*), Lydekker's boar (*Sus* cf. *lydekkeri*), Pleistocene muntjak (*Hydropotes inermis pleistocenica*), Gray's Japanese deer (*Cervus nippon grayi*), flat-antlered giant deer (*Megaloceros flabellatus*), Teilhard's buffalo (*Bubalus* cf. *teilhardi*), and robust macaque (*Macacus robustus*)—thirty-seven species altogether.

The above fauna indicate proportionally greater ratios of extinct genera (11.11 per cent) and extinct species (66.64 per cent)

than the fauna at Locality 1 of Zhoukoudian. This, in turn, testifies to an earlier dating for Locality 13, which ranks in time with the Kehe site in Ruicheng County, Shanxi Province. The Kehe site dates back to the Günz-Mindel interglacial period. Judging by the ecology of such fauna, this must have been an area of grassland and forests with a climate similar to our own, or somewhat colder.

Though the site has yielded no human remains, it has given other evidence of human activities. A small chopper made from a worn flint pebble shows that it was worked on both sides by hammering. A small quantity of worked quartz fragments and some ash and charred bones were also found. The paper by Teilhard and Pei did not attempt to elaborate on the identity of those who made these early artifacts, but just stated that they might have been *Homo* (*Sinanthropus?*). They also said that the artifacts found in Locality 13 are "so far the earliest traces of human activities known in China."

In 1958, we dug at three places at the Peking Man site. The first was the East Cavity at the base of the east slope. This area is part of the fossil-bearing deposits lying on the northeast corner and is conjectured to have been the cave en-

Top and *bottom*: Working Locality 13. (*Photo by Jia Lanpo, November 20, 1933*)

Digging at Locality 13. Pei Wenzhong is in the lower right corner, and Bian Meinian in light-coloured garb in the centre. (*Photo by Jia Lanpo, November 20, 1933*)

trance for Peking Man. Our purpose was twofold. One was to locate the passage through which Peking Man went in and out of the cave; the other was to find more fossils, artifacts, and traces of human activity that would help us to reconstruct Peking Man's life in this area near the cave entrance.

The second place we dug at was at the middle section of the cave deposits. The purpose was to penetrate all the way to the basal part so as to gain a better understanding of all the stratifications.

The third place was in the western section of the cave roof at Pigeon Hall. The purpose was to recover more Peking Man remains and artifacts, which, as already proved, abounded in the deposits extending westward or downward from here.

Work in the East Cavity, however, had to be suspended because of frequent landslides. And excavation in the middle part of the cave was suspended on August 19, thirteen days after it had begun, because a layer of pebbles was mistaken for the base of the deposits. Now all hands turned to the area west of Pigeon Hall. The first phase was started on August 8, from the top of the deposits, and ended on September 30 when the ninth layer was reached. The work was a joint effort by the Academy of Sciences and the Archaeological Section of the Department of History at Beijing University. The second phase began

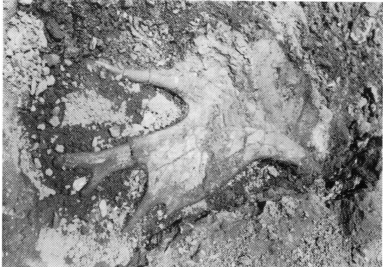

Top: Remains of a flat-antlered giant deer at Layer 13. (*Photo by Jia Lanpo, June 7, 1934*) *Bottom*: When the bottom of Locality 13 was reached, thick stalagmites could be seen. (*Photo by Jia Lanpo, June 1936*)

1951, and 1958. It is worth noting that these three lowest layers were unproductive—ash was absent and fossils scant. The twelfth layer was about two metres deep, of red coarse sandy structure. The fossils found here were whitish, fragmented, few in number and thoroughly water-worn. Some of the teeth were so water-worn that they were as thin as a fingernail.

The coarse sand sediment at this depth in the site is much like that at Locality 12 on the south slope of Dragon Bone Hill, a site that dates back to lower Pleistocene times. The fossils here, however, were more water-worn than those at Locality 12, and even a broad classification of their species was difficult

on October 2 and ended on November 28, when the digging of the tenth layer was completed. The number of workdays totalled 85, and 1800 cubic metres of earth were removed.

The more-than-40-metre-deep deposits at the Peking Man site had been demarcated into thirteen layers prior to 1958, with the first ten layers delineated by Teilhard and Yang Zhongjian, while the other three were a result of further digging in 1949,

to determine. The eleventh layer was composed of breccia, approximately two metres deep. The thirteenth layer, composed of sandy clay, had the same depth. It provided even fewer fossil remains, but a thick layer of hyena excretion was found on top of it. The remains of flat-antlered giant deer and *Myospalax epitingi*, which are representative species of the Locality 13 fauna, led Jia Lanpo to say, in his paper on the 1958 excavation at Zhoukoudian: "The site should be considered as ranking in time with the Middle Pleistocene base of Locality 13, lying about one kilometre to the south."[1]

A flint-flake implement was found in the thirteenth layer. It had a thick coating of white stone rust. Judging from the radiating cracks and concentric waves on its bullar face, this flake was hammered into a triangular shape from a corner of a big chunk. One side remained thick but polished and probably served as a handle.

The scanty remains at the site indicate that human occupancy was brief. But strong evidence shows that hyenas moved in soon after the departure of the humans. Two metres above the flint-flake artifact was a 40-centimetre thick pile of hyena excretion. This is a species that defecates in a fixed place.

At the western end of the Pigeon Hall site was a huge chunk of limestone beneath the third layer. It was 5 metres thick at its widest part and extended 12 metres to the east from the western end of the site. It was not directly attached to the south and north walls, but its position was astride them, which suggests that it had once been part of a cave roof that had collapsed. The deposits on its top, the third layer, were no doubt formed after the collapse when the cave was in the open. Peking Man had not gone away. The deposits yielded human remains, artifacts, and a great variety of animal bone fossils. Although most of the cave was in the open after the collapse, the remaining part could still have served as eaves for sheltering human occupants.

Worth special note was the ash overlaying the huge chunk of limestone mentioned above. The ash at one point was heaped up to one metre in height. A large number of burnt bone fragments and stones were found in it. This shows, on the one hand, that the rock had once been the floor of a human habitat and, on the other, that the occupant could control fire in that early age.

---

[1] *Paleontologia Sinica*, Vol. 1, No. 1, 1959.

14

The Expansion of Peking Man's Living Quarters

The latest dating methods show that the Peking Man cave was the home of early humans for 500 000 years. From Layer 13, the early humans may have moved to Locality 13, as the mammalian fossils there prove the two sites to be of the same age.

About 300 000 years ago, or later, the time of Layer 3, Peking Man's living quarters were on top of the limestone chunk that had fallen from the roof of the cave. Meanwhile, probably because of an increasing number of people in the tribe, Locality 15 was added to their living areas. This site was discovered in 1932 when an effort was made to determine the boundaries of the Peking Man site. Deep trenches were dug at that time on top of Dragon Bone Hill to the south of the Upper Cave site, and rocks, weeds and lime wastes were cleared away.

The area had been a lime quarry. Thus the deposits at Locality 15 and Locality 4 were all exposed. The latter was obviously a north-south fissure, but the identity of Locality 15 was not so clear. There is no way for us to tell whether it was a cave with a roof. The local old-timers could offer little help. They could not even tell us when the lime quarry was in use. Probably it was because of the presence of too much breccia and clay that the quarry was abandoned. Fossil-bearing deposits in a cave or fissure always add to the cost of quarrying, for explosives then have to be used and the work slows down. In fact, before the

scientific excavation, all quarries in the area had gone out of business. Market conditions may have been one factor, but the cave deposits were certainly another.

The exposed part of Locality 15 was quite small at first, and only after the discovery of some of the fossils was the area explored further. It was costly to clear away the quarry wastes in terms of labour and expenditure, but it proved worthwhile because over this hillock no fewer than nine sites of scientific value were brought to light.

The first few bone fossils sighted at the site failed to attract much attention because in the Zhoukoudian limestone area such objects were commonplace. But the international recognition given to the stone artifacts and ash remains unearthed at Locality 1 (the Peking Man site) helped put Locality 15 in a new light.

After that, the team leader Pei Wen-zhong frequently took Bian Meinian and Jia Lanpo to scout the area. It was on one of these reconnaissance trips that they came across a black substance at Locality 15 similar to that found at the Peking Man site. Vein quartz flakes were also sighted. On the strength of such evidence, a plan for the exploration of Locality 15 was initiated.

Observation over the years has led us to believe that the giant cave that Dragon Bone Hill once housed may never be thoroughly known. At present, we have no evidence to resolve the question of whether the two sites, Locality 1 and Locality 15, were connected. We only know that Locality 15 was probably related to Locality 4 at the base, although their upper parts are now separated and blocked by a limestone wall.

Locality 4 has a 10-by-20-metre room that was found in 1967 by some children who crawled inside through a gap between a big boulder and a rock wall. The tunnel between the gap and the room is 10 metres long and 3 metres wide. This is the only known cave in the whole area without deposits of human artifacts and with a roof well preserved. When we learned of the youngsters' adventure, we followed their steps and sighted fossil-bearing deposits occupying one quarter of the room space along the east wall. Later this site was referred to as the New Cave.

Though the possibility of a passage between Localities 1 and 15 cannot

Top: Locality 3. Bian Meinian standing on top. (*Photo by Jia Lanpo, June 3, 1933*)
Bottom: Fossil remains of a tiger at Locality 3. (*Photo by Jia Lanpo, June 20, 1933*)

yet be determined, there is sufficient ground to say that the deposits above Layer 3 at Locality 1 and the visible part of the deposits at Locality 15 are of the same period. The fossiliferous breccia of Layer 3, Locality 1, is reddish in colour, and the limestone fragments are distinctly angular. The huge 3-metre-thick limestone chunk on the floor indicates frequent collapses of the cave roof. The first two layers at the site are composed of the same breccia struc-

ture, but are yellowish, and the fragments have been weathered to such a degree that their angles are no longer clear.

The deposits in the lower part of Locality 15 are structurally the same as those of Layer 3, Locality 1. Since the digging has not yet reached the bottom, the thickness of the deposits remains unknown. The upper part of the deposits possesses the same characteristics as Layer 1, Locality 1.

The deposits above Layer 3, Locality 1,

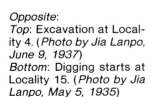

Digging further down at Locality 15. (*Photos by Jia Lanpo, May 31* (*top*), *October 4* (*bottom*), *1935*)

Opposite:
Top: Excavation at Locality 4. (*Photo by Jia Lanpo, June 9, 1937*)
Bottom: Digging starts at Locality 15. (*Photo by Jia Lanpo, May 5, 1935*)

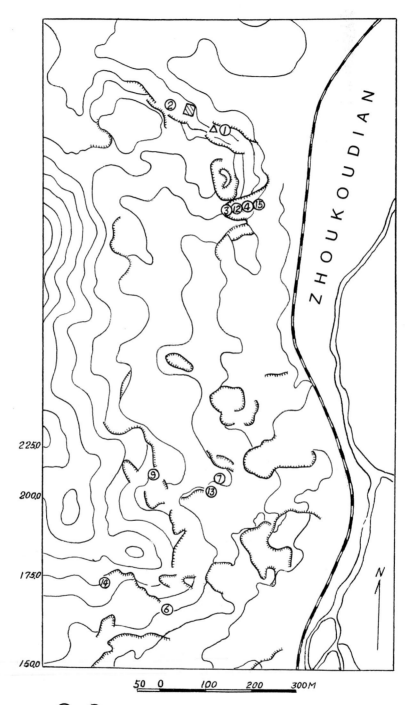

①—⑮   Fossiliferous Localities

△   Upper Cave Site

Map of the Zhoukoudian area (with the indications of the main fossiliferous locations)

Top: Huge rocks abound at the lower part of Locality 15, and its deposits are similar to those of Layer 3 of the Peking Man site. (*Photo by Jia Lanpo, April 18, 1937*)

Bottom: The last picture taken at Locality 15 on the eve of the war. (*Photo by Jia Lanpo, 9 a.m., June 21, 1937*)

have yielded fossils of middle Pleistocene mammals such as thick-jawed deer (*Megaloceros pachyosteus*), and red deer (*Cervus elaphus*)—that often appear in late Pleistocene deposits. The two mammalian species have been found in the lower part of the deposits at Locality 15, too, giving proof of the contemporaneity of the two sites.

Locality 15 was found in 1932, but excavation did not take place there until three years later. Jia Lanpo headed a group of labourers who arrived at Zhoukoudian on April 2, 1935, and began working the following day at the top-level deposits of Locality 1. As excavations at Locality 15 were included in their plan of operation, the number of workers totalled as many as 117. Work at Locality 15 started on May 3. Fifty square metres of the deposit surface were cleared for digging, which began on May 7. On that very day, a large number of quartz fragments and flakes were unearthed. Of particular interest were two chert implements uncovered on May 13. One showed clear signs of secondary working and was very small. The Peking Man site had seldom yielded artifacts with such characteristics.

Excavation at both sites was then conducted using the new technique of trenching. The target ground was marked into squares with limewash, and a 1:100 sketch map was made. The next step was to dig a trench 1 metre deep, after which a cross-section sketch was made. Every block was 4 square metres in area. Two workers, one skilled and the other unskilled, were assigned to do the digging of each block, with more men assisting in the removal of the soil. For a time, the total number of workers reached 130.

The two sites yielded a profusion of fossils. On June 9, Locality 15 alone yielded more than 400 stone implements and flakes, predominantly of vein quartz. The first batch of specimens was boxed into eighteen crates and shipped to Beijing by train on June 10. That day also saw the recovery of an artifact made of vein quartz, somewhat like one found at the Peking Man site.

The first animal fossil was unearthed on June 22 at Locality 15—a thick-jawed deer antler. As this species has always been taken as representative of Middle Pleistocene fauna, the deposits were determined to be of the same dating as those of the upper part of Locality 1. Another significant find was a thick layer of ash underneath the whitish upper breccia stratum. Burnt rodent bones were embedded in this ash layer. This find tallied with the conditions at Locality 1 too.

Taking stock, the 114 days' working at Locality 15 resulted in excavating 882 cubic metres of breccia and 130 boxes of specimens. The mammalian fossils that came to light were mostly fragmented, and some had been made into implements, but they were better preserved than those found at the Peking Man site.

The fieldwork at Zhoukoudian was carried on up to the end of 1936 and continued during the first half of 1937. Excavation at Locality 15 started on January 1 and ended on April 2.

Here is a list of the stone artifacts found at Locality 15: a polyhedral nucleus of chert, triangular flakes of chert, stone hammers, scrapers made from quartz pebbles, small scraping blades of quartz, small bifaces made from quartz flakes, pointed side-scrapers of quartz, bipolar flakes of quartz, burins of quartz or chert, microliths of vein quartz or quartz crystal, and large choppers or chopping tools made of igneous rock flakes. The last were of much better workmanship than similar tools found at the Peking Man site. One of the platform ends was trimmed into a convenient heel at its thick edge, and the opposite end was very sharp with traces of its having been used, but no sign of its having been worked upon.

It is not difficult to recognize the striking similarities between the above assemblage and the stone artifacts found in the top stratum at Locality 1. Both consist mostly of microliths and both share almost the same raw materials. The only difference is that the Locality 15 group has fewer artifacts of sandstone and more of chert. Indeed, the two assemblages are so much alike that no one can identify the site from which they were retrieved when they are put side by side. The fauna and stone artifacts at Locality 15 were so well represented by the specimens recovered in the 1930s that excavations undertaken in the early 1950s by students of two seminar courses on the excavation and restoration of vertebrate fossils recovered nothing new in terms of types.

The similarities of the finds from the two sites indicate that Peking Man's shelter area had been extended from Locality 1 to Locality 15, and possibly to Locality 4 (including the New Cave) as well. This last site is situated only a few paces west of Locality 15. It had been excavated by a small number of workers for 140 days in 1935, and great quantities of mammalian fossils were then recovered. Thus the site was designated as such in spite of the lack of traces of human activity. The New Cave site was explored again in 1972 and also in 1973. Again it yielded mammalian fossils in profusion. Finally some stone artifacts, ash, and one human tooth were found at this site.

We believe it is quite possible that Localities 15 and 4 were once connected and that the New Cave was an integral part of Locality 4. These three sites were, in fact, probably one. Therefore the discovery of the New Cave has given new significance to Locality 4.

The tooth found at the New Cave is a left upper first premolar representing, according to anthropologist Gu Yumin, the human species between Peking Man and Upper Cave Man. It represents Peking Man with more advanced characteristics, as do the human remains found in Layer 3 of Locality 1, which possess more progressive features than those of finds unearthed in lower layers.

It can be said that during the latter half of the Peking Man period, the human's living quarters were not only extended to Locality 15, but spread to any corner of Dragon Bone Hill where they could make their home.

15

Fossil Fish
at Zhoukoudian

In November 1933, a fish fossil site was found on a hilltop 70 metres above the present local riverbed. The site is near the Upper Cave where Bian Meinian and Jia Lanpo were working. They learned of it from a kiln worker, who told them where they could find 'live fish in stone.' Later the two, with Pei Wenzhong, went to take a look.

The site is on a ridge to the southwest of Locality 13 and 1.5 kilometres south of the Peking Man site. The place was called Siheyao, the name of an old kiln which was still in business, but the hill was called Fish Ridge after fish fossils were found there in quantity. It was later given the serial number of Locality 14 by the excavation team.

The fossils had become known to the local people a few months before, but the kiln workers had kept it a secret for fear that the fossil hunters might interfere with their operation. The worker who revealed this to the scientists knew that the kiln was soon going out of business and he wanted a new job.

When the three scientists arrived at the site, the kiln was practically abandoned, and there were only a few men clearing the ground and carting the remaining lime downhill. Due to quarrying, the ridge was now U-shaped, but in its middle there was a sandstone formation that rose above the ground. Viewed from certain angles, it looked like a pinnacle. This formation was composed of fossiliferous deposits left by the kiln workers.

The three scientists made careful observations of the rock and fragments scattered on the ground. The evidence was clear, abundant, and well preserved. A decision was made to excavate the site.

Most of the deposits were embedded in a bathtub-shaped area 26 metres long, 10 metres wide and 8 metres deep. The original length might have been 2 metres larger had the kiln workers left the structure alone. Geologically, the area was of Ordovician limestone. The fossil-bearing deposit was of yellowish sandstone, a thin stratum of coarse reddish-brown sand and pebbles. There was another red layer between the sandstone and the surface soil, obviously a weathered crust. The fish fossils were found in the fine sandstone structure from the middle part down.

Digging started on November 16, 1933. The *Daily Journal* of Zhoukoudian field-work has this entry for that day: "Start to excavate another locality to the south of Locality 9 where many fish fossils have been found."

Four masons and seven labourers were added to the already big team for this new operation. Such help could be recruited locally because many Zhoukoudian villagers were skilled at digging for 'dragon bones'. There were some father-and-son teams that worked year-round for us.

The supervising staff from the office in

Beijing at no time exceeded three in number, namely Pei Wenzhong, Bian Meinian and Jia Lanpo. They were in charge of all sorts of routine activities including fossil digging and selection, bookkeeping, wage payment, and packing of specimens for shipment.

They worked like bees. Sometimes they had to dispatch workers to look for new fossil-bearing sites. Many workers were, in fact, so experienced that they searched for new fossils independently and became highly skilled in extracting them.

On the very first day of operation at this site a mason sifted a complete fish fossil out from its surrounding sandstone. The next day a technician was assigned to work with this team.

It was an important year in terms of results and morale. Often meals and sleep were ignored. Excavation was conducted simultaneously at several sites. One of these was Locality 12, situated between Localities 3 and 4. Here, coarse sand deposits yielded mammalian fossils of early Pleistocene dating. Another was the Upper Cave site. Locality 13 was a third, and the fish fossil site, Locality 14, was a fourth.

Pei, who was in charge of the entire team, gave his attention to the entire project at Zhoukoudian and the Upper Cave excavation. Bian, who was formally trained in both geology and biology at Yanjing University, supervised the work at Locality 12. Jia, as a trainee, looked after the work at Localities 13 and 14, and learned more about fossil digging. Pei, of course, made inspection rounds of all the sites, and whenever the Upper Cave site yielded something extraordinary, Bian and Jia would go there to help with the digging to set their minds at ease.

In the autumn of 1949, after Liberation, excavation at Zhoukoudian was resumed with Jia Lanpo heading the team, which was now officially referred to as the Geo-

logical Survey and Excavation Team instead of the Zhoukoudian Excavation Office. Jia arrived at the village with the paleoichthyologist Liu Xianting and, after spending a few days on the preparatory work, went to visit Locality 14. Although they heard the thundering noises of blasting from a cement company quarry to the west, the fish fossil site did not look very different from the way it had appeared in 1933, except for overgrown weeds.

Under Liu's direction, digging at the site resumed on a small scale in 1951, and was greatly expanded in 1953. The area excavated covered approximately 28 square metres, 8 metres from south to north and 3.5 metres from east to west, on the east side at the north end of the deposits. It reached a depth of 10.2 metres, with 285 cubic metres of deposits removed from July 11 to November 6.

Altogether (1933, 1951 and 1953) the site yielded 2000 freshwater fish fossils, mostly well preserved and some still exhibiting scales. The fish had apparently gathered in a depression as water receded and died *en masse* when the hole went dry. Most of the fish fossils were found lying flat, some with their tails turned up as if in the throes of death. It is not an exaggeration to say that they looked almost alive. The fish varied in size and there were some egg fossils as well, showing that they must have lived in the hole for a considerable length of time.

Studies by Zhang Xizhi (Hsichih) and Liu Xianting, the two paleoichthyologists, revealed that the fish fossils included *Cyprinidae* of the genus Szechuan barbel (*Barbus szechuanensis*), Yunnan barbel (*Barbus yunnanensis*), short-head barbel (*Barbus brevicephalus*), and Hsichih's matsya (*Matsya hsichihi*). Sediments and altitude indicated that this site is of greater antiquity than other sites in the area, and the fauna also proved this. Three of the

Top: Locality 14 prior to excavation, where fossil fish occurred. (*Photo by Jia Lanpo, November 16, 1933*)
Bottom: The slender part of the deposits containing fossil fish.

above species are extinct, and the living one can now be found only south of the Changjiang (Yangtze River). From these data, Zhang and Liu dated the fish fossils as early Pliocene.[1] Fish of the genus *Barbus* are found today in a variety of species in the tropical and subtropical zones of the old continents, especially Africa. Those found in China all live south of the Changjiang, specifically in Sichuan, Guangdong, Hainan, Guangxi, Fujian and Taiwan Provinces. This indicates that 10 million years ago the Zhoukoudian area was warmer and wetter than it is now.

The discovery of Locality 14 is not only significant for the study of fish, but helps us to understand the geological structure of the Western Hills of Beijing.

---

[1] A similar depression on a hillside north of Locality 4, with a similar fine sand structure and at a similar height, yielded no fauna evidence.

The abundance of fish on a hilltop 70 metres above the present riverbed shows that the site must once have been part of the river system. The topography today is the result of deformation of the earth's crust over the last 10 million years.

The late Director of the Institute of Vertebrate Paleontology and Paleoanthropology, Dr Yang Zhongjian, investigated the tectonic processes of uplift and deformation of the Western Hills region that includes the Zhoukoudian area. Basing the study on the type of rock, he and Bian Meinian co-authored a paper in 1936[1] in which they observed that in the Middle and Upper Pliocene, as a result of the uplift of the western section, faults occurred along the Western Hills near Beijing. Localities which had formerly been of the same elevation were dislocated into regions that varied in height to the extent of several hundred metres. This can be seen, the authors asserted, in the characteristics of the

[1] *Bulletin of the Geological Society of China*, Vol. 15, No. 2.

rock structures at Chaoyangdong, Mentougou, and Dragon Bone Hill at Zhoukoudian, two cave sites and one hilltop which at present rise above the North China Plain by 70 to 800 metres.

The first trip to Chaoyangdong was in the autumn of 1935. Yang Zhongjian, Bian Meinian, and Jia Lanpo found a few deer toe fossils and other fragmental objects that were of little significance. But they did notice round pebbles, the size of apples or chestnuts, embedded in the cave wall. The fossiliferous deposits were at the base, 70 millimetres thick, consisting of reddish-yellow clay and limestone fragments. The soil was soft, obviously formed much later than the pebbles, which Yang and Bian concluded were of the Pliocene period, in their characteristics much like those found at the top of Dragon Bone Hill. Chaoyangdong is 800 metres above the North China Plain and some 300 metres above the present river valley nearby, but it has never been part of the river system as judged by the different characteristics of the pebbles found at the cave and at the valley bottom.

A 'fish wall' decorated with fish fossils unearthed at Locality 14.

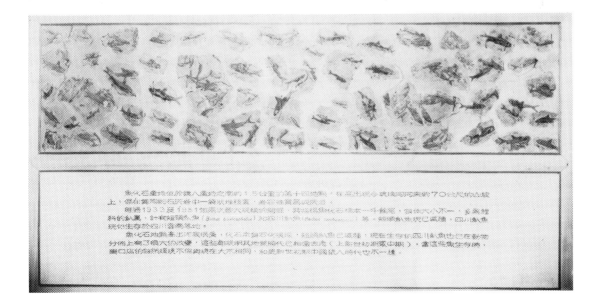

The Mentougou pebble deposits are 100 metres above the North China Plain. They share common characteristics with the pebbles at the other two sites, seeming to prove that they once shared the same elevation.

Almost 40 years later, Yang Zhongjian, at the age of 76, began to have doubts about this conclusion. In May 1973 he invited his colleagues—geologist Tang Yinjun, engineer Wang Zhefu, and Jia Lanpo—on a trip to Fangshan, a county 20 kilometres southwest of Zhoukoudian and the place where Yunshuidong, the biggest cave in North China, is situated. They would have to pass the Chaoyangdong site on the way. Although Yang did not disclose his reasons for the trip, Jia Lanpo recalled conversations of the past and guessed what was on the old scholar's mind. He apparently wanted to revisit Chaoyangdong to see if the pebbles were glacier deposits. To do so involved a long trek as well as a few hundred steps of the 'Ladder in the Clouds'. In the end, the group had to turn back after having covered only about a quarter of the Ladder steps, for the sun was setting and the old scientist was thoroughly exhausted. His wish thus remained unfulfilled. But if his doubts are eventually confirmed and the pebbles at Chaoyangdong are found to be glacial in origin, then how can the warm-climate fish fossils at Locality 14 of Zhoukoudian, which was believed to be of the same elevation as Chaoyangdong in the past, be explained? Perhaps the Chaoyangdong pebbles should be considered as of Quaternary dating. The problem can be resolved only by further studies.

16

After the Low Ebb, an Upsurge

As of July 1934, the 122 workers at Zhoukoudian (28 technicians, 26 masons and 68 hired hands), following the suspension of digging at the other two sites, concentrated on Locality 1, the Peking Man site. Every day, many basketfuls of material would be carried into the office, but only common artifacts and mammalian fossils were found, and we felt we were making much ado about nothing significant. The entries of the *Daily Journal* grew so monotonous that even a few flint flakes were considered important enough to be mentioned. "Many pieces of fragmental quartz, a few chert flakes, and one worked pebble were discovered at the top deposits at Locality 1," says a record made on November 1, and it is typical.

Not until May 7, 1935 had the dig at Locality 15 begun, and the next day the site yielded charred bones and fragmentary quartz, which put us on our toes in anticipation. But the increasing quantity of finds served only to prove more convincingly that they were identical to the material at the Peking Man site from Layer 3 up. When a fragmentary thick-jawed deer skull was unearthed on May 22, the contemporaneity of the two deposits was all the more convincingly confirmed.

Adding to the unproductive-

A monkey mandible (in white circle) was unearthed. (*Photo by Jia Lanpo, April 6, 1936*)

Top: An almost complete mandible of Peking Man occurred here (white circle) on October 22, 1936.
Bottom: The mandible was found at the spot indicated by the rule, or Locus K. (*Photo by Jia Lanpo*)

Opposite:
Top: Layer 7 was all fine sand without a trace of human remains or stone artifacts, but it yielded fossils of giant beavers, otters, buffaloes and other waterborne species or species taking to water. (*Photo by Jia Lanpo, June 7, 1936*)
Bottom: Layers 8-9 were rich in human remains. The ground was demarcated into blocks for systematic digging. (*Photo by Jia Lanpo, October 19, 1936*)

Top: Jia Lanpo at the Peking Man site, November 11, 1936.
Bottom: At Zhoukoudian, Jia Lanpo receiving a party of visitors from the Peking Union Medical College led by Professor Stevenson (*rear middle*) from the United States, October 31, 1936.

ness of the sites, the three leaders of the team at Zhoukoudian were no longer together—Pei Wenzhong was to go to France for advanced study and Bian Meinian was to go to Borneo (Kalimantan) with two American scientists. The growing number of 'commonplace' objects helped little to inspire the team, and it seemed that the good old times would never come back again. Now alone at the supervision level, Jia Lanpo felt the melancholic weight of his job, but he was steadfast in spite of his low spirits. He wished for some extraordinary finds to cheer him up, but when these were not forthcoming, he kept reminding himself that the possibility was always there and negligence on his part might cause irretrievable losses. Every day he shuttled between the two localities, 15 and 1, seeking new inspiration.

From the autumn of 1935, Jia tried to make a breakthrough elsewhere, for he had never believed that Peking Man had lived exclusively at Dragon Bone Hill. He had a cherished wish to explore all the caves within a 100-kilometre radius of Zhoukoudian in three years, provided such a project would not interfere with the one at Zhoukoudian. His wish might have been fulfilled had it not been for the Sino-Japanese War of 1937-45. As it turned out, he made only one reconnaissance trip along the Yongding River and prospected for specimens at two cave sites. One of these was the Huiyu, 40 kilometres from Zhoukoudian in terms of air distance. The site yielded twenty-seven mammalian fossil remains and was dated as

Mr and Mrs Weidenreich and their daughter at the Peking Man site. Two other friends are unidentified. (*Photo by Jia Lanpo*)

Early Pliocene by Pierre Teilhard de Chardin.[1] The reason that a site at such a distance had to be given a serial number in line with the sites at Zhoukoudian was entirely financial. The grant from the Rockefeller Foundation was for the Zhoukoudian project, and all expenditures had to be cleared with documents stamped 'CKT' (initials for Choukoutien); thus the serial number system was sometimes applied to localities elsewhere. Once in 1937 it had almost covered a site in Yunnan Province, but thanks to Weng Wenhao, who managed to have the project funded from other sources, the idea was dropped.

There was another site of potential value to Jia, who in September 1935, driven by the same desire to make a breakthrough elsewhere, took along three technicians and explored a cave site west of Zhoukoudian. The space in the cave was 25 metres long and 8 metres wide, and the floor was of yellowish deposits. They dug about one cubic metre on the first try, and forty-four fragmentary pieces of quartz were found which, though bearing no distinct signs of

having been worked, gave food for thought because of their presence in this cave. There were also two stone flakes and a few horse and sheep teeth. Earthenware fragments occurred near the surface. Whether relics of greater antiquity could be found deeper down remained unknown; the lack of funds forced the team to leave the site unexplored.

At Locality 1, the dig reached Layer 6 on June 6, 1935. The breccia structure of the layer made the going extremely difficult. There was no way, not even blasting, that would help to extricate the numerous embedded objects. For a time, a few monkey's teeth served to alleviate somewhat the anxiety of the fossil hunters. However, the heaps of small mammal remains, including species of the orders *Insectivora* (insect eaters), *Chiroptera* (bats) and *Rodentia* (rodents), most of them burnt like those which had occurred in Layer 4, led us to believe that these were leftovers from Peking Man's meals. Based on these finds, Jia wrote that rats had been served on Peking Man's dinner tables. There have been objections to this view, but Jia has stood his ground.

In 1935, during the winter lull in field-

[1] 'Fossils at Locality 18 near Peking', *Paleontologia Sinica*, New Ser. C, No. 9, 1940.

work at Zhoukoudian, Jia was overjoyed to accept an assignment from the Cenozoic Laboratory to go to Yichang, Hubei Province, and Wanxian County, Sichuan Province. He was intensely interested in finding more human fossil sites in China, but ended up with more boxes of mammalian remains. He and a technician returned to Beijing in March for the preparatory work at Zhoukoudian.

When the excavation season started in the spring of 1936, two college graduates, one a geologist, the other a biologist, came to work at Zhoukoudian. They were competent hands, and so prospects for the fieldwork looked bright for a time. But neither stayed long, and when the work

season ended in July, Jia found himself a loner on the job again.

Actually the team did not do badly during these months. On June 1, work had begun on the lower section of Layer 7, which was of loose sand composition. Two monkey teeth (teeth of *Macacus robustus*) were unearthed—not very significant, but something new to the workers, for a change. A lower monkey mandible occurred on the 3rd of June; two more mandibles and a few more teeth followed on the 6th. The red-letter day fell on the 10th when work started at Layers 8 and 9 and an almost complete monkey skull occurred. It was considered to be so significant that Jia Lanpo made a special trip to

Staff and labourers at the grounds where Peking Man lived. First from the left in the front row is Li Yueyan. Second from the left and first from the right are the martyrs Dong Zhongyuan and Zhao Wanhua, who were killed by the Japanese occupation troops at Zhoukoudian. Jia Lanpo is first from the right in the back row. (*Photo by Sun Shusen, June 15, 1936*)

the city to deliver the specimen, the first of its kind to have occurred at Zhoukoudian, to the Cenozoic Research Laboratory. On the train, he encountered none other than Yang Zhongjian, who was on the way to Beijing from his native place. Jia wasted no time in breaking the news of the find to him, and delighted, Yang insisted on unwrapping the thing to take a look. His excitement was perfectly understandable, and it was he who later determined the scientific name for the skull. It is a tragedy for science that this specimen, together with another fragmentary one, was lost at the same time as were the Peking Man fossils, just before the bombing of Pearl Harbour in 1941. This complete skull had not yet been studied, and not even a photo had been taken of it.

Layers 8 and 9 yielded a considerable number of stone artifacts. Microliths abounded, and implements of sandstone, especially choppers, were more numerous than at any other layer at the site.

June 20 brought great expectations when two Peking Man incisors and a fragmentary skullcap were found, together with three monkey upper mandibles. As monkey fossils had often preceded human remains, a phenomenon that so far has defied explanation, and since a few human teeth had also been found, the team knew that significant finds were in the offing. What happened in the ensuing days strengthened this belief. Two human upper molars were found on the 28th, two fragments of a Peking Man skullcap on the 29th and another two on July 2, and another upper molar was found on the 4th. Spirits at the site were high, but the rainy season intervened and the great expectations had to wait for the next fieldwork season, to be fulfilled. Work was suspended for that season on July 7.

17

The Culmination

The excavations at the middle section of Locality 1 began in April 1934, and by July 7, 1936, 451 fieldwork days had been devoted to the site. In that period the site yielded more than 500 boxes of specimens, mostly stone artifacts, which accounted for some 70 000 pieces. Mammalian fossils also occurred in quantity. Human remains, however, had all along been scarce. The site had yielded only a few teeth and bone fragments until the closing days of the autumn season in 1936.

The fieldwork for that season began on September 16, the day after Jia Lanpo and a group of technicians arrived in Zhoukoudian. They carried on the dig left off at Layers 8 and 9, on the 32nd level. Right from the beginning some fine liths occurred, and flint implements appeared in increasing number. Every day mammalian remains were found, which included a lower mandible of Merck's rhinoceros, horn-cores of argali, and an almost complete thick-jawed deer antler. There was a whole layer of crushed hackberry seed, a few thousands of which were undamaged, but charred like the crushed ones.

Never had the team suffered from such tension as it experienced during this season. Financial stress and the hope of significant finds were the cause, as indicated by correspondence between the field and the office in Beijing.

Mr Qiao Shisheng to Mr Jia Lanpo
October 2, 1936

. . . A telegram [has come] from New York informing the office of additional funds made available for half a year, and any further grant shall be decided afterwards. Mr Yang Zhongjian wrote to Dr Weidenreich today advising him not to limit the monthly expenses at Choukoutien to one thousand dollars, so that more work could be done and soil would not be piled up without being sifted.

Mr Bian Meinian to Mr Jia Lanpo
October 5, 1936

The Cenozoic Laboratory has received the grant from the Rockefeller Foundation for this six months' expenditure, but the old gentleman [meaning Weidenreich] is so possessive that he would appropriate only one thousand dollars for the fieldwork each month. You need not worry, however, if you have to spend more, say, two, three or five hundred more. I'll fight the battle at the front for you. The old gentleman has a notion that the fieldwork has to be done slowly and cautiously, oblivious of the fact that the piled-up soil has to be sifted, and that [this] costs money. You should just go ahead and have the soil sifted.

Dr Yang Zhongjian wrote to the old gentleman today protesting vehemently against his complaint about the study and reconstruction of the dinosaur. There might be a scene in a couple of days. Weidenreich is so preoccupied with controlling expenditures that he gives no thought to the fact that money unspent has to be handed back. He is anxious also to search for a new site

Top: At 9.30 a.m., November 15, 1936, at Block J-3 of Level 25 (corresponding to layers 8-9), a fairly complete skullcap was unearthed. The spot was designated Locus L. (*Photo by Jia Lanpo*)

Bottom: Fragments of a skullcap were sighted and retrieved. When glued together, they turned out to be the complete skullcap of an adult male. (*Photo by Jia Lanpo*)

and anticipates [*sic*] us to possess eyes sharp enough to tell sites that may yield human fossil remains.

Actually, Weidenreich was probably more anxiety-ridden those days than we were, for he made trips to Zhoukoudian frequently. He came by car with Teilhard, Yang and Bian again on October 12, and before anything was said, he inquired if there were any new finds. Jia briefed the group on the increasing amount of materi-al recovered, which gladdened them. They stayed until the next day, visiting the site and discussing the work in progress.

An extraordinary find was made on October 15. As many as forty thick-jawed deer lower mandibles occurred near the south wall of the Peking Man cave. The following few days, however, were uneventful. Then on October 22, a Peking Man left lower mandible was sighted at the centre of Level 24, Layers 8-9, 24 metres

down from Layer 3. This was approximately 6 metres above and 10 metres south of Locus E where the complete skullcap was found by Pei Wenzhong in 1929. It was a little after 10 o'clock in the morning. At first, only a front molar was spotted by a labourer named Liu Er. Jia Lanpo at once identified it as a human fossil and did the digging personally with a hand hook. Presently, the mandible emerged, but due to the pressure of the limestone above and below the object, it came out in fragments and the whole thing was friable. With great care, the specimen was taken into the office, where it was dried on a charcoal fire, solidified, and glued together until it was reconstructed. Only a molar and an incisor were missing, and these had not been found. It was a female mandible. A technician was dispatched the next day to deliver the object to the office in the city. As a mandible in such well-preserved condition was new, it attracted wide attention in academic circles, both Chinese and foreign.

The first group of visitors was from the Cenozoic Laboratory and the Peking Union Medical College, including Teilhard de Chardin, Olga Hempel Gowen, Assistant Professor (of anatomy) Paul H. Stevenson and Bian Meinian, who all came by train to inspect the *in situ* position of the mandible. They enquired about the details of the finding and took photographs. With everything done, they left for the city that same day. More visitors came in their wake in those few days. Weidenreich himself arrived at the scene with four others on November 11. Upon seeing Jia Lanpo, his first utterance was "Anything new? A skull may be lying below!" "Entirely possible," Jia responded, "in a day or two." "I hope so," said Weidenreich, "but I'm sorry I can't stay long. I have to go back to the city this afternoon."

The job at Level 24, Layers 8-9 (breccia layers), was over on November 14. The ground was thoroughly cleared, since the fieldwork was to be suspended for the season. Overcast skies and freezing weather were working against continuation of

the job. But the discovery of the lower mandible had been so electrifying that no one wanted to give up at that moment. After long deliberation, Jia made the decision to go on with digging at Level 25. Blocks were demarcated and a plane map was drawn that afternoon.

November 15 was a Sunday. There had been a heavy snowfall the previous night, and the team waited until 9 a.m. to make sure of the weather before beginning work. Ever since the day of the recovery of the mandible Jia Lanpo had never stayed away from the site for fear of missing something. And on that day when everybody was busy, he noticed a fragmentary bone in the hand of a technician, Zhang Haiquan, who was 5 metres from him; Zhang had just retrieved the bone from the porous sandy soil deposits about 1 metre below and 4 metres to the north of the *in situ* position of the mandible. When Zhang was routinely putting it into his wicker basket, the shape of the piece impressed Jia as part of a human skullcap. He rushed over, took a second look, and found himself right. He immediately checked the time by his pocket watch—it

Human fossils being dried and glued together. Technicians Cai Fengshan (*left*), Xue Qing'en (*middle*), and Du Linchun (*right*). (*Photo by Jia Lanpo, November 15, 1936*)

Pei Wenzhong sent a message of congratulation from Paris to Jia Lanpo on November 21, 1936, on the November 15 discovery of two Peking Man skullcaps.

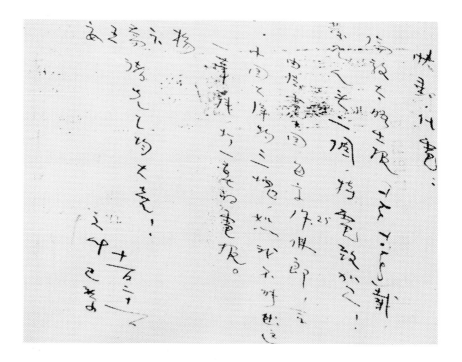

Top: The greater part of the third Peking Man skullcap unearthed at the site is exposed.
Bottom: All hands at work are asked to search carefully for human remains. (*November 26, 1936*)

was half past nine.

He gave orders to mark a 6-square-metre zone as a special area and selected several of the ablest men to work with him in that zone. In an area of half a square metre, they found fragments of human skull; occipital bone, brow ridge (supraorbital bone), and ear bones were also sighted. It was certain now that the skullcap was embedded. Fortunately the deposit was of loose sandy soil. Only one piece was coalesced with the limestone and it took them a few hours to get it out.

That afternoon, in the deposit half a metre below and one metre to the north of the position of the first skull, another turned up. It was also fragmented. Although the pieces could be seen clearly, it was too late in the day to remove them. Besides, it was a good opportunity for people in the office to have a view of Peking Man fossils in their original position. So they were left intact, and six persons were assigned to guard the site around the clock.

Not until Monday morning did the telephone message from Zhoukoudian reach Weidenreich, who, as related by his wife, got so excited that he put his pants on inside out. That afternoon when he came to Zhoukoudian and held the first skull, which it had taken four people the whole night to glue together, his hands were shaking, and he uttered the words "Wonderful! Wonderful!"

This skull was serial-numbered LI, and

Jia Lanpo looking for additional fragments of the third Peking Man skullcap discovered at the site.

Fieldwork team members. (*November 26, 1936*)

The Peking Man skullcap unearthed on November 26, 1936 was better preserved than any of the previous finds.

the one found next followed with LII. Both were fairly complete, but LII had a brow ridge missing.

On November 23, a letter from the office informed Jia Lanpo of a press conference to be held the following day at Weiden-reich's office at the Union Medical College to announce the news of the finding of the skulls. And on the 25th, newspapers the world over carried the story. After the first discovery of a skull at Zhoukoudian in 1929 under the supervision of Pei Wen-zhong, the repeat of the spectacular find again shook academic circles on an inter-national scale. A London Fleet Street clip-ping service wrote to Jia Lanpo offering him news accounts related to the new find

at a bargain price of 10 pounds 10 shillings for each 2000 items, covering newspapers in Europe and America. But he did not have the money.

On Thursday November 26, night snow again delayed the digging. But at 9 a.m. another, much better preserved skull oc-curred in the hard breccia deposits 1 metre below and 3 metres south of the position that had yielded a mandible. This was giv-en the number LIII.

Reconstruction of the specimen was not as painstaking as for the other two as this skull was complete with nasal bones, parts of the foramen magnum and orbital plate. It was taken to the city by Jia Lanpo. The hurry was due to considerations of safety, since now that the valuable human fossils had become common knowledge, people might be tempted to steal them.

It should be mentioned in passing that a large quantity of stone implements was found in the deposits of Level 24 between Layers 8 and 9 where the Peking Man left lower mandible had occurred. Most of the stone artifacts bear signs of having been worked. But strangely enough, in the deposits of Level 25 where three Peking Man skullcaps were unearthed, few stone implements were found. The reason is still unknown. Nevertheless, the many fragmented animal bones found there, many of which show signs of secondary work, are evidently stone and antler implements once used by the ancient human beings.

After the recovery of the LIII skull, the Beijing Branch of the Geological Society of China held a special conference on December 19 at which Weidenreich and Jia Lanpo briefed the more than one hundred scholars from various countries on the new discovery and its significance.

In early 1937, on the initiative of Weng Wenhao, Director of the Geological Survey of China, a team was dispatched to the far southwestern region of China to search for traces of early humans. The team members were Jia Lanpo, Bian Meinian and Du Linchun. The last was one of the ablest technicians working at Zhoukoudian. The undertaking was inspired by the theory of Professor H. Osborn, a United States paleontologist, which suggested that the central Asian plateau might well be the earliest home of human beings, from which Java Man and Peking Man had emanated. The teams re-investigated the fossiliferous site of Heshandong in Yunnan Province. The site had been explored twice without success, and the team now fared no better and had to give up. As the excavation season at Zhoukoudian was near, Jia Lanpo hurried back north, leaving Bian Meinian and Du

Linchun to work at another hopeful site at Qiubei County, Yunnan Province which had been known to scientists. They found only some charred hackberry seed in a rock shelter.

When the fieldwork at Zhoukoudian was resumed at the beginning of April, preparations were made first for the further exploration of the peripheral site at Huiyu, or Locality 18. Then from April 12, full-scale work was launched at Localities 1, 15 and 4. Before the month was over, Level 26 of Layers 8-9, Locality 1 yielded more Peking Man fossils, which included a premolar, two skull fragments, a skullcap, a fragmentary mandible, and a brow ridge. Although meticulous attention was paid to each, the degree of excitement was not as intense as at the end of the previous season. But it occurred to Jia that the brow ridge was something special—could it be a part of the skullcap found on November 15?

The specimens were sent to Beijing through the postal service, together with a letter about the brow ridge. On April 29, Weidenreich wrote to Jia:

> I wish to thank you for sending me the material. The predicted jaw arrived. I believe that you will find additional pieces pertaining thereto.
>
> The supraorbital fragment fits exactly to Skull II of Locus L. I have already placed it to its place. Here also, it seems to me, that there are possibilities to find more, perhaps some teeth.

How right he was. Before the end of May, five individual teeth, one fragmentary mandible, and one left maxilla with six teeth (one lateral incisor, two premolars and three molars) attached were unearthed. This last, discovered at Level 29, was of special significance, for with such a maxilla, or upper jaw, the reconstruction of Peking Man's face would have a scientific basis to go on. Thus the season saw another bumper harvest. Mammalian remains and stone artifacts, too, occurred in great numbers. Among them were skeletons of one Gray's sika deer and two thick-jawed deer, all almost complete. This was the very first time that the site had yielded such fossils.

When work at Level 29 was concluded on July 9, the season drew to a close. Due to the discovery of three almost complete Peking Man skullcaps in November 1936, the Rockefeller Foundation had made more funds available for the project to go on. But the war in China prevented this from happening, and not until 12 years later, in 1949, after a revolution that brought the socialist system to China, was the excavation at Zhoukoudian resumed.[1] Thus that day, July 9, 1937 marked the end of an era in the fieldwork at the Peking Man site, and in paleontological and paleoanthropological studies in China.

*　　　*　　　*

Franz Weidenreich

Franz Weidenreich (1873-1948) came from a Jewish family in Germany, but took up American nationality later. A kind man, he was of medium height, and was always well turned out. He had the bearing of a scholar. He did not talk much, but when he did he was articulate. After Jia Lanpo resumed excavation work at Zhoukoudian, the two began to have frequent contact with each other. Weidenreich made many trips to the Peking Man site at Zhoukoudian; Jia would either travel with him, or else meet him at Zhoukoudian.

Weidenreich had mentioned more than once that before coming to China he had serious doubts about the excavation work being conducted at Zhoukoudian. As many Peking Man skull bones but only a few body bones had been discovered at Zhoukoudian, Weidenreich assumed that the majority of the body bones had been thrown away unrecognized. After several visits to Zhoukoudian, however, his doubts disappeared. He came to realize that the excavation work at Zhoukoudian was scientific and was being carried out with the greatest of care.

So there had to be some other reason for the apparent scarcity of body bones in the area. Weidenreich explained this phenomenon as evidence that Peking Man had practised cannibalism. Although some people did not agree with him they could raise no evidence to support their own arguments.

---

[1] When organized exploration was resumed 12 years later, the scale had grown much larger, and significant evidence continued to accumulate, with the Chinese Government alone providing the resources—*Tr.*

18

Unknown Heroes at Zhoukoudian

Due to the nature of the work, injuries were common at the work site, and everyone was good at giving first aid. Fatal accidents were, however, rare. The most tragic one happened on October 2, 1934 to a labourer named Li Guangcai. He was one of the 115 technicians, quarry workers and labourers working at the site that day. Pei was not at the site when the accident took place, at about 9 o'clock, as he had gone to the office to receive a visitor. Jia, however, was standing near the man who was to plunge to his death a few minutes later. With his face to the hill and his back to the

A letter from Weidenreich informing Jia Lanpo that the brow ridge (supraorbital bone) unearthed in 1937 belonged to the No. 2 skullcap that had come to light in 1936.

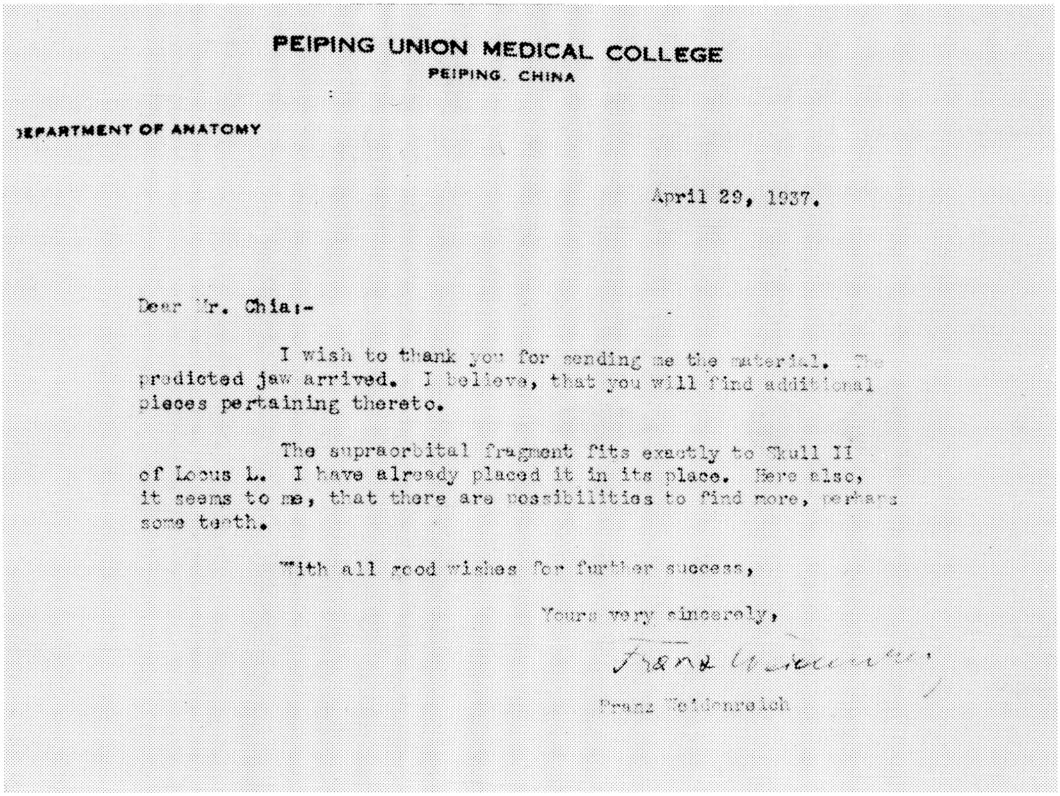

PEIPING UNION MEDICAL COLLEGE
PEIPING, CHINA

DEPARTMENT OF ANATOMY

April 29, 1937.

Dear Mr. Chia:-

I wish to thank you for sending me the material. The predicted jaw arrived. I believe, that you will find additional pieces pertaining thereto.

The supraorbital fragment fits exactly to Skull II of Locus L. I have already placed it in its place. Here also, it seems to me, that there are possibilities to find more, perhaps some teeth.

With all good wishes for further success,

Yours very sincerely,

Franz Weidenreich

edge of the cliff, the man was working with a long rod to pry loose a big chunk of limestone. Jia warned him that he must turn around lest the rock roll down on him. It was actually an order. Others were yelling at him too: "Are you trying to kill yourself?"

This turned out to be a bad omen. While Jia was on his way down the hill to join Pei and the visitor at the office, he heard voices cry in alarm and saw from afar a figure dropping from the cliff. Li's fellow workers gathered along the edge in horrified silence. Jia was certain who it was. He rushed to where the man had fallen and heard cries of agony from a deep pit where the first Peking Man skullcap had appeared.

The rescue operation got underway immediately, but nothing could save Li's life. For three days and nights, we could occasionally hear his moans, which ceased only at his death. His wife and his father received a modest compensation from the Geological Survey of China, but a donation from all who had known him enabled his family to buy 10 *mu* of land, sufficient for them to make a living.

Li had worked as a boy with Dr Andersson and had joined the Zhoukoudian team under Li Jie in 1927. He had always been a conscientious worker, and his accidental death at the age of 30 was a great pity.

A grimmer story than this involved three Zhoukoudian workers who died at

The last photo taken at the Zhoukoudian site prior to the War of Resistance Against Japan. On July 5, 1937, three days before the war broke out, an upper jaw with six teeth attached were found at the H-4 block of Level 29. The spot was designated Locus N. (*Photo by Jia Lanpo, afternoon, July 5, 1937*)

Opposite:
Top: Work at Level 28 (Natural Layer 10) is about to be completed. (*Photo by Jia Lanpo, June 12, 1937*)
Bottom: A rhino mandible was unearthed at Level 29. Worked stone flakes were found around the mandible. (*Photo by Jia Lanpo, June 27, 1937*)

One of the letters Yang Zhongjian wrote to Jia Lanpo showing his concern over the work at Zhoukoudian. This one was sent in May 1937, when he was out of Beijing.

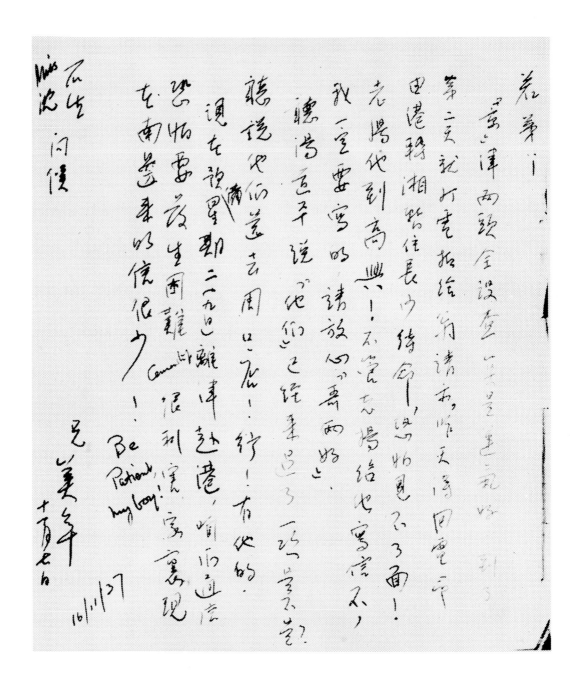

The war interrupted the Zhoukoudian project and drove the members of the staff to flee from the area. This is the first letter from Bian Meinian to Jia Lanpo. Jia used a pseudonym to avoid trouble from censors, so here Bian addressed Jia Brother Ruo.

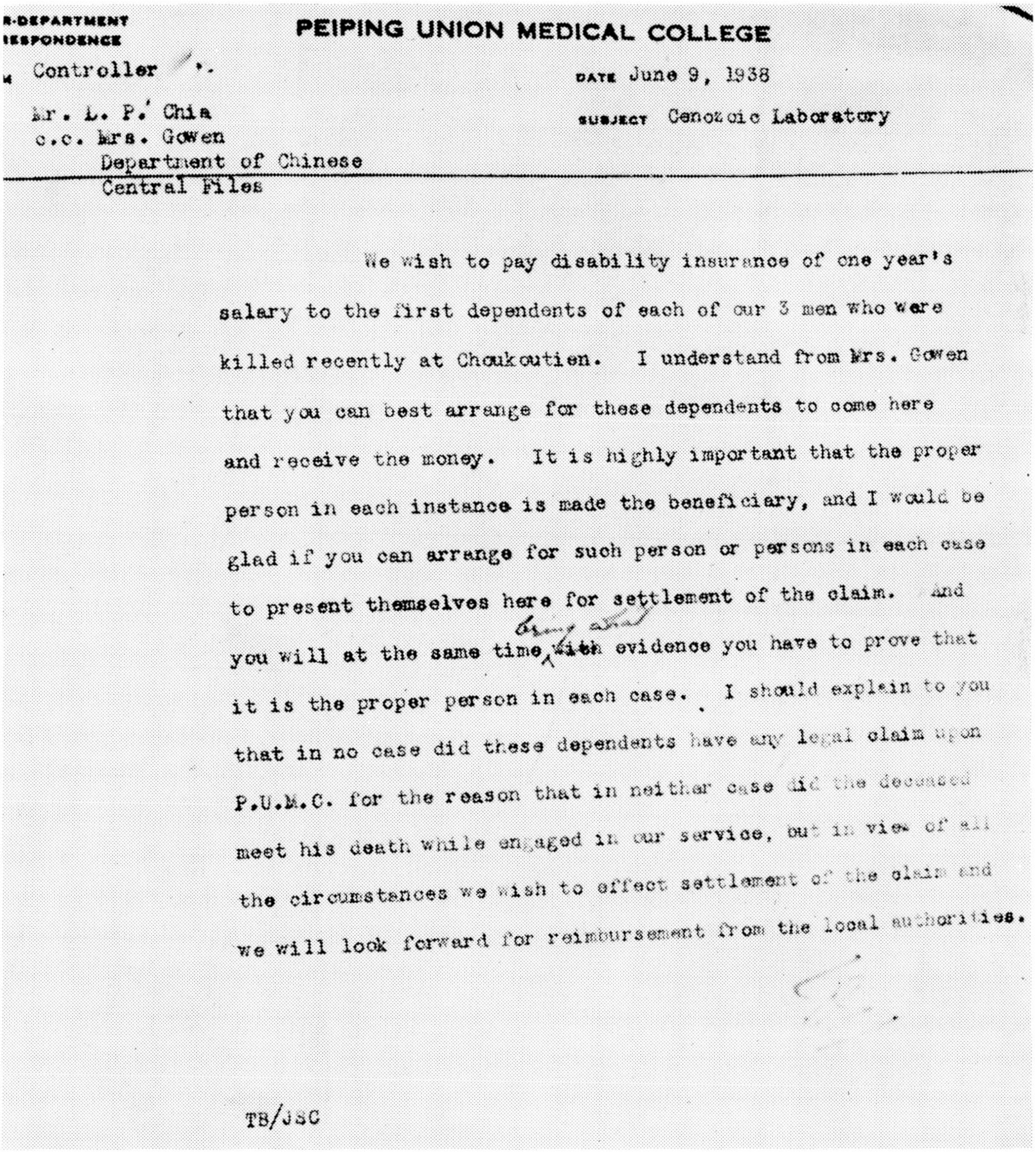

PEIPING UNION MEDICAL COLLEGE

R-DEPARTMENT
IESPONDENCE

Controller
hr. L. P. Chia
c.c. hrs. Gowen
Department of Chinese
Central Files

DATE June 9, 1938
SUBJECT Cenozoic Laboratory

We wish to pay disability insurance of one year's salary to the first dependents of each of our 3 men who were killed recently at Choukoutien. I understand from Mrs. Gowen that you can best arrange for these dependents to come here and receive the money. It is highly important that the proper person in each instance is made the beneficiary, and I would be glad if you can arrange for such person or persons in each case to present themselves here for settlement of the claim. And you will at the same time, with evidence you have to prove that it is the proper person in each case. I should explain to you that in no case did these dependents have any legal claim upon P.U.M.C. for the reason that in neither case did the deceased meet his death while engaged in our service, but in view of all the circumstances we wish to effect settlement of the claim and we will look forward for reimbursement from the local authorities.

TB/JSC

The letter from the Controller of the Peking Union Medical College regarding compensation for the three Zhoukoudian workers killed by Japanese troops.

the hands of Japanese invaders in 1938.

After the occurrence of the July 7th Incident in 1937, the fieldwork at Zhoukoudian, being near to the battle zone, was suspended and workers discharged. But a few technicians went with Jia Lanpo, who was then in charge, to Beijing, while another twenty-six men remained behind, being local people or permanent residents of the area. Records show that they were still on the payroll in December 1937.

There had been a tradition at the Zhoukoudian site that during off season, some workers would stay on to keep an eye on the field and installations, to make trial diggings at sites considered to be not significant, or, more important, to sift the earth again for overlooked fossils, especially those of very small size. Rodent teeth, jawbones and limbs had often been found in this way.

A 54-year-old technician named Zhao Wanhua, who was to become one of the three martyrs, was heading the team that remained at the site during this difficult time. The other two were Dong Zhongyuan and Xiao Yuanchang. Zhao corresponded regularly with the Beijing office, where Jia was, but because of the war, an item of mail now took half a month to reach its destination.

Zhoukoudian was soon under Japanese occupation, and the Beijing office time and again urged Zhao Wanhua and the team to abandon the site and transfer to the city in separate groups so as not to attract the attention of the Japanese troops. Zhao wrote that they had taken heed of this and had begun transferring members to Beijing in groups of three on September 30. But a letter from Zhao to Jia dated November 10, 1937 reads:

> Three truckloads of Japanese soldiers and six Japanese civilians in Western attire came to the site looking around. The six-

man group wanted to lodge here and we told them that there was no place to accommodate so many people and that those in charge had gone to Beijing. Then they enquired after Mr Pei and Mr Jia. We said we did not know the whereabout of Mr Pei, but that Mr Jia was in Beijing. The group then made a close observation at Locality 1, taking more than ten photos and measuring the length and breadth of the site. They brought with them a number of journals and books, including the *Journal of the Chinese Geological Society*, Vol. 13, No. 3, and *An Outline of the History of Ape-Man in China*. After stamping about the entire area, they had a picnic lunch at the entrance of Locality 1 and took off.

Battles were at their fiercest in August that year. The battlefield was nearby and local residents suffered the most. In the Dragon Bone Hill area, more than a hundred troops were billeted in a temple and other buildings. Zhao's letter had not made clear whether these were Japanese or puppet troops, or guerrillas under the Chinese Communist Party. Jia considered that in any event, the safety of the workers was in jeopardy and again urged them to abandon everything and evacuate. In the beginning of 1938, only a few of them remained, and they were advised to come to the city at once. But Zhao replied that they'd better wait until the trip to Beijing would be safer. He did not want to leave the site unattended.

In all the eight years that Jia Lanpo had known them, these men had been dedicated workers who never shirked a day's work or uttered a disgruntled word. But alas, he was never to see them again. In April, he received two messages from Zhao informing him that plainclothes troops were at the site and no work could be done; otherwise things were quiet. But on May 4, an unsigned note dated May 3 brought the bad news that Zhao and two other workers had been seized by the Japanese troops and taken to the county seat of Fangshan.

Rescue efforts were in vain, and in the middle of May, a messenger from Zhoukoudian told Jia that the three, together with some thirty others, had been bayoneted to death by Japanese. Later it was learned that guerrillas had indeed billeted in the Dragon Bone Hill area to fight against the Japanese, but they had retreated after several fierce encounters. The three men, who had been ordered to serve in their kitchen, were then taken captive by the Japanese, who hoped to learn from them where the guerrillas had gone and what their names and addresses were, since many were local people and quite a few had worked for the excavation project. The captives were tortured but revealed nothing to the enemy. We wish to pay tribute to them with this brief account.

19

Stealing the Drawings

After the July 7th Incident all the technicians returned from the Zhoukoudian project except the group of three who stayed. They and employees of the Cenozoic Research Laboratory, as well as an American paleontologist, A. W. Grabau, who worked for Beijing University, were paid out of the fund provided by the Rockefeller Foundation. Although they kept themselves busy with sifting the specimens collected at Zhoukoudian, a sense of despair and precariousness dominated their minds. As the clouds were gathering in 1941, when US-Japanese relations were worsening, Yang Zhongjian and Bian Meinian sneaked out of Beijing and went via a

Staff members of the Cenozoic Research Laboraory and the Anatomy Section of the Peking Union Medical College gathered for a farewell party for Mrs Olga Hempel Gowen (*eighth from left*), who was leaving China for the United States. At the party were (*from left, front row*) Jia Lanpo (*first*), Pei Wenzhong (*sixth*), Weidenreich (*seventh*), Pan Mingzi (*tenth*), Teilhard de Chardin (*behind Weidenreich*), A. B. D. Fortuyn (*behind Mrs Gowen*). Hu Chengzhi is second from the right in the back row.

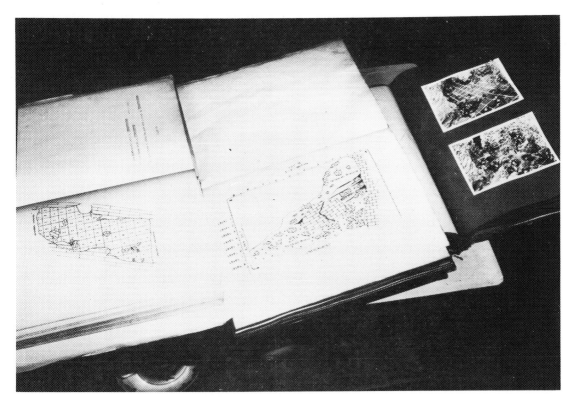

Duplicates of the Peking Man site sketch maps were smuggled out of Lockhart Hall of the Peking Union Medical College by Jia Lanpo for safekeeping when Beijing was under Japanese occupation. (*Photo by Wang Zhefu, July 1981*)

roundabout way to Chongqing, the wartime capital of China, to which the headquarters of the Geological Survey of China had transferred.

Before Yang's departure Jia was entrusted to head the remaining personnel and was told to stick around as long as he could, expecting that the situation would soon take a turn for the better. Jia was also told to go to the south if things turned worse. When at last he had to leave too and had in fact reached Nanjing, it was a day after the Japanese attack on Pearl Harbour. All sea routes leading to the interior of China via Hong Kong and Hanoi were cut off, and he had to turn back to Beijing.

Home again, Jia planned to write something on the digging at Zhoukoudian, and so he had to go to the office to get information on the subject. On the first day after his arrival, he visited the Cenozoic Laboratory, where he met Pei Wenzhong, who had just returned from France and was now Director of the Laboratory, and together they pondered the uncertain future of their work.

The building that housed the Laboratory was now guarded by Japanese occupation troops. The doorman was the same familiar one, but upon seeing Jia, he made no sign of recognition. Jia had the proper credentials and had little trouble entering the building, but he knew the Japanese would search him thoroughly before they allowed him to leave.

Jia had a feeling that the very existence

of the institution was in doubt, and it impelled him to try to save whatever he could of the scientific treasure of China. The first objects that came to mind were the drawings of the Peking Man site without which all marks on the specimens indicating their *in situ* positions would become useless.

Duplicates of the original size would be too conspicuous to escape the search of the guards, so Jia cut the proportion from 1:100 down to 1:200. Using the thinnest kind of paper, which would pass for toilet tissue, he made rough sketches in the office, which had to be worked over at night, at home. The originals had been his own handiwork, so it was easy for him to make the copies. Still, he couldn't finish more than two a day, and it was two months before he got all the drawings copied and bound into a book.

Jia had also taken most of the photographs showing the work in progress at Zhoukoudian. Each day he also smuggled out a few negatives to have them printed at a studio. These were also bound into a volume.

The book on the excavation at Zhoukoudian that he intended to write failed to materialize, but the materials collected for this purpose proved to be highly useful in the ensuing years. Indeed they have been indispensable, as these copies carry more detailed information than the originals. Years later, photocopies were made of them and they are still in use.

20

Specimens Boxed
for Shipment

Human remains as well as some higher primate fossils were kept in Franz Weidenreich's office safe in the anatomy section of the Peking Union Medical College. As US-Japanese relations worsened in 1941, many of the US citizens in China were leaving for their homeland. Those who worked in the Union Medical College felt the oncoming storm. Weidenreich was due to leave in April for the United States, where he would continue his work on Peking Man as a visiting scholar at the Museum of Natural History in New York. He asked his able assistant Hu Chengzhi (now an engineer at

The old front gate of Peking Union Medical College. The building near the gate, Building B, housed the Anatomy Section of the College, where fossils from Zhoukoudian were kept on the ground floor. Davidson Black and Franz Weidenreich were here at different times, studying Peking Man fossils. The building is now a part of the Chinese Academy of Medical Science. (*Photo by Wang Zhefu, August 1981*)

Lockhart Hall, built in 1904, housed the vertebrate fossils from Zhoukoudian. Yang Zhongjian, Pei Wenzhong, Bian Meinian, Teilhard de Chardin and Jia Lanpo all worked here. (*Photo by Wang Zhefu, August 1981*)

Hu Chengzhi briefs Japanese visitors on how the Peking Man fossils were packed for shipment to a safe place during World War II. (*Photo taken in 1980*)

the Museum of Geology of the Ministry of Geology of China) to make copies of all the Peking Man fossils for him. Hu hesitated. This would be no simple task, and would take a long time. "It's urgent," Weidenreich said, "so get started. The new finds first, then the older ones. If you run out of time, well, just do as much as you can."

Weidenreich knew that the valuable Peking Man fossils would not be safe in the Japanese-occupied zone. He said he would confer with Weng Wenhao about transferring them elsewhere.

Soon after a farewell party held in his honour in Lockhart Hall at the Union Med-

ical College, Weidenreich made his departure. Three months later, Hu was told by Pei Wenzhong that all the Peking Man fossils were to be boxed for shipment and he was asked to make preparations. The US Embassy was said to have been approached by the Chinese authorities to ship the fossils to America for temporary custody. The embassy hesitated, for the Agreement (1927) between the National Geological Survey of China and the Peking Union Medical College had stipulated that all collections of specimens should belong entirely to the Survey and 'nothing will be exported out of China' (Art. III).

There has been some confusion about

A farewell party for Franz Weidenreich (*middle of the front row*) who was leaving for the United States in the autumn of 1941. Pei Wenzhong (*sixth from left, front row*) and Jia Lanpo (*middle of the second row*) were among the group. This picture has been referred to by the group as a memento of their 'dissolution'.

who packed the specimens. In the book *Searching for Peking Man* by Christopher G. Janus and William Brashler published in 1975 in New York, the authors state that Claire Taschdjian was the last person to see the Peking Man fossils when at the Peking Union Medical College, and she packed them for shipment. But in fact the job was done by two Chinese specialists, Hu Chengzhi and Ji Yanqing. Hu was an expert in making moulds and had rich experience in the reconstruction of these fossils, and Ji was a technician in the anatomy section of the College. They had the skills for preparing these delicate objects for shipment.

Hu recalled that Ms Taschdjian, known as Hirschberg, had been working in the Cenozoic Research unit for eight months. Her father, a doctor, had known Weidenreich in Nanjing, and the young woman was also his secretary. In 1977 she wrote a book on the missing Peking Man fossils, but the work is fictional and the details are therefore exaggerated.

A long letter dated March 4, 1977 from Hu Chengzhi to Jia Lanpo relates the following reliable information concerning the episode:

> I heard that you are writing a book on the excavations at Zhoukoudian. This is quite necessary and must be done before you join Karl Marx in the Other World. You know more on many matters than I do, and it should be easy for you to give an account of them. Upon your request, I present here what I had come to know:
>
> Dr Davidson Black died at his desk on March 15, 1934. You know that he had a habit of working at night and retiring during the day. At 5 p.m. while working on an Upper Cave Man fossil, I went to his office to borrow a needle, but I turned back upon hearing that he was animatedly talking with Yang Zhongjian. When I came to the office the next morning, I was told he had passed away during the night due to his heart condition.

Professor Weidenreich, a German Jew and later a naturalized American, succeeded him in the research on Peking Man fossils. He was invited to be Honorary Director of the Cenozoic Laboratory when he was teaching anatomy at an American university. And he did not come to China until more than a year later, after he had fulfilled his contract at the university.

After the July 7th Incident of 1937, the Geological Survey of China kept functioning in Beijing in the name of the Cenozoic Laboratory until 1941 when Japan attacked Pearl Harbour.

In the spring of 1939 or thereabouts, the German (later Dutch) paleontologist G. H. R. von Koenigswald brought to Beijing many human remains found in Java, to study with Weidenreich. He stayed for over two months and we all worried about the safety of the specimens he brought along and disapproved of his incautiousness.

In the summer of 1941 when Franz Weidenreich was about to return to the United States, he gave instructions to have copies made of all the fossil specimens of human skulls and [have them sent] to him in America. He also said that the originals should be transferred from the Japanese-occupied area for safety and that he would consult with Weng Wenhao on the matter. He left for the United States shortly after. About three months later, Mr Pei Wenzhong said to me that all Peking Man fossils were to be shipped off. I asked him when, and he told me to wait for further instructions. Two or three months passed before Weidenreich's secretary told me that all specimens were to be boxed. I confirmed this with Pei Wenzhong, who had succeeded Yang Zhongjian as the Director of the Cenozoic Laboratory. He urged me to get the job done as quickly as possible.

The next day, with the help of a technician from the anatomy section, Mr Ji Yanqing, the job was done. We wrapped every fossil in white tissue paper, cushioned it with cotton and gauze and then overwrapped them with white sheet paper. The packages were placed in a small wooden box with several layers of corrugated board on all sides for further protection. These boxes were then put into two big unpainted wooden crates, one the size of an office desk, the other slightly smaller. We delivered the two cases to the head of Controller T. Bowen's Office, at the Peking Union Medical College, and from then on none of the Chinese knew what happened to them.

After the Pearl Harbour attack on December 8 [Beijing time], 1941, we were all paid off. The day after the Japanese took over the College, Mr Pei told me that according to S. K. Wang (Wang Sih-tze), then head of the hospital attached to the Peking Union Medical College, the fossils had been moved into the No. 4 strong room in Building F of the medical college on the day we delivered them, but were transferred to an unknown place the next day. I had tried to recollect with Professor Pei the date of delivery to Building F from Building B where the specimens had been kept in two safes, and we had placed it 18 to 21 days prior to Pearl Harbour.

Not long after, the paleontologist Dr Hasebe Kotondo of Japan came to Beijing for studies on Peking Man and discovered the removal of the fossils.

After V-J Day, in September or October, I happened to be in Nanjing and noticed in a news dispatch that Weng Wenhao had just flown in to town. I looked him up the next day at his office and asked him about the whereabouts of the fossils. "They are missing," he said. "One source had it that they were taken on board a US ship that was evacuating American residents in China, and the vessel was captured by the Japanese on December 8 soon after embarkation. . ."

Mr Yang Zhongjian and I came to Beijing on business in 1947 and bumped into Taschdjian Hirschberg in the street. She told us that she had been taken prisoner by the Japanese military police and escorted to Tianjin (Tientsin) to search for the two Peking Man fossil boxes at many warehouses, but the search was in vain and she was released. That was the last I saw of her.

Hu also said that these Japanese military police were in such earnest that they interrogated anyone they suspected. Professor Ma Wenzhao of the anatomy section of the Union Medical College and one labourer who had wheelbarrowed the two boxes into the No. 4 room in Building F were among those who were grilled.

He concluded:

I can only provide information concerning the packing of the fossils. Other matters are known to all. What I say here may be inaccurate in some details owing to such a long lag of time, but the essence cannot be wide of the mark.

There had been a list of items packed in the two cases, but it was lost in the 'cultural revolution'. Fortunately, the list had been recorded in a paper by Jia Lanpo published in 1951[1] and republished in the book *Early Man in China* by the same author.[2]

It is known that on the day following the packing, the fossils were delivered to the US Embassy located at Dongjiaominxiang in Beijing, and since then they have been missing.

The list of lost items is again copied here in the hope that these missing objects will someday be located.

LIST OF THE ITEMS BOXED

Case 1 containing seven boxes of specimens:

Box 1:
Teeth of Peking Man (in 74 small boxes)
Teeth of Peking Man (in 5 small boxes)
  9 thighbone fragments of Peking Man
  2 fragmented humeri of Peking Man
  2 upper jaws of Peking Man

[1] 'The Missing Remains of the *Sinanthropus Pekinensis* and the Losses of the Cenozoic Laboratory During the War of Resistance Against Japan.'
[2] Foreign Languages Press, Beijing, 1980, pp. 32-33.

1 upper jaw of Peking Man from below Upper Cave
1 collar bone of Peking Man
1 carpal bone of Peking Man
1 nasal bone of Peking Man
1 palate bone of Peking Man
1 first cervical vertebra of Peking Man
15 fragmentary skulls of Peking Man
1 box of Peking Man skull fragments of skulls Nos. 1 and 2 from Locus L
2 boxes of toe bones unlikely to have belonged to Peking Man
3 boxes of orangutan teeth
13 fragmentary mandibles of Peking Man

Box 2:
Peking Man skull No. 2 from Locus L

Box 3:
Peking Man skull No. 3 from Locus L

Box 4:
Peking Man skull No. 1 from Locus L

Box 5:
Peking Man skull discovered in 1929 at Locus E

Box 6:
Skull of a female of Upper Cave Man

Box 7:
Same

Case 2 containing the following:

Peking Man skull from Site D
Upper Cave Man skull of an aged male
2 macaque skulls
5 macaque mandibles
3 macaque upper jawbone fragments
1 small box of macaque skull fragments
4 mandibles of Upper Cave Man
1 big box of vertebrae
7 pelvic bones
3 shoulder-blades
3 kneecaps
3 skull fragments
6 metatarsal bones
2 sacra

1 glass tube of teeth
3 mandible fragments

There were other losses of fossils collected by the Cenozoic Laboratory, mainly mammalian remains packed to be shipped off for safety towards the end of spring 1937. The boxes were divided into three groups. The first group, totalling twenty-eight boxes, each marked with an upside-down V over the serial number, contained the following fossils:

1. *Cervus (Euryceros) pachyosteus*
   386 upper jaws
   Loc. 1

2. *Cervus (Euryceros) pachyosteus*
   310 lower jaws
   Loc. 1

3. *Cervus (Euryceros) pachyosteus*
   285 lower jaws
   Loc. 1

4. *Pseudaxis grayi*
   676 lower jaws, 47 broken antlers
   Loc. 1

5. *Rhinoceros*
   13 humeri, 13 radii and 2 femora
   Loc. 1

6. *Rhinoceros*
   14 ulnae, 15 tibiae and 58 foot bones
   Loc. 1

7. *Cervus (Euryceros) pachyosteus* and *Pseudaxis grayi*
   Broken teeth, some broken upper and lower jaws
   Loc. 1

8. *Cervus (Euryceros) pachyosteus*
   19 broken skulls
   Pseudaxis grayi
   84 broken antlers
   Rhinoceros
   Broken teeth and limb bones
   Loc. 1

9. *Hyena*
388 broken limb bones
Loc. 1

10. *Hyena*
154 broken lower jaws
Loc. 1

11. *Hyena*
77 broken upper jaws
Loc. 1

12. *Hyena*
206 canines
42 broken jaws
590 broken teeth
Loc. 1

13. Some small fossils
Loc. 1

14. *Cervus*
Limb bones
Loc. 13

15. *Cervus*
Limb bones
Loc. 12

16. *Cervus*
Limb bones
Loc. 1

17. *Cervus*
Limb bones
Rhinoceros
Limb bones
Loc. 13

18. *Cervus* and *Bubalus*
Vertebrae
Loc. 13

19. *Cervus*
Foot bones
Rhinoceros
Foot bones
Loc. 13

20. *Cervus*
Scapulae, sternum, vertebrae, pelvis and fragmentary limb bones
Loc. 13

21. Fossil bones from Loc. 1 of Zhoukoudian
(packed in a small wooden box)

22. Fossil bones from Loc. 1 of Zhoukoudian
(packed in a small wooden box)

23. *Cervus*
Limb bones, vertebrae, phalanges and pelvis
Rhinoceros
Limb bones and foot bones
Loc. 1

24. *Cervus*
Antlers, broken skulls, scapulae, ribs, vertebrae and pelvis
Loc. 13

25. *Hyena*
Upper and lower jaws, postcranial bones
Loc. 1
Cervus
Antlers and limb bones
Loc. 13

26. *Hyena*
Teeth and limb bones
Loc. 1

27. *Hyena*
Skulls, lower jaws and postcranial bones
Loc. 1

28. Shells of molluscs (packed by M. N. Bien)

The second group consisted of nine boxes, each marked with a circle around the serial number. The contents were stone implements:

(1)-(2) Stone implements from Loc. 15 of Zhoukoudian

(3)-(4) Quartz artifacts from Loc. 15 of Zhoukoudian

(5) Flint artifacts from Loc. 15 of Zhoukoudian

(6)–(9) Stone implements from Loc. 15 of Zhoukoudian

The third group had thirty boxes, mostly non-mammalian, but a small part consisted of mammalian fossils unearthed from various areas in China. The letter C was marked before the serial number on each box. The contents were as follows:

C1–C6 Fossil fish from Loc. 14 of Zhoukoudian
Barbus brevicephalus chang and *Barbus szechuanensis tchang*

C7 *Endinoceras* cf. *Kholobolchiensis* Osb. and Granger. Left half part of skull with 4 upper teeth and 3 isolated fragmentary teeth. From Ichang, Hupei (Yichang, Hubei Province)
Spirocerus peii young
Skull fragment with complete left and fragmentary right side antlers. From Loc. 1 of Zhoukoudian (with mounting: iron frame and wooden board)
Geoclemys reevesii
One nearly complete shell from Loc. 3 of Zhoukoudian
Ocadia sinensis
One complete shell from Anyang, Henan
Geoclemys reevesii
Skull with shell and skeleton from Anyang, Henan

C8 *Plesiaceratherium gracile*
Limb bones from Shanwang, Shandong (Loc. 37)

C9 Mounting boards (wooden) and iron frames for the limb bones packed in C8

C10–C11 Fossil fish from Loc. 14 of Zhoukoudian

C12 Fossil fish from Loc. 14 of Zhoukoudian
Protitanothere mongoliense, 1 left lower jaw, from Yuanqu, Shanxi

C13 *Cervus elephas*
Left antler, from Upper Cave of Zhoukoudian
Sinokennemyeria pearsoni
8 vertebrae, from Wuxiangxian, Shanxi

C14 *Bubalus brevicornis*
Skull with 2 complete antlers, from Mianshixian, Henan

C15 *Pseudaxis grayi*
Antlers, from Loc. 9;
Eudinoceras kholobolchiensis
Atlas, from Yichang, Hubei
Sinokennemyeria pearsoni
Humerus, femur and pelvis, from Wuxiang, Shanxi

C16–C17 Fossil plant from Shanwang, Shandong

C18 *Cervus*
Limb bones
Rhinoceros
Foot bones
Loc. 9 of Zhoukoudian

C19 *Cervus*
Limb bones
Rhinoceros
Foot bones
Equus
Lower jaw
Lepus
Limb bones
Loc. 9

C20 *Cervus* and *Rhinoceros*
Limb bones
Loc. 9

C21 *Cervus* and *Rhinoceros*
Postcranial bones
Loc. 9

C22 *Rhinoceros* and *Cervus*
Foot bones
Loc. 9

C23 *Bubalus*
Fragmentary jawbone
Cervus
Limb bones
Rhinoceros
Phalanges
Vulpus
Limb bones and foot bones
Loc. 9

C24 *Ursus* and *Felis*
Postcranial bones
Upper Cave of Zhoukoudian

C25 *Meles* and *Lepus*
Limb bones
Upper Cave of Zhoukoudian

C26 *Cervus*
Postcranial bones
Upper Cave of Zhoukoudian

C27-C28 *Cervus*
Postcranial bones
Upper Cave of Zhoukoudian

C29-C30 *Cervus, Canis, Vulpus, Ursus, Felix*
and *Lepus*
Skulls and postcranial bones
Upper Cave of Zhoukoudian

The Cenozoic Laboratory had its offices in the Union Medical College in East Beijing and at 9 Bingmasi and 3 Fengsheng Hutong in the west of the city. The 67 boxes of fossils and artifacts listed above, together with 30 boxes of books published by the institution, were left in the storeroom of Lockhart Hall at the College. Also kept there were more than ten boxes of Xinjiang reptile fossils left by Professor Yuan Fuli of Qinghua University, and some personal scripts.

Until the end of January 1942, the Japanese authorities merely guarded the gates of the building so that nothing could be taken out. When all the employees were discharged on the first of February, the specimens, books and equipment were left undisturbed. The place was later the headquarters of the Japanese military police, and it was then that the remaining items suffered their worst fate—some were shipped away, some burnt, and some thrown into a storeroom of the College.

In May 1942, books of the Cenozoic Laboratory suddenly appeared in many book stalls in Beijing. They had been salvaged by local people when Japanese soldiers were burning them and had been sold to dealers.

At the end of 1950, the Chinese Academy of Sciences miraculously received four pieces of fossil from a man named Han Deshan in Xi'an. Upon receiving these objects, Yang Zhongjian, then Director of the Cenozoic Laboratory, wrote to Mr Han enquiring how the remains had come into his possession. Han replied on January 22, 1951. The following is his account in part:

I had been an employee of the Union Medical College from January 1931, to January 31, 1942, when I was discharged with all other employees by the Japanese authorities. I got a job at the Beijing Research Institute of Hygiene afterwards. While working at the Medical College, I heard about the important and rare Zhoukoudian fossils of the Cenozoic Laboratory, but I had never seen one. In April 1942, the Japanese military police were in a hurry to vacate the rooms of Lockhart Hall and ordered the books and 'bones' shipped off and destroyed. On my way home after work, I heard about the burning of books and went to see. It was true, but most of the books were carried off by local residents, who were later seen selling these books to second-hand book dealers. There were great numbers of bones on the ground, scattered and smashed, so I ventured to pick some up. Japanese soldiers were still there watching, so I only took four pieces furtively. I brought them with me to Xi'an in April 1949, when I began to work here. That is what happened.

After V-J Day, the Beijing Branch of the Geological Survey of China and the Cenozoic Laboratory, which was under its direction, resumed work. In November 1946 the Union Medical College discovered specimens from the Laboratory on its premises and notified the Geological Survey. These were fossils, new bones and moulds all jumbled up in a room. The damage was serious and irreparable, according to Jia Lanpo and the paleoichthyologist Liu Xianting, who were in charge of regrouping them.

21

The Disappearance of the Human Remains

The two big boxes containing the Peking Man, Upper Cave Man and some other primate remains were said to have been delivered to the US Embassy at the end of November 1941 by T. Bowen of the Controller's Office of the Union Medical College. The fossils have been missing ever since.

There have been many speculations on what happened to them, but so far, nobody has been able to give solid evidence on their whereabouts. The only credible account is that a vessel which had sailed from Manila to Qinhuangdao (Hebei Province) to fetch US marines was sunk by Japanese forces off the Changjiang (Yangtze River) on December 8 when Japan declared war on the United States. Considering the time factor, the two boxes could not have been shipped out of China and most probably had been in one of the warehouses of the US military either in Tianjin or at Qinhuangdao.

In the beginning, the news of the missing fossils was kept secret, but later it became the talk of the world as magazines, newspapers and books offered various interesting accounts of what had happened. A few examples follow.

The *Peking Chronicle*, an English daily, reported on August 23, 1942:

Sinanthropus Pekinensis
Skull Remains
Kept in P.U.M.C. Stolen
Famous Peking Man replaced

by mere copy
American staff suspected of theft

(Chung Hwa-Domei)—It is learned that the famous skull remains of the *Sinanthropus pekinensis* primitive man, an ancestor of mankind who lived approximately 200 000 years ago near Peking, was discovered to have been carried away and replaced by a mere copy which was found in its place.

The amazing discovery was made by two scholars, Professor Kotondo Hasebe of the Geological Department of the Tokyo Imperial University accompanied by Mr Fuyuji Takai, assistant in the same department of the same university who arrived in Peking on August 19 and commenced their researches in Choukoutien.

When the two scholars visited the Peking Union Medical College where the precious remains of the primitive man were kept, they found to their amazement that the skull had been replaced by a mere copy. An American staff member of the college was suspected to have [sic] removed the skull remains upon the outbreak of the Greater East Asia War in anticipation that the university would be occupied by the Japanese forces.

Stolen Two Years Ago?

Several implements of the Stone Age and some human bones belonging to a transitional period between the Stone and Bronze Ages also were genuine specimens which were left, Dr Hasebe asserted. It is also learned that on the other hand, Lieutenant Tamotsu Matsuhashi, a graduate of the Nippon Medical College who had actually seen the skull remains of *Sinanthropus pekinensis* on one of his visits to the Peking Union Medical College for anthropological studies, declared that when he took several Japanese scholars in 1940 to the University, he discovered that the only article remaining in the college depository was a model *Pithecanthropus erectus* of Java. According to Lieutenant Matsuhashi, there was a contract prohibiting the removal of the skull remains of the *Sinanthropus pekinensis* from the college.

According to a dispatch of the Associated Press of the United States, we know what happened to some of the finds from Zhoukoudian. The following news dispatch was issued by AP on November 19, 1945:

Save Peking Man Relics
—Geological Treasure Included in
Loot Discovered in Japan

Tokyo, Nov. 19 (AP)—In the plunder sent to Japan by her army and recovered by occupation authorities are priceless scientific treasures that came from the cave of the Peking Man, one of man's earliest known ancestors.

The recovered loot, it was learned today, included crude tools, carved tooth jewelry and charts showing where the articles were discovered originally in a limestone cave in Choukoutien, near Peiping, in 1929. They had been kept at the Peiping Union Medical College.

The bones of the Peking Man (*Sinanthropus pekinensis*) were well hidden by the Chinese and escaped a three-year search by Japanese scientists, seized letters revealed. The articles were found at Tokyo Imperial University after Japanese authorities had informed Allied headquarters.

Dr Frank C. Whitmore Jr, scientific consultant of the United States Geological Survey attached to Allied Headquarters, took custody of the relics pending their return to the National Geographic Survey [should

Floor plan of the Anatomy Section on the ground floor of Building B of the Peking Union Medical College. Peking Man fossils were kept in safes in Rooms 111 and 112. (1) Office of Black and Weidenreich; (2) lab where Black worked on the fossils; (3) Weidenreich's worktable; (4) Teilhard occasionally worked here; (5) where Hu Chengzhi made copies of the Peking Man fossils; (6) where Chen Zhinong and Jiang Hancheng made sketches; (7) Mrs Gowen and Miss Hirschberg worked here at different times; (8) and (9) safes in which Peking Man fossils were kept; (10) the wooden case in which the Upper Cave Man fossils were kept; (11) lab room; (12) office of Fortuyn; (13) stairway; (14) worktables.

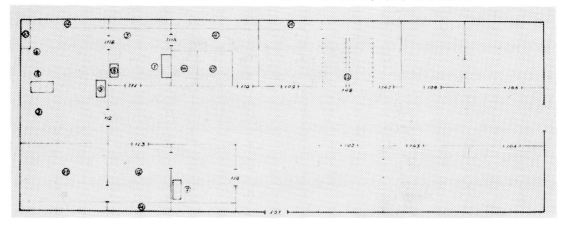

read Geological Survey—the authors] of China.

On January 2, 1946 the *Peiping Chronicle* carried a news item saying that the Peking Man remains were found in Japan:

Shanghai, Jan. 1 (Reuter):—The 'Peking Man' taken to Japan by the Japanese Army as loot during the occupation is to be re-

turned to the National Geographical Survey Society [should read Geological Survey —the authors] of China. The Tokyo University is reported already to have carried these priceless bones together with the implements to the Allied Authorities.

Japanese Army scientists found the 'Peking Man' in Peiping after three years' search and a specialist supervised the removal to Tokyo. None of the bones and the charts or other documents accompanying the relics appears to have been damaged in Japanese hands.

The 'Peking Man' was discovered by Chinese scientists in co-operation with American anthropologists under the Rockefeller Foundation in 1929. For some time a controversy raged as to whether the 'Peking Man' or the 'Java Man' was older. Finally scientists agreed that 'Java Man' was probably older, but that the 'Peking Man' was of more value to science because he was more like a human being.

It is known that during the occupation Japanese scientists made new finds, but failed to make new discoveries.

The 'Peking Man' is the first of China's looted treasures to be returned, but Chinese patriotic organizations are trying to obtain the return of other Chinese antiques and art treasures seized by the Japanese.

Top: Dr Harry L. Shapiro, American anthropologist and Honorary Chairman of the Anthropological Department of the American Museum of Natural History. His book *Peking Man* (1974) relates the finding and disappearance of the fossils and the subsequent search for them. He visited China in 1980 for the specific purpose of locating the precious relics.
Bottom: Barracks of the US Marine Corps at Chinwangtao (Qinhuangdao), where the Peking Man fossils were alleged to have been stored in 1941 for shipping out of China (*Photos from Shapiro: Peking Man*)

But among the items the Allied Head-quarters passed on to China there was no Peking Man specimen, as a letter from Dr Li Ji to Dr Pei Wenzhong, dated May 24, 1946 indicates. The text of the letter and its enclo-sures—a memorandum of the Chinese del-egation and a list of the items returned —follows.

I have received your letter dated May 21st. I was back on May 5th but I have been so busy writing a report that I found no time to answer letters until now. While in Tokyo, I tried five times to search for 'Pe-king Man', all in vain. However, the stone and bone implements kept at the Tokyo Imperial University have been repossessed (I have checked and identified that they are yours) and are in the custody of the Allied Headquarters. Prior to my departure I had completed the formalities for their return to China (a newspaper reported that they had already been returned to China on April 15th). The enclosed copy of our Memoran-dum to the Allied Headquarters may relate the main happenings and I will give you the detailed account when I see you.

Memorandum:

To: Maj. Gen. C. A. Willoughby
    Assistant Chief of Staff, G-2, GHQ, SCAP
Subject: Return of Anthropological Materials from Choukoutien and Research Records of *Sinanthropus* Projects
    1. The following articles from the Ce-nozoic Laboratory, Geological Survey of China, Peiping, were reported to be taken to Japan during the war:
    a) Specimens of 'Peking Man', consisting of seven skulls, twelve lower jaws, a num-ber of teeth and skeletal materials;
    b) Stone and bone implements as well as animal remains from Loc. 1, Loc. 15 and Upper Cave of Choukoutien;
    c) Records, photographs, and documents concerning excavations at Choukoutien;
    d) Mammalian fossils of dogs and wolves from Anyang;
    e) Books and pamphlets on anthropolo-gy of Professor Black and Professor Wei-denreich.
    2. It is understood that Peking Union Medical College which cooperated with the Geological Survey of China in the excava-tion of Choukoutien and founding of the Cenozoic Laboratory has already requested SCAP to make inquiries about the loss as listed above, and subsequently some speci-mens under items (b) and (c) have been restored, now under the custody of the Natural Resources Sections, GHQ. Dr Li Chi (Li Ji), Adviser of the Chinese Mission, has been asked by the Chinese Ministry of Economics to make further inquiries about these highly important scientific specimens and has received upon request, from G.I.E. Section, the list of the articles recovered. Attached is a copy of the list.
    3. It is hereby requested that GHQ, SCAP instruct the Foreign and Miscellaneous Property Division, Office of Civil Property Custodian, to deliver the recovered spe-cimens of anthropological material from Choukoutien and research records of *Sinan-thropus* projects to Dr Li Chi, representing the Chinese Mission. It is further requested that search of the unrecovered materials be continued by the SCAP.
    4. Your attention to these requests will be highly appreciated.

Chu Shih-ming
Chief, Chinese Mission in Japan

The list of restored materials is as fol-lows:

Anthropological Material from Upper Cave, Choukoutien, and Research Records of *Sinanthropus* Project, Peking Union Medi-cal College
Plans and sections of different levels of Locality 1 of Choukoutien 1
The summary reports and accounts of field office .... 11 sets
Lists of mammalian fossils from Choukou-tien given abroad .... 1 set
Films of views of Choukoutien (already re-troceded to the Section of Anatomy of

the Peiping Union Medical College)

.... 7 albums

Polished antler from Upper Cave ...... 1 PC.

Canines of fox and moles (44 pieces) from Upper Cave .... 1 PC.

Canines of fox and moles (37 pieces) and 3 stone beads from Upper Cave, not polished .... 1 box

Stone pendant, bone needle, limestone fragment with red colour and canines of large deer from Upper Cave .... 1 box

Canines of fox (type) from Upper Cave

.... 1 box

Artificially perforated shells of *Arca* sp., bird bone pendant, fish bones, fish vertebrae and stone bead from Upper Cave

.... 1 box

Stone implements, 4 pieces, from Upper Cave .... 1 box

Stone implements, 3 pieces, from Locality 1 .... 1 box

Burnt antler fragment from Locality 1

.... 1 box

Stone implements from Locality 15, 5 pieces

.... 2 box

Stone implements from Locality 15, 1 piece

.... 1 box

Documents (English) .... 3 vol.

Chinese Mission in Japan, Tokyo
30 April, 1946

The search was, however, still inconclusive. A letter to Pei Wenzhong from Frank C. Whitmore Jr of the Geological Survey of the United States Department of the Interior may show this. He had been the Acting Geologist in Charge, Military Geology Unit of the Allied Headquarters in Tokyo. The letter from Washington dated July 12, 1946 reads:

Dear Dr Pei:

You have probably already received the collection and documents from Choukoutien which were found by US Army authorities at Tokyo Imperial University.

At the request of Dr Weidenreich, I enclose a list of the material.

While in Tokyo last winter I endeavored to find traces of the *Sinanthropus* remains, but was unable to do so.

If you have any suggestions as to further sources of information in Tokyo concerning any material which was taken by the Japanese, I suggest that you communicate with Lt. Col. H. G. Schenck, Natural Resources Section, GHQ, SCAP, APO 500, Tokyo Interisland Mail.

Sincerely Yours,
Frank C. Whitmore Jr,
Acting Geologist in Charge
Military Geology Unit

An authoritative account had also been given by Pei Wenzhong when he talked to a reporter from *Da Gong Bao*, a Beijing daily, in March 1950. An extract of that interview follows.

Long before the Pearl Harbour attack, Kotondo Hasebe and Fuyuji Takai, both scholars from Tokyo Imperial University, had come to Beijing. After the Union Medical College was taken over by the Japanese army, they hurried to find the Peking Man fossils. When they ordered the safe opened and saw that there was a copy of the skullcap, they left without a word.

A few days later, a captain of the Japanese army made an appointment with Dr Pei during which the captain said they knew that the genuine fossils in the safe were gone and that it was Americans who had smuggled them away. He asked whether Pei knew their whereabouts. Pei's answer was that because his office was far away from the College premises, he knew nothing. The captain said to him, encouragingly, "You have nothing to worry about. We'll look after you after occupation, for we know you are a scholar, not a politician." While taking his leave, he added: "If the Army authorities decide not to press the search, you may go on working as usual; if they do, you can't get away by pleading ignorance." He confiscated Pei's resident ID card, a necessary credential for any Chinese who wanted to leave the city or even to go beyond the city limit.

After a half year (in April or May 1942), someone called on Pei telling him that visitors from Tokyo wanted to have a talk with him. It was learned much later that in the beginning, the Japanese military authorities were aware of the Medical College only for its importance in the field of medicine and paid only incidental attention to the problem of the Peking Man fossils. The scholars Kotondo Hasebe and Fuyuji Takai, however, submitted a report to the Ministry of Education, which forwarded the message to the Emperor—and it was he who ordered the headquarters of the North China Expeditionary Force of Japan to search for the fossils. When summoned to Hotel Beijing, Pei gave the same answer. The Japanese expressed the hope that Pei would co-operate with them in the future.

Arriving home, Pei was told a Japanese by the name of Josha had visited him. The man came again on the following day. He spoke fluent English, stating that he was a detective working for the North China Headquarters, and he had orders from the Supreme Command to search for Peking Man fossils. Pei gave the same answer once again, and the officer raised a few questions —When had he seen the objects last? Who was in charge of them? etc.—before he took off. He warned Pei not to leave home in the two coming weeks so that he would be available for further questioning. Sharp and efficient, the Japanese officer had probed into the matter with all concerned in three days. In the meantime, Dr Kotondo Hasebe and a few army officers had taken Pei to Zhoukoudian and expressed bewilderment over the lost fossils. They said they were contemplating resumption of excavation at the Peking Man site.

Two months later, news suddenly came that the fossil was found in Tianjin (Tientsin) and the Japanese authorities were looking for someone to identify the authenticity of the object. They had indeed summoned Miss Heisenberg, former secretary of Dr Weidenreich, to the city, but as soon as she arrived there by train, she was told to go back, as the object found had nothing to do with the Peking Man fossil. After that, the Japanese dropped the matter completely, and under the pretext of lack of funds, Dr Hasebe and company gave up their project of excavation at Zhoukoudian and left China for Japan.

22

Charge and Counthercharge

The search for the Peking Man remains turned dramatic in the 1950s as more and more scholars of various countries became involved. At the beginning of the decade, a feud developed between the Chinese scientists and their American colleagues caused by a misunderstanding conveyed in a letter from Dr Walter Kühne, a paleontologist at Humboldt University, Berlin, German Democratic Republic, to Yang Zhongjian, the late Director of the Institute of Vertebrate Paleontology and Paleoanthropology of the Chinese Academy of Sciences (then the Cenozoic and Vertebrate Paleontological Department of the Institute of Paleontology of the Academy). Dated October 6, 1951, the letter reads:

> At a high tea in the faculty lounge of the Department of Zoology of University College, London, this spring, I was told by the Head of the Biology Department, the vertebrate paleontologist Dr D. M. S. Walson, that the Skullcap II of Zhoukoudian is now in the American Museum of Natural History, turned over to it by Franz Weidenreich prior to his death. When he last visited New York, he saw the specimen in the hands of Weidenreich . . . The specimen was taken by an American GI from the Imperial Museum of Japan . . . I wonder if you have come to know this already, but I was astounded upon hearing it. I did not ask Walson further about this then or later, but just put it down in my notebook. From what I heard from him, I am certain that the fact is undoubtedly true.

With this evidence, Yang Zhongjian and Pei Wenzhong believed that the object had been in the hands of Americans. Thus on January 1, 1952 they published an article in the *People's Daily* urging the return of the fossil to its rightful owner, the People's Republic of China. However, a letter dated April 29, 1952 from Dr Joseph Needham, President of the Britain-China Friendship Association, to the late Guo Moruo, President of the Chinese Academy of Sciences, proves that Walson was mistaken about the identity of the skullcap. The letter from Needham reads:

> I have pleasure in transmitting to you herewith a letter from my friend, Dr K. P. Oakley of the British Museum of Natural History, addressed to Dr Pei Wen-chung, the eminent paleontologist. You will see that it concerns the problem of the whereabouts of the Choukoutien skulls.

And the enclosed letter from Dr Oakley reads:

> I have often wondered how your work is progressing and I hope very much that your new excavations at Choukoutien are yielding important material.
>
> My friend Dr Needham showed me the report that one of the Choukoutien skulls was in the American Museum of Natural History. Professor Walson told me the same story in 1949 that he told Dr Walter Kühne in 1951. I have since discovered that Professor Walson was mistaken in thinking that the fossil skull which Professor Weidenreich showed to him in the American Mu-

seum was Choukoutien No. XI. When I was in New York in 1950, I repeated his story to Dr Shapiro. He said that the skull which Weidenreich showed to Walson was not Choukoutien XI; it was Solo XI. I now find that Professor von Koenigswald published an article in *Natural History*, Vol. 56, No. 1, January 1947, in which he mentions that one of the Solo skulls was sent to the Emperor of Japan as a birthday present during the Japanese occupation of Java, and that it was subsequently recovered from the Palace.

The American Museum has now returned Solo XI to the Dutch custodians.

The Editor of the British magazine *Antiquity*, O. G. Crawford, in an article entitled 'The Fate of the Chinese Skulls' (Notes and News, pp. 226-7, December 1954), had this to say:

About a quarter of a century ago the fragmentary remains of extremely ancient human skulls were found at Choukoutien near Peking. The first finds were later added to and implements found also. During the war of 1939-45 all these remains disappeared, and all efforts to rediscover them have so far failed. Fortunately casts were made of all the more important specimens, and these are still available for study in Europe and America.

Chinese journalists have recently accused the Americans of having stolen them. It all began with an unfortunate mistake made by Professor D. M. S. Walson, of London University, who, when visiting the American Museum of Natural History in 1945, saw another ancient skull which was found in Java and bears the name of Solo XI, and which he mistook for the skull called Choukoutien XI. He spoke about the matter to his friends, and in 1951 he repeated the story to Dr Walter Kühne who is described as "faculty member of Berlin's Humboldt University in the German Democratic (i.e. Communist) Republic." Dr Kühne repeated the statement of Professor Walson in a letter he wrote to Dr Yang of the Chinese Academy of Sciences . . .

The plain fact is that an honest mistake was made, and Professor Walson has admitted it, in a letter which he allows me to print; it is dated August 30, 1954 from the Department of Zoology of University College, London, and runs as follows:

"The statement that I saw a skull of Peking Man in the American Museum of Natural History in 1954 is an error. What I did see there was a skull from Java, one of the Solo series, which had been found in Japan after the war."

Two accounts are given of the movements of the skulls and other objects immediately before their disappearance. The New China News Agency (15 January 1952) states that originally the entire Peking Man collection, including the No. XI skull, belonged to the Cenozoic Research Laboratory of the Geological Survey of China . . . It was kept in the custody of the Peking Union Medical College, then an American subsidized institution. In November 1941, shortly after the Pacific War broke out, T. Bowen, American Controller of the College, removed the prehistoric fossil to the former American Embassy, preparatory to shipping it to the United States. At that time the fossil was to be 'evacuated' together with the American marines via Chinwangtao. But the war broke out and the American Embassy, together with the warehouses in Peking, Tientsin and Chinwangtao, was occupied by the Japanese invading army. Since then the 'Peking Man' has been missing.

Professor Walson's account is quite different. "Weidenreich," he says (in the same letter to me), "told me not long before his death that he had been particularly careful to place them in Chinese custody, and that they were being taken to Tientsin by Chinese when they were lost to sight." It would appear from this statement that the responsibility for their disappearance rests upon the Chinese.

Professor Walson adds: "You might perhaps in any *Note* point out that the whole discovery and publication of the 'Peking Man' was done at vast expense by the Rockefeller Trustees; and that not a single

American scientist had any part in it. The men were Canadian, French, Austrian, German, Swedish and Chinese!"

A detailed account of the disappearance of the skulls and of the post-war search for them is given in Ruth Moore's *Men, Time and Fossils* (1954). Moore's account in the above-mentioned book is as follows:

. . . But the times were growing increasingly uneasy. There were threats and reports of Japanese troop movements. By late November and early December those living at the centre of the gathering storm could no longer misread the signs.

Weidenreich was in the United States on a visit. Dr Wong Wen-hao, Director of the Geological Survey, appealed to Dr Henry S. Houghton, President of the Peking Union Medical College, to have the priceless Peking Man collection taken to safety. Wong was the custodian of the remains and wanted to save them from capture if the Japanese should move into Peking.

Somewhat reluctantly, Dr Houghton asked Colonel William W. Ashurst, commander of the Marine detachment at the American Embassy in Peking, to send the Peking Man collection to safety in the United States with a Marine detachment leaving within a few days.

Dr Houghton personally took the bones —scarcely more than a few handful packed in glass jars—to the Colonel. The instructions were to handle them as 'secret' material. Despite the hectic rush of departure, the Colonel personally packed them in one of his footlockers, along with some of the most valuable documents of the Embassy.

At five o'clock in the morning of December 5 the marines' special train, bearing the hidden bones of Peking Man, pulled out of Peking. It was to proceed via the Japanese-owned Manchuria railroad to the tiny Chinese coastal town of Chinwangtao. There it was to meet the American liner *S.S. President Harrison*, which was steaming north from Shanghai.

That rendezvous was never kept. On December 7 bombs crashed on Pearl Harbour. Total war instantly ripped the Far East.

To prevent the capture of the *Harrison*, her crew grounded her at the mouth of the Yangtze River. The marine train with its special cargo and guards was captured at Chinwangtao.

What happened from that moment on is clouded by rumour and the confusion of war. Only one fact is certain. From that day the remains of Peking Man disappeared completely. Despite the efforts of three governments to find them, they have vanished from the world as completely as during the centuries when they lay hidden in the earth of Dragon Bone Hill.

According to one account, the Japanese loaded all the cases taken from the train on a lighter that was to take them to a freighter lying off Tientsin. The lighter, it is said, capsized, and the remains of Peking Man drifted away or sank to the bottom of the sea.

The other story is that the Japanese who looted the train knew nothing of the value of the scraps of bone and either threw them away or sold them to Chinese traders as 'dragon bones'. If so, they may long since have been ground into medicine.

The nine marines who had been on the train were later returned to Peking and, with Colonel Ashurst and the 250 men of his command, were sent to prisoner-of-war camps in Japan.

By roundabout means Colonel Ashurst learned that the Japanese had taken millions of rounds of ammunition from the train and must have gone through everything aboard.

"Perhaps they found the remains and just threw them away," said the Colonel. "Like canned foods. The Japanese had no use for our goods they captured, so they just dumped them off the train. The Peking relics must not have looked like much. I hardly realized what they were."

A marine sergeant, interned in a concentration camp near Tientsin, reported that he later saw blankets and other marine equipment that had been on the same train. This too would indicate that the baggage had been captured by the Japanese . . .

Another sample of speculation appeared in the *Hongkong Standard*, a daily, on November 22, 1954:

The 'Peking Man' (or more properly —woman) is in Western hands . . . and he's only 50 000 years old.

This is revealed in a letter to the *Standard* by Dr J. J. Markey, President of the San Luis Bay Historical Society of Oceanside, California, the man mainly responsible for 'collecting' the remains of the Peking Man.

Dr Markey spent some time in Hong Kong two years ago following up reports stating that the Peking Man fossils were smuggled out of China during the Pacific War.

In this letter, Dr Markey writes that all 70 fragments of fossil *Sinanthropus* were recovered in Calcutta after having reposed in Macao for eight years.

"All are now quite safe in Western hands," he added. "Chemists who have been working on them for more than a year have now determined that they are not 400 000 years old, a date given them as a guess by Black in Peking, but only 50 000 years old."

He said that this new age has been determined by fluorine absorption tests, and adds that "our own calcium conversion test has eliminated all guess work as to the age of the Peking Man."

While in Hong Kong in the summer of 1952, Dr Markey denied persistent reports emanating from Peking at the time that fossil fragments of the Peking Man were in communist hands.

There have been countless such speculations published over the years; the portion we have collected, covering the period to 1959, is insignificant in size, but sufficient to show how academic circles the world over have been concerned with the problem. The story would be incomplete without mentioning the reaction of the Americans. The following article[1] is one of the two samples we quote in this chapter.

Where Is Peking Man?

Anthropologists are still speculating about the war-lost specimens.

The whereabouts of 'Peking Man', the world-famous anthropological collection that disappeared during World War II, is still the subject of hopeful speculation. Composed of specimens that are among the earliest traces of mankind, the collection was excavated from the floor of a limestone cave at Choukoutien, about 40 miles southeast of Peking, China, between 1928-37.

According to the best information available, the remains of Peking Man escaped the first onrush of the Japanese forces in North China in 1937 because they were stored in an American institution, the Peking Union Medical College. An agreement had been reached with the Chinese that the *Sinanthropus* material should remain in China permanently, and there be available to scholars of all nations for study. A few weeks before the United States became involved in World War II, negotiations were completed with Chungking for shipping the specimens to the United States for the duration of the war. Peking Man and all other associated specimens were packed in three cases and turned over to the US Marines, who were being evacuated from Chingwangtao on the American Dollar liner *President Harrison*. On December 8, 1941 the liner was run aground off the Yangtze River near Shanghai and the Marines were captured, and with them the three cases of *Sinanthropus* material. From that point on there is no definite knowledge about what happened to the remains.

Frank Whitmore, Chief of the Military Geology Branch, US Geological Survey, has been accused many times during the past decade of knowing more than he would tell about the whereabouts of *Sinanthropus*. Recently, he reaffirmed an earlier statement

---

[1] *Science*, Vol. 129, No. 3352, pp. 825-827, March 1959.

that denied any secret knowledge. He believes, as do others, that the collection is at the bottom of the Yangtze.

In 1942, the Japanese anthropologist Kotondo Hasebe went to Peking to study *Sinanthropus*, but when the vaults at the College were opened, only plaster casts were found. A year later, Japanese police made a thorough search, questioning everyone known to have had any connection, but all to no avail.

In 1945, Whitmore was detailed from Headquarters of the Allied Powers' Supreme Command to examine certain fossils and archaeological material from Choukoutien, China, at Tokyo University. However, most of the material that he was shown was from the Upper Cave at Choukoutien, belonging to an age much younger than that of *Sinanthropus*. In a statement about these specimens, Whitmore says in part: 'Most of the material recovered was from the Upper Cave, which is much younger than the strata in which *Sinanthropus* was found. There are a few stone implements of questionable nature from Loc. 15, which is probably paleolithic and is older than the Upper Cave material. From Loc. 1, which includes the strata in which *Sinanthropus* was found, there are only three questionable stone implements and no bone remains. This material was returned to the Cenozoic Laboratory (in Peking) in early 1946. Nothing was learned of the fate of the missing *Sinanthropus* specimens.'

According to Whitmore, the best hope for restoring Peking Man to anthropologists at first hand lies in the resumption of excavations at Choukoutien cave. Although excellent plaster casts of the skeletal material are available, these obviously do not have the same value for researchers as the original specimens.

Authoritative as this article may sound regarding the whereabouts of the Peking fossil, the issue remained as wide open as usual when the same magazine later published a note from Corald L. Beeman of the Cleveland Museum of Natural History contradicting Whitmore's assertion. It reads:[1]

As a former member of the American Embassy guard at Peking, China, at the outbreak of World War II, I would like to rule out the theory that the Peking Man may be at the bottom of the Yangtze River.

The *S.S. Harrison* had just taken the 4th Marines from Shanghai to the Philippine Islands and was returning to China for those of us who were still in North China. The war caught the ship just off the coast of China near Shanghai, and the captain ran it aground. This was hundreds of miles from Chinwangtao, and thus the Peking Man never went aboard the *Harrison*.

I recall seeing some cases in Peking marked for Johns Hopkins University and believe these contained the collection. If so, I am fairly certain they arrived safely in Chinwangtao.

Since we were preparing to leave China on Thursday December 11, 1941 we had packed up all our guns, ammunition and other equipment and had sent it to Chinwangtao. Because of the facilities in that small Marine outpost, it is quite likely that the Peking Man was stored with our things.

When the war broke out, the approximately 35 stationed in Chinwangtao were moved to Tientsin, and we were moved from Peking to Tientsin.

It may be that the Peking Man was discarded as unimportant in the looting of our supplies—that it was thrown out with the usual debris of such looting. If this was the case, there is a good chance that the collection is still in the vicinity of the camp at Chinwangtao or that it fell into the hands of the Chinese and was used for medicine, as was the practice.

Since the Japanese at the time had a great need for military supplies and since our equipment was all packed and ready to go, it may be that the Peking Man was shipped out with our equipment to some point within the Japanese war theatre. If this is the case, the collection could still be in existence in any one of a number of

---

[1] *Science*, Vol. 130, No. 3373, p. 416, Aug. 21, 1959.

places, from the Aleutians to Borneo.

It seems that a check with Japanese Army records, to locate the soldiers who were stationed at Chinwangtao would be a logical step in trying to locate the collection. Perhaps the men who were there could tell what happened to it.

One thing is certain: the Peking Man was not on the *S.S. Harrison.*

The above sampling of views, instead of clarifying the facts, simply adds to the confusion. Sheer rumours and guesswork are naturally filled with contradictions. Some of the 'facts' presented in these writings are simply fabrications, for example Markey's assertion about the dating of the Peking Man remains (50 000 years), and Moore's statement that the skullcap was contained in a glass jar.

Even more absurd speculations have come to our attention. They are good only for fiction, and we choose to ignore them in this book.

23

A Decade Later, Exciting New Clues

On October 21, 1971 the *New York Times* News Agency flashed a dispatch about a doctor, William T. Foley, who claimed he was the person last entrusted to take the Peking Man remains to the United States for safety and that he knew where he had left them. This news had been announced by Dr Harry L. Shapiro, Honorary Curator of the American Museum of Natural History in New York.

Subsequently, in his book *Peking Man* published in 1974, Shapiro devoted 20 per cent of the text to the problem of the missing fossils, in which a detailed account is given of the William Foley episode.

> Then one morning in April of 1971, almost thirty years after the loss, Dr Walter Fairservis came into my office with an air of excitement to announce that he had just received a telephone call from a Mr Herman Davis. Davis worked in the office of Dr William T. Foley, a prominent heart specialist in New York City, and was calling on Dr Foley's behalf. Dr Foley, apparently in preparing the memoirs of his career serving in the Marine Corps in China, had come across Fairservis' name in the records in Washington. These were concerned with Weidenreich's efforts in 1946-7 to have Fairservis assigned to the task of searching out the facts that might have led to the recovery of the fossils, and Dr Foley now hoped to get from Fairservis the names of others who had been involved in the correspondence. From the conversation with Davis, Fairservis had reached the conclusion that Dr Foley knew something about the loss of the Peking fossils that the rest of us did not know. He wanted to report this to me at once, knowing my deep professional concern over the fate of the fossils and being aware in particular of my personal involvement in the matter through my close association with Weidenreich and his efforts. And he knew of my implication as the alleged custodian of the fossils, for I had been publicly charged with harbouring them.
>
> As Fairservis no doubt anticipated, I reacted immediately by calling Dr Foley's office to make an appointment to see him and Davis. Davis answered, and from his brief account on the telephone, I knew at once that I was on the trail of some critical information. Though where it might lead was, of course, unpredictable at this point, it was obvious that I had to follow it. We made arrangements to meet, and they also agreed to permit me to tape their stories in their own words.
>
> I distinctly recall the feeling of excitement I experienced as, clutching my tape recorder, I went across town to East 68th Street, where Dr Foley's office was situated. When I arrived, Dr Foley was occupied, but Mr Davis was free and we retired to an unoccupied office to talk.
>
> Essentially, Davis's story was as follows: In the autumn of 1941, he was a pharmacist's mate in the US Navy stationed at Camp Holcomb in Chinwangtao . . . In his charge were seventeen Marines who formed a medical unit under the command of Dr Foley, a Marine medical officer who was himself living in Tientsin.

At that time, conditions in China had become distinctly ominous. As an expansion of Japanese military activity was anticipated momentarily, it was decided to transfer the entire Marine detachment stationed in the Peking area—which included Tientsin and Chinwangtao to the Philippines, where we were strongly based. The departure was scheduled for December 8, on the *S.S. President Harrison.*

Late in November, Davis received word from Dr Foley that some footlockers labelled with his name were being sent to Camp Holcomb from Peking. These, he was told, were personal baggage and were to be carefully guarded and held for shipment on December 8. Shortly thereafter, a freight train from Peking pulled into the siding at the camp, and Dr Foley's boxes were unloaded. Davis stacked them in his own room for safety, along with other baggage that had been made ready for shipment.

Davis related that when he awoke on the morning of December 8 (December 7, New York time), he looked out his window and discovered that the camp was surrounded by Japanese soldiers . . . Davis told me that he immediately mounted a machine gun on the pile of boxes in his room and began getting ready to shoot it out—but a call was put through at once to the top command in Peking to report the situation. Davis was ordered not to offer resistance since the situation was hopeless, but to surrender.

The Japanese straight away placed the Marines under arrest. Before herding them off to Tientsin for temporary imprisonment, they permitted each man to pack a single bag of personal belongings. The rest of the luggage, including the footlockers sent from Peking in Dr Foley's name, remained behind, apparently for inspection, and was then to be forwarded to Tientsin. A week or two later, the boxes of the Marines were delivered to them in their prison camp at Tientsin.

The boxes bearing Dr Foley's name were not sent to Davis and his companions in the prison camp at Tientsin, but were delivered to Dr Foley himself . . . The footlockers

containing the fossils were labelled as Foley's personal luggage and were the boxes that he had alerted Davis to receive at Camp Holcomb and guard with care.

At this point, the author tried to reconcile the allegation that Foley had seen the fossils contained in large glass jars with what Mrs Taschdjian, Weidenreich's secretary who had seen the packing, told him —that she had no recollection of such a glass jar. Shapiro expressed his bewilderment, but comforted himself with the thought that how the fossil was packed was perhaps unimportant. But anyone with experience knows that it is indeed important, for fossils are too fragile to be put into a glass jar. We had only used medicine glass tubes for human teeth or rodent specimens wrapped in cotton; we never used glassware for human fossils, not even for exhibition, let alone long-distance transportation.

This bizarre allegation had appeared in *The New York Times* on January 4, 1952 in an article on the missing fossils, and now Dr Foley claimed to have 'seen' that "some fossils were in large glass jars," which were then packed in military bags. Shapiro went on in his book:

On the day that the war broke out—December 8—Dr Foley also was immediately placed under arrest. He was transferred to the Marine barracks for about a week, but was then permitted to return to his home in the British Concession. At first he was allowed semi-diplomatic status, which gave him freedom to move around the city, though not beyond its limits. This lasted for about a week, and while still enjoying the privileged arrest, he received his boxes from Camp Holcomb, those containing the fossils sent from Peking as well as his personal luggage, apparently unopened and intact. I asked Dr Foley why the boxes bearing his name were delivered in this fashion while those belonging to the other Marines from Camp Holcomb had been opened and rifled and their contents mixed up. He replied that when he opened his personal boxes he had found that several skulls he had kept as anatomical specimens and a Chinese Buddha figure were missing. He had not opened the footlockers assigned to him from Peking. The fact that the boxes had been sent to him instead of to the Marines he attributed to the customary Japanese courtesy and respect for rank.

Faced as he was with the prospect of an extended internment (which, in fact, began shortly and lasted for four years), Dr Foley decided to distribute the Peking footlockers to various depositories for safekeeping. Some went to the Swiss Warehouse and the Pasteur Institute, both in Tientsin, and some were placed in the care of two Chinese friends on whom he felt he could rely.

A discrepancy appears at this point which may be due to the tricks of memory after thirty years. At a minimum, there would have been four boxes distributed in the fashion Dr Foley describes. And to this number one would have to add a fifth—the footlocker bearing Colonel Ashurst's name, which also, according to Dr Foley, contained fossils. But Mrs Taschdjian firmly recalled that only two footlockers were used for packing the fossils. Dr Pei, in his account, also specifically refers to only two boxes . . .

When Ashurst and Foley arrived at the prison camp, they managed to keep this footlocker under their own surveillance and prevent it from being opened and inspected. Subsequently, the group of US Marine officers, including Ashurst and Foley, was removed to another prison camp at Chung Wan, somewhat near Shanghai, and they were again successful in protecting the box from routine inspection that such a change of camps might entail.

Then in June 1945, the prisoners and their effects were transferred once more. This time to Fungtai, near Peking. Once again they somehow managed to save the box, presumably containing the fossils, from inspection. In retrospect, this three-fold success seems miraculous, but Dr Foley was very convincing about the strategems employed to achieve it.

After all these narrow escapes, it is tragic to have to relate that at the end of the war, this box, which had survived so many moves and so many hazards, disappeared with its secrets. According to Dr Foley, the last he saw of it was when he and Colonel Ashurst parted company, the former being sent to an abandoned iron mine in northern Japan, and the latter to Hokkaido. There they remained until arrangements could be made to return to the United States.

In the latter part of the book, Shapiro related another episode concerning Christopher G. Janus, a stockbroker from Chicago, who in the early summer of 1972 invited Shapiro for luncheon, claiming he had just returned to the United States from hunting the Peking Man fossils in China and wanted to tell him the story. They were strangers.

Janus had also lost no time in calling a press conference at which he gave an account of his China trip and announced a $5000 prize for anyone who might provide information leading to the finding of the Peking Man fossil collection.

Shapiro expressed misgivings about such a prize offer, for he believed that the fossils were still in China and that the prize would invite nuisance letters and phone calls. His prediction turned out to be correct, as Janus told him at their second meeting. From the United States alone, several hundred letters were received shortly after the prize was offered. The most bizarre incident was a phone call from a woman who claimed that the lost fossils were in her possession; she proposed to meet Janus at the top of the Empire State Building.

Janus went and met a good-looking middle-aged woman who related that after the war, her late husband had brought back from China a box he described as a 'trophy', containing Peking Man fossils. He repeatedly told her that the things inside were hazardous but extremely valuable and bade her be cautious lest there would be serious trouble.

She showed Janus a photograph to prove her point. The picture, reprinted in Shapiro's book, showed bones lying in disorderly fashion at the bottom of a box, cushioned by a layer of grass. One glance is proof that these were no Peking Man fossils, for there seemed to be finger and pelvic bones, which had never occurred at the Zhoukoudian Peking Man site. Yet for what she had in possession, she demanded a half million dollars in ransom. At one point during their talk, she panicked and ran for the door at the sight of some men with cameras in their hands. These were obviously only sightseers as the tower is a tourist favourite. Janus told reporters of the whole incident, and an account was duly published in the American newspapers.

If this mysterious woman had given cause for us to doubt, Janus himself gave cause for alarm as an alleged fraud. On February 26, 1981 *The New York Times* carried a news item with the headline 'Financier Is Charged with Fraud in Search for Bones of Peking Man'. It runs:

> Chicago, Feb. 25 (Reuter)—An international search for the missing bones of the prehistoric Peking Man by the Chicago financier Christopher G. Janus was a $640 000 fraud, Federal prosecutors charged today.
>
> A Federal grand jury indicted Mr Janus, 69 years old, on 37 counts, charging that he funnelled most of the money raised for the search to his personal use.

The indictment alleges that Mr Janus, a retired investment banker, fraudulently obtained $520 000 in bank loans and $120 000 from investors to finance the search and make a film about the Peking Man.

Harry Shapiro, a noted American anthropologist, however, made a serious search in 1980 when he and his daughter visited China (September 17 to October 1) and fulfilled his wish to take a look at the Pasteur Institute and the Swiss Warehouse and to meet with the Chinese colleagues.

Accompanied by Dong Xingren, a young anthropologist, Shapiro visited Tianjin. With information provided by his friends in America, the scholar knew precisely where to look for the hidden treasure—the ground beneath the wooden floor of the cellar in Building No. 6 of the former barracks of the US Marine Corps. He had a photograph of the barracks taken in 1939. With the co-operation of the Tianjin Museum of Nature, the place was quickly located. It is now the campus of the Public Health School of Tianjin, but still unmistakably identifiable with the picture Dr Shapiro had in hand. Unfortunately, however, the Building No. 6 had collapsed as a result of an earthquake in 1976, and the area now is a sports ground. According to the recollection of people in the school, there had not been any wooden floor over the concrete ground. But this proved nothing even if true, as before the Public Health School, several units had occupied the building at different times. Hence the search was again fruitless.

24

Getting in Touch with William Foley

Dr William Foley, a heart specialist, was born in 1912 and had been a researcher at the Peking Union Medical College prior to the Pearl Harbour attack. After being drafted, he served in the US Marine Corps at Tianjin as a medical officer. In November 1941, when the Chinese and American sides decided to transfer the Peking Man fossil remains to safety abroad, it was he, according to his own account, who was entrusted by Colonel Ashurst of the US Marines to carry out the plan.

Until 1980, the authors had no direct contact with Foley, although we knew about him through Shapiro's book and other accounts. We were aware that in spite of his intimate knowledge and extraordinary importance in the case, he had to be wary and, over the years, had turned silent each time key points were mentioned.

On March 4, 1980 the Swiss Embassy in China gave a cocktail party in honour of the well-known archaeologist Professor H. G. Bandi of Bern University and his associates who had come for a visit. Jia Lanpo, Huang Weiwen, and two other Chinese colleagues were present, as we had been a host group who had received Professor Bandi in September 1977, introducing him to many palaeolithic finds unearthed in China and discussing with him their significance.

At the cocktail party that evening, the Swiss Ambassador, Dr Werner Sigg, talked at length with Jia Lanpo on a wide range of subjects from the expeditions in western Asia to the more recent discoveries in China, and from the excavations at Zhoukoudian to the missing Peking Man remains. He told Jia that Dr Foley was his close friend and a reliable person who was in a key position to help in the search for the missing objects, and he expressed the wish that Chinese authorities would pay sufficient attention to this clue.

Jia Lanpo later sent the Ambassador the English version of two of his books, *Early Man in China* and *Cave Home of Peking Man*, and on March 17 Ambassador Sigg wrote a letter to thank him. On March 20 another, much longer letter followed to reaffirm the credibility of Dr Foley. The letter reads in part:

> Having in the meantime studied the book you had obligingly sent to me, I regret even more that when I met you I was unaware of the important part you took in the discoveries of Peking Man at Zhoukoudian.
>
> Had I known that, I would have brought into discussion one topic which I still have in mind and which was brought afresh to my attention at page 31 of your book *Early Man in China* about the mysterious disappearance of Peking Man fossils.
>
> When still in New York, I became acquainted with and later a good friend of Dr William Foley who told me the following:
>
> Working as a medical doctor in Tianjin, he was supposed to return to the United

States on a ship (this must have been in 1941) when his friend and neighbour Pierre Teilhard de Chardin, afraid of the advance of Japanese troops, asked him to shelter in his house the cases containing the famous fossils. Before Dr Foley was able to move these cases to the ship, together with his own belongings, he had himself to flee in a hurry, leaving everything behind in his house which was immediately occupied by Japanese Army men. According to Dr Foley, these Japanese had been the last to see the valuable cases with the fossils, and his guess is that the cases were shipped to Japan later on, when the house was totally emptied by the Japanese. His further guess is that the cases arrived in Japan—provided the carrying ship was not sunk—and his hope was that they are still stored in some army depot and will ultimately still be found.

I thought it might interest you to hear this version of things. Personally, based on the friendly and good relations, I have no reason to doubt the sincerity of the sayings of Dr Foley. Did you possibly know him yourself at that time, as he was a friend of Teilhard?

At the time we were contemplating writing this book and were interested in any such clues about the whereabouts of the missing Peking Man fossils. Jia Lanpo therefore wrote back to ask permission to quote the above letter in the forthcoming book. Permission was granted in a reply on May 5 in which the Ambassador also mentioned that he had the conversation with Dr Foley three years ago and had suggested to Dr Foley that he exchange correspondence with Jia and visit China to meet the Chinese scientists. He enclosed a letter from Foley accepting the invitation for some time in the coming fall. Foley's letter runs, in part:

Kindly tell Professor Jia Lanpo that I still entertain the possibility of finding the long lost specimens. Ask him to communicate with me directly and perhaps we can develop a *modus operandi* . . .

So Jia wrote to Dr Foley, hoping that he could provide more clues leading to the rediscovery of the fossils. The reply came in early June from New York. It runs:

Dear Professor Jia Lanpo,
Your charming letter arrived. Finally, after all these years, the scientist who last dealt with the specimens is introduced to an officer who was entrusted with their transportation to safety, through our mutual friend, Swiss Ambassador Werner Sigg. For many years I have hoped for such a happening. One of my aims has been to see their safe return to P.U.M.C. before I pass on from this life.

The care and precision that you gave to ensuring the proper packing of the specimens [actually it was Hu Chengzhi and Ji Yanqing who did it.—Authors], convinces me that they have not been discarded, but are being safely and carefully guarded awaiting the proper moment for their disclosure.

For reasons that must be obvious to you, I hesitated to write to or to contact our former colleagues. Your warm and friendly letter reassures me. Two weeks ago, our medical school was visited by a group from Peking who are interested in medical education, under the leadership of Dr Shen Qizhen. Two of the group, Dr Fan Chi and Dr Li Siqiao, visited my family at home the next day. I was impressed by their friendliness and asked them to bring to you my respects when they return to Peking. Meeting them indicates to me that the atmosphere of P.U.M.C. has returned to what it was when I last left it.

A few years ago I wrote a small thesis about our role in the handling of the specimens. It is enclosed and summarizes many happenings that would take too long in this letter.

Separately, you may receive a letter from our Bursar discussing certain features of the possibility of assisting you in relocating the specimens.

The 'small thesis' he referred to appeared in the *Alumnus Quarterly*, Winter

1971-72 issue, Medical College, Cornell University. In it, Foley recounted his experience in 1938-45 as a medical doctor for the US Marines and at the same time as a scholar engaged in research in medical colleges in Hong Kong and Beijing. He stated that he could speak fluent Chinese and therefore had extensive contact with his Chinese as well as European colleagues, and that he had been a prisoner of war from Pearl Harbour Day until 1945. He described the Peking Man fossils as few in number and said they were contained in a dozen glass jars.

What Foley recalled about the packing was completely different from the facts on record furnished by the two men who did the packing. Glass jars were unlikely to contain Peking Man fossils. Moreover, the entire body of specimens could not possibly have been put into one footlocker.

The Bursar's letter mentioned by Foley reached Jia Lanpo the same day, with a photo copy of Ambassador Sigg's invitation enclosed. It is concerned with the expenses of the proposed trip.

> Your recent letter to Dr Foley has brought up the possibility of Dr Foley's assistance in locating the missing specimens of 'Peking Man'.
>
> Dr Foley has requested leave for the month of September . . .
>
> The office of the People's Republic of China was contacted in New York for information concerning a proper entrance visa on Dr Foley's passport . . . valid until 1982 . . .
>
> Expenses for such a visit have not been included in our yearly budget. Hence it would be appreciated if your organization or your government would send the necessary tickets. Ambassador Sigg has offered his hospitality in Peking, but travel to Tientsin, Fengtai, and Chiang Wan (Jiangwan) may also be necessary in the search.

(Signed) Rosmarie Gianella, Bursar

Dr Foley's trip did not materialize as he had wished, for during those few months Jia Lanpo had been committed to go to Japan as a member of a Chinese delegation and again to lecture at Meiji University. He asked Foley to postpone the visit.

At the end of October 1980, Mr C. C. Chiu, Senior Vice President of the American Express International Banking Corporation called Jia Lanpo from Beijing Hotel, saying that he was a close friend of Dr Foley, that Foley had asked him to convey a message, and that he wished to meet Jia. Mr Chiu said that Foley and he had read Jia's letter together and had tried to understand the meaning between the lines. They had come to the conclusion that for some reason China was not ready to receive Foley. He explained that Foley would have no difficulty in paying for the trip himself. It was the invitation from the Chinese Government that he really cared about, according to Chiu, and he had expressed the same thought to the Chinese medical group in the United States.

Chiu took a personal interest in the case. Not only had he tried to bring about an agreement for Foley to visit China, but he went to Tianjin himself and, with help from his friends, located the house that was once Foley's home. It was exactly as Foley had described it to him.

In March 1981, Chiu paid another visit to China and met with the authors. He recounted what he had seen at Tianjin on his last trip and told us that when he talked to Foley about the well-preserved residence, the doctor expressed a sort of excitement. But when he was asked whether he had placed the missing fossils there, Foley made no comment.

While an exhibition on Zhoukoudian finds was being held in Japan, the country's second largest daily, *Yomiuri*, assigned reporters to interview Pei Wenzhong, Jia Lanpo and Hu Chengzhi in Beijing and

William Foley in New York on the topic of the missing fossils. Foley's account appeared in *Yomiuri* on July 10, 1980:

> It was Henry S. Houghton of the Peking Union Medical College who conferred with Colonel Ashurst, Military Attaché of the US Embassy, and the latter was asked to help to transfer the fossils to safety. This negotiation between the two went on for some time and finally Houghton agreed. [But the truth is that the decision was made on a higher level, between Dr Weng Wenhao representing the Kuomintang Government and the US Ambassador to China.—Authors] Secret orders were given to have the fossils shipped to the United States under the escort of the US Marines . . . which had detachments stationed at Shanghai, Tianjin, and Qinhuangdao (Chinwangtao), totally about 200 men . . .

> It was decided to put the fossils in my bag, to leave Beijing on December 9 for Qinhuangdao marine base, and from there to get on board *S.S. President Harrison* via Manila to the United States. The plan was top secret and only Colonel Ashurst and I knew about it and no third person knew about this secret mission.

> From then on, the fate of the Peking Man fossils was in the hands of the two Americans.

Thus the problem remains unresolved. In the hope that it might be of help to those who are still concerned about the missing fossils, we have once again presented all the relevant information we have on hand.

25

Sorting Through
the Specimens

After the surrender of Japan in 1945, the Beijing office of the Geological Survey was returned to the Chinese Government, and the Cenozoic Research Laboratory, which had directed the Zhoukoudian project, resumed its activities. But lack of funds ruled out the possibility of further exploiting the Peking Man site. Not even a geological survey of the related areas in the Western Hills was affordable, let alone the much more costly activity of excavation. As it was no longer feasible in 1947 to obtain funds from the Rockefeller Foundation, the Cenozoic Laboratory had turned to Beijing University for support. The University made financial contributions, but they were inadequate for operations at Zhoukoudian.

However, sorting over the specimens which had been collected over the years and which had been scattered and thoroughly disturbed during the war was necessary preparatory work for future undertakings at Zhoukoudian. Jia Lanpo and the paleoichthyologist Liu Xianting set out to do the job, which was to last for two full years—1947 and 1948.

Since the Cenozoic Laboratory was no longer related to the Union Medical College, it asked that institution for permission to remove specimens and other property to its own office building on the premises of the Beijing Division of the Geological Survey of China, its parent organization. Lockhart Hall and Building B were the two places where specimens had been stored, but there was no trace of them there now. An exhaustive search resulted in finding some mammalian fossils, modern vertebrate bones and what was left of the Zhoukoudian material in a large storage room outside of the College. They had been removed from Lockhart Hall by the Japanese. Neolithic and later human remains and the academically valuable modern human skulls from Building B were found jumbled up together in the space under the roof of the room.

It took the entire staff of the Cenozoic Laboratory a whole winter to sort out and move these specimens to their new home. Some were put into boxes and carted away, but many complete ones, such as antlers and skeletons, had to be carried in full view through the busy streets. The grotesque objects transported in this fashion frequently startled the passers-by.

When the move was completed, the specimens occupied a whole floor. Although they had been sorted roughly for the move, everything was still a mess —many of the larger skeletons were separated, plaster casts were no longer in their sets, and fossils from distant regions of the country were mixed up with those from Zhoukoudian. Later, it was discovered that one rhino skeleton unearthed at Locality 13 of Zhoukoudian and formerly kept in a building at 3 Fengsheng Hutong in West Beijing had even found its way to a biological research institute unrelated to the Cenozoic Laboratory. It was two years before Jia Lanpo and Liu Xianting had all the specimens sorted out and registered. The catalogue came to 59 pages typed in English. The section listing human remains of the neolithic age and later, alone, took 14 pages. These remains had been unearthed at sites in Yangshao, Xindian, Shajing, Machang, Zhujiazhai, etc.

The thoroughness of the work is indicated by one entry from the *List of Prehistorical Human Remains Found in North China*:

> Serial number: 157
> Place: Village of Yangshao
> Specimens: bone fragments, 8; parietal bones, 12; lower jaw bones, near complete, 15; lower jaw bones, frontal part, 10; lower jaw bones, left part, 18; lower jaw bones, right side, 12; left collar bones, 41; right collar bones, 35; right radia, 2; vertebrae, 2.

The original serial numbers of the assemblage totaled 145. The specimens were probably collected by Andersson and Black at sites in Henan, Gansu, and Qinghai Provinces. We first arranged them according to the serial number on each item and registered what had survived the war. Some put under the serial number are new ones.

The most trying job was to put together the plaster casts of human remains. Casts for one skull can run to a dozen, and when they are scattered among other casts, it takes gargantuan effort to locate them all and match them up. Serial numbers for this group had to be assigned anew, as many old numbers were illegible and some casts were not numbered at all. The new numbers were headed with the letters AN, standing for 'anthropology', and all casts are so marked. There are 516 numbers all told on the list of plaster casts of human remains consisting of casts of the Peking Man and Upper Cave Man remains, nearly all of which were made by the expert Hu Chengzhi.

More important still are the casts exchanged with or purchased from foreign countries. Among these are casts of bones of 'Cro-Magnon', Solo Man, Java Man, 'Heidelberg', 'Swanscombe', 'Ehringsdorf', 'Krapina', 'Gibraltar' and 'Obercassel'.

Casts of artifacts came to 105 pieces, and they too, were given new serial numbers preceded by the letter A, indicating 'archaeology'. Among them the ones from Zhoukoudian are stone artifacts: 17 from Loc. 1; 1 from Loc. 13; 11 from Loc. 15; and worked antlers, perforated shells, scrapers, bone needles, bone implements, perforated animal teeth, fish bones and stone earrings from the Upper Cave.

There are also casts of artwork of the late paleolithic age in Europe, such as stone and ivory carvings of a horse's head, a bison and a woman. And there are 57 pieces of stone artifacts and implements of the typical Solutrian type. These casts mentioned above are as highly regarded as casts of the Zhoukoudian objects whose originals had disappeared during the war, for they are difficult to obtain.

The sorting and classification covered specimens from various other localities in China as well. Piles of them littered the floor of the storage room. Some were in fragments; some bore no label and their places of origin had to be verified. The most painstaking of all the jobs was to gather the scattered fragments of a specimen and glue them together. We were short of skilled lab workers at the time, and the amount of work for each of the scientists was formidable. When the fragments were finally in good order and put into separate cabinets according to place of occurrence, they were serial-numbered and identified in detail, down to the name and issue of the journal in which the relevant papers had been published.

The extant cards of the specimens were also worked over, and all the specimens that had passed through the sorting were registered. Thus a solid foundation was laid for continued research and for the resumption of excavation at Zhoukoudian.

26

Zhoukoudian Busy Again

After the Liberation of Beijing in 1949, the People's Government sent its representative, the geologist Zhao Xinzhai, to complete the official transfer of the administration of the Beijing Division of the National Geological Survey of China. Henceforth the institution was to be the Beijing Geological Survey; for some time it would be under the leadership of the Economic Commission of the North China People's Government. The few staff members of the Cenozoic Laboratory, in the meantime, were also transferred to the new Survey organization.

In retrospect, these Cenozoic Lab workers, in the early years after Liberation, accomplished three things: (1) the sorting of the specimens of the exhibition hall of the old Geological Survey (at 3 Fengsheng Hutong); (2) making the transfer of property to the new government; and (3) resuming and conducting the excavation at Zhoukoudian.

The first of these was a continuation of unfinished work which had started prior to 1949. Now Jia Lanpo and Liu Xianting were carrying on the job in the office building where Teilhard de Chardin and the abbé Henry Breuil, both pioneers from France in the study of fossils unearthed in China, and Chinese scientists Bian Meinian and Jia Lanpo used to work before the anti-Japanese war.

The bulk of the specimens here consisted of stone artifacts and bone fragments (mostly bone implements) which had

Old field office built in 1932 at Zhoukoudian demolished by Japanese troops for building ramparts during the war. (*Photo by Jia Lanpo, 1933*)

Top: Ming temple destroyed by Japanese troops for war purposes. (*Photo by Jia Lanpo, 1933*)
Bottom: View of Dragon Bone Hill and Zhoukoudian from the gate of the temple. (*Photo by Jia Lanpo, 1933*)

facts of Peking Man' came into circulation. The actual figure might far exceed this; Jia Lanpo recalls that the bipolar flakes alone accounted for more than 50 000 items.

Item 2 was the official transfer of the property of the Cenozoic Laboratory. This involved mainly the specimens, especially those which had been found at Zhoukoudian. The 98-page list of assets was handed from Jia's left hand to his right one, and the legal procedure was thereby completed. A copy of this list can still be found in Jia's files.

Item 3 was the resumption of excavation at Zhoukoudian. In July or August of 1949 the geologist Zhao Xinzhai, representative of the new government, came to Jia Lanpo's office in the Cenozoic Laboratory and asked him to draw up a plan for the project as soon as possible. These glad tidings of course delighted Jia, as for quite a few years he and his colleagues had been occupied with nothing but sorting specimens, and the job had sometimes been very monotonous. He had made an occasional trip with Pei Wen-

been badly disturbed in the war years. Some of them were jumbled up in boxes and drawers; the rest just littered the floor. The amount of work needing to be done was so prohibitive that it was only possible roughly to sort out the specimens on the floor and put them into drawers. By estimating the average number in each drawer, an approximate total was obtained. This was how the saying '100 000 stone arti-

zhong to the Babaoshan area in the western suburbs of Beijing to study pottery pieces on the ground and to look at Han tombs exposed by torrential rains. But this could hardly give him the gratification of 'fieldwork', and he felt like an actor playing at home with friends, not on stage for an audience. The invitation to resume excavation came at a time when the Government had many more urgent matters to deal with and had really been a surprise. More unexpectedly still, the plan was approved a few days after its submission.

Excavation at Zhoukoudian had been suspended for twelve long years during which all connections with the locality had been severed. To prepare for the excavation, it was now imperative to gain a first-hand understanding of the changed local conditions. To this end, Jia Lanpo and Liu Xianting visited the village twice. As soon as they arrived on their first trip, they rented a large room from a quarry establishment (later, for a long time, the room was used as the office from which the excavation was conducted) Surviving old-timers who had worked as technicians for the Peking Man project came to see them. It was a sentimental reunion; all hearts were filled with joy and excitement—and with deep grief, too, when missing faces were noticed. They talked about Tang Liang, a highly skilled fossil hunter who had worked with Yang Zhongjian for years, and who had died of starvation as a rickshaw coolie after being discharged from the job at Zhoukoudian.

The environment was no more cheerful. The hills, now devoid of trees, were bleak, and the whole village looked more desolate than ever. There were only a few new dwellings owned by the quarry, which belonged to a cement factory, among the old, dilapidated huts of the peasants. The view from the top of the hills was no longer pleasing, as all the trees that had been planted had later been cut down by the Japanese troops for fear of guerrilla fighters. The trenches along the hillsides were a reminder of the war. Gone also was the office building compound erected by the Cenozoic Laboratory in 1932 at a cost of 5000 silver yuan; the Japanese had needed the building material for their fortifications. Further off, a temple built in the Ming Dynasty on the slope opposite the north side of Dragon Bone Hill was devastated, together with the few square kilometres of scenic woods surrounding it With so many ruins near and far, and only the chirping of insects to punctuate the stillness, the atmosphere conveyed a feeling that was unsettling, indeed even lowering.

The plan for the excavation in 1949

Work at Zhoukoudian resumed soon after the founding of New China in 1949. The interruption had lasted 12 years. The project is now funded by the Chinese Government.

Top: Yang Zhongjian, Liu Dongsheng, Liu Xianting and Jia Lanpo accompanied Zhu Kezhen, Deputy Director of the Chinese Academy of Sciences, on his visit to Zhoukoudian on October 7, 1951. Work was going on at Level 32 at the time.

Bottom: Excavation at the Peking Man site in November 1951.

prescribed the continuation of work left off in 1937, or from Level 30 on down. At the time the work was discontinued because of the war, the work face had been covered with a layer of earth and rubble 30 centimetres thick to prevent disturbance by the enemy. This 'camouflage' had evidently worked, for although the Japanese had tried to do something here, they had given up when they saw the futility of their efforts.

The digging began on September 27 under the direction of Jia Lanpo and Liu Xianting. While the work was in progress, the Director of the Cenozoic Laboratory Pei Wenzhong, the archaeologist Su Binqi, and some experts from the Soviet Union came to observe.

It took some twenty days to clear away the earth and rubble. This could have been done sooner if half a molar had not been found in the 'artificial deposit' three days after the digging had begun. On the same day, September 29, another half of the tooth was found; thus a slightly damaged lower molar was complete. And again on the same day, at a distance less than one metre away from where this tooth had occurred, another lower molar and an upper central incisor were covered. We had to go slowly. All three teeth were found in a deposit of hard, fine sandstone and ashes. The teeth had coalesced with the sandstone, which seemed to confirm their *in situ* position—the thin layer of fine sandstone 2.6 metres above Level 30, or the 27th Level. The deposits here had collapsed under torrential rains. There are still such collapsed original deposits at the southern fissure of the Peking Man site.

But the *in situ* position of the three teeth might also have been in the 26th Level, for in the spring of 1937, four teeth, two mandible fragments, two skull fragments—all of Peking Man—had been found at the F-2 Zone, which was designated as Locus M. This zone could also have been the original location of the three newly found teeth.

With the covering cleared, the digging began formally on October 16. Following the practice established before the Sino-Japanese War, a 1:100 sketch map was drawn first, on which the *in situ* location of significant finds would be noted.

With a shortage of skilled workers, the work was done on a limited scale, that is, one zone at a time. Up to November 18 when the weather was too cold for the work to go on, the five zones M, N, L, K and J were dug. Deposits removed came to 125 cubic metres plus the covering cleared, the result of 721 worker-days, 13.6 mandays on the average per day.

Apart from the above-mentioned three teeth, the material recovered in this season consisted of single teeth of horses, rhinoceroses, pigs, deer, etc., but mostly of the fossilized dung of carnivores, bone flake fragments and truncated antlers. Judging from the marks left on the bone flake and antler fragments, it is certain that some of them were implements made by humans.

The operation did not seem worthwhile as the only significant finds were the three Peking Man teeth. Yet these attracted great attention as the only real specimens we had, all the others having been lost during the war.

While the season's work was coming to an end and the plan for the following year was in the making, we contemplated conducting excavations at many other prospective sites within a few kilometres, such as Badger Cave at Shuiyu and Scorpion Cave at Biandanwo, in addition to deepening the same site at Zhoukoudian.

27

The Significance of
the Zhoukoudian Finds

Zhoukoudian, once a forlorn village, is now a bustling centre of paleontological studies with a special highway connection. The area has been designated as one of China's major government-protected cultural sites and attracts thousands of visitors each year. There are several reasons for its prominence.

1. There are twenty-four sites within the 2-square-kilometre area of Dragon Bone Hill at Zhoukoudian. Although Locations 17 and 18 are not within this sphere, there are two sites, the hilltop deposits and the Upper Cave, which are not serially numbered, so the actual number is still 24.

In spite of the highly concentrated distribution of these sites, they have yielded specimens of great antiquity as well as of more recent times. Vertebrate fauna unearthed represent all periods from Early Pliocene (beginning more than 10 million years ago) to Late Pleistocene (10 000 years ago). Thus the area is quite rare in the world.

The assortment of fauna represents various Quaternary periods and provides indispensable information for scientists the world over on the occurrence, development and migration of mammals. Mammalian fossils are reliable records in the study of environments of the remote past, and also in determining the geological age of a site or an object. As faunas are different in different ages, the relative antiquity of a given fossil can be determined by its char-

acteristics—its degree of primitiveness or advancement. That is why the faunas from Zhoukoudian, with its sites of different dating, are taken as 'models' for researchers everywhere.

2. The area has also yielded great numbers of human remains of varying dating, and many artifacts have occurred in association with them. Among these, the Peking Man fossils are of special significance. In terms of antiquity, Locality 13 is the most ancient, being 600 000 to 700 000 years old. The Peking Man site (Locality 1) comes next, and Localities 15, 4 and 3 follow, in that order. The Upper Cave site is of the most recent dating so far known.

The Peking Man remains may seem insufficient and even fragmentary, but as a whole they represent upwards of forty persons, nearly all parts of the human frame, male and female, old and young, providing adequate materials for the reconstruction of a fairly accurate portrait of Peking Man.

3. The area still tops all other sites in the world in the abundance of stone artifacts and traces of the use of fire; the presence of these traces at Locality 13 has greatly updated the earliest known use of fire on record. Before 1930, the earliest known fire users were the Neanderthals, who lived 100 000 years ago, but Locality 13 dates back to 700 000 years, while the Peking Man site (Locality 1), where such traces occurred in profusion, is 500 000 years

old. A few other sites in China of much earlier dating have yielded the same traces —ashes and charred bones.[1] These and the Zhoukoudian finds are all valuable evidence on the subject of this important development in human history.

4. The discovery of Peking Man settled a great controversy which had lasted for decades in paleoanthropological circles over the identity of *Pithecanthropus erectus*, or Java Man. When the Dutch medical doctor Eugene Dubois found the fossils of Java Man in 1891, he identified them as a species between man and ape on Darwin's evolutionary ladder, and he duly established the species name. Later, however, he became the centre of a bitter controversy in Europe as people from powerful circles challenged his view and insisted that the skullcap among his finds belonged to a deformed long-arm ape and the thighbone to a modern human, the two specimens not being related at all. Under the pressure, Dubois eventually gave in and stated that what he had found were indeed the remains of an extinct species of 'giant gibbon'.

The discovery of Peking Man once again confirmed the ape-to-human scientific hypothesis. Not only were the human remains at Zhoukoudian similar to *Pithecan-thropus erectus*, or Java Man, but also artifacts and traces of the use of fire had occurred in association. The sceptics opposing Dubois were thus silenced.

But it is common among paleontologists to differ in views that are based on the same evidence, and Peking Man was no exception. One of the causes of the Java Man controversy was a morphological incongruity—a primitive skull on a developed frame, indicated by the thighbone with straight shaft and prominent ridge, characteristics that led Dubois to name the species 'erect apeman' and later to retract. The fact that Peking Man possessed similar features had settled this problem, but not once and for all. Commenting on Weidenreich's hypothesis that cannibalism prevailed in Peking Man's community, the noted French paleoanthropologist Dr H. Boule in the book *Homme Fossiles* asserted that two species of creatures lived at Zhoukoudian, one the hunters, the other their prey. Only the hunters were human beings, and the stone and bone implements occurring in association were theirs; the Chinese 'apemen' were their prey. This theory cannot hold water, for the sites at Zhoukoudian have yielded no such 'real human' fossil.

---

[1] These are the Xihoudu and Kehe sites in Shanxi Province, the Lantian Man site in Shaanxi Province, and the Yuanmou Man site in Yunnan Province. Geologist Qian Fang of the Institute of Geodynamics of the Academy of Geological Sciences has provided data indicating that the dating determined by the paleomagnetic method for the Yuanmou Man site is 1 700 000 years, and for the Xihoudu site, 1 800 000 years.

28

Environmental Changes in the Last 500 000 Years

There has been much discussion since the 1930s on the environmental changes of the Zhoukoudian area, but owing to the fact that most participants considered the more-than-40-metre-thick deposits to be a one-layer mass formed in the same geological age, the inferences made were not necessarily valid. Some authorities held that the climate then was colder than now; others stated that the contrary was true. Some also suggested that the area then was well watered but near a desert region.

Sporopollen analysis of the cave deposits made by paleobotanists Xu Ren and Sun Mengrong did not cover the entire cross-section of the fossil-yielding strata due to incomplete sampling, but it did reveal that climatic changes had occurred when the stratigraphic layers were formed. A study made by Jia Lanpo on the living habits of the mammals represented by specimens confirmed what Xu and Sun had deduced through the sporopollen analysis.

Before going on to the subject of climatic change, it is necessary to have an understanding of the duration of Peking Man's habitation at the Zhoukoudian cave. Over the years, fauna has been relied on to determine the geological age of the area. Through analyzing the data obtained from animal fossils, Jia estimated that the interval of Peking Man's habitation was 300 000 years, off and on, or from 500 000 years B.P. to 200 000 years B.P. Data obtained subsequently by newer

methods approximately tallied with this range of time.[1] However, if Locality 13 is taken to be the earliest home of Peking Man, the dating would have to be 700 000 years B.P., according to the data obtained by the paleomagnetic method.

Another view held by Jia Lanpo was that the uppermost deposits, or the upper part of Layer 1, cannot be older than 200 000 years (this part had been removed in 1934), and the samples that can be collected there now are not the same as those from the uppermost part in the past. That is to say, the interval of human habitation would have to have been 500 000 years, instead of 300 000 years.

Could habitation have lasted for so many millennia? It is entirely possible. Instances abound in Europe. The Acheulean period of the latter half of the Early Old Stone Age had lasted for 300 000 years, from 430 000 B.P. to 130 000 B.P. The Clactonian period had been as long, from 540 000 B.P. to 240 000 B.P., a total of 300 000 years. Over such long periods,

---

[1] The geologist Yin Zanxun in a speech made at the closing of the conference commemorating the fiftieth anniversary of the finding of the Peking Man remains said: 'In the co-ordinated research conducted this time, the methods employed included spontaneous fission track dating, uranium-series dating, paleomagnetic dating, amino acid dating, and thermoluminescence dating to determine the antiquity of the Zhoukoudian site. The conclusion based on the data obtained indicates that it is at least 500 000 years ago that human activities had begun in the cave, and the site was abandoned more than 200 000 years ago.'

Years B.P.	Geol. Sub Divisions	Localities
-10,000	Holocene	
-100,000	Upper Pleistocene	Upper Cave (Human Fossils, Cultural Remains)
-200,000 -300,000 -400,000 -500,000 -600,000 -1,000,000	Middle Pleistocene	Loc. 3 (Animal Fossils, Charred Bones, Ashes) Loc. 4 (Animal Fossils, Human Tooth, Stone Artifacts) Loc. 15 (Animal Fossils, Cultural remains, Traces of Using Fire) Loc. 19 Loc. 20 Loc. 21 Loc. 22 Loc. 23 Loc. 24 Loc. 2 } (Fossils of Vertebrate) Loc. 5 Loc. 6 Loc. 7 Loc. 8 Loc. 9 Loc. 13 (Cultural Remains, Animal Fossils) —Loc. 1 (Human Fossils, Cultural Remains, Traces of Using Fire) Peking Man Site
-3,000,000	Lower Pleistocene	Loc. 12 (Fossils of Vertebrate)
-10,000,000	Pliocene	Cap Travertine (Fossils of Vertebrate) - - - - - - - - - - - - - - - - - - - Loc. 14 (Fossils of Fish)

Environmental changes of the Zhoukoudian area.

environmental changes were inevitable. There had been a few glacial periods during the Pleistocene, with temperatures dropping sharply; during the subsequent interglacial epochs, the temperatures would rise again. Such tremendous changes in climate must have left records in the fauna and flora of the Zhoukoudian area.

Indeed, the site had yielded remains of paleovertebrates of more than one hundred species, yet as a body for statistical counting, they are unreliable because most of them belong to species which are highly adaptable to climatic change. Among the rest, there are some whose genus cannot be determined, while the *in situ* positions of still others are unknown. The damage and destruction during the war added to the difficulties, making verification impossible. The following analysis is based on only 20 per cent of the specimens unearthed from the site.

Layers 11 and 10 contain mammalian fossils of cold-climate species such as the bobak marmot (*Marmota bobak*), complex-toothed marmot (*Marmota complicidens*), cave bear (*Ursus* cf. *speleus*), Teilhard's wildcat (*Felis teilhardi*), and the Chinese short-faced hyena (*Hyaena brevirostris sinensis*). Of the warm-climate species, only Merck's rhinoceros (*Dicerorhinus kirchbergensis*) occurred. Layers 8 and 9 saw the increase of warm-climate species such as robust macaque (*Macacus robustus*), Asian straight-tusked elephant (*Paleoloxodon nomadicus*), Teilhard's buffalo (*Bubalus teilhardi*), porcupine (*Hystrix* cf. *subcristata*), and Koken's black bear (*Ursus tibetanus Kokeni*). Of the cold-climate species, only the thick-boned giant deer (*Megaceros pachyosteus*) was added to the earlier group. The proportion of cold- and warm-climate animals was half and half, indicating a transition period in climate. At Layer 4, the proportion of cold-climate fos-

sils was only one in four, indicating that the climate was at its warmest during Peking Man's colonization. In the three uppermost layers, remains of cold-climate animals are outnumbered by the warm-climate group, indicating a temperate climate.

Some writings on the ancient landforms around Zhoukoudian state definitely that there were both forest and grassland in the area. This is attested by both sporopollen analysis and the occurrence of mammalian fossils of macaques, bison, ancient dholes, tigers, brown bears and black bears, which are forest dwellers, and horses, cheetahs and woolly rhinoceroses, which are typically grassland species.

Discovery of remains of aquatic animals at the site has given rise to a consensus among many authors that there must have been a large lake or river in the vicinity. But at what period of time and in what precise location? From the papers published, the amphibious mammalian remains found at the site include European giant beaver (*Trogontherium cuvieri*), beaver (*Castor* sp.), and otter (*Lutra molina*). Although the European giant beavers were extinct in the middle stage of the Pleistocene, the fact that many of their remains were uncovered from lacustrine and fluviatile deposits, as well as their morphological features, indicate that they were an amphibian species. The beaver is a species of large amphibian rodent known as a 'dike builder'. The otter lives in a hole at the water margin and dives into the water at night to prey on fish and crabs. It has a long tail that controls its pace of movement while in the water. These creatures could not possibly have survived in a stream the size of the present-day Ba'er River in the locality. These fossils occurred in the sand layers in the middle and upper part of the cave deposits, namely Layer 7 (a sand layer), Layers 8 and 9, and Layer 6 (a breccia structure). A more complete buffalo skull had occurred at Layer 7, indicating that the area was most abundant in water when this layer and the structure adjacent to it were formed, and that in the long process of the formation of the rock series of the site, this was the stage in which the lake or river here was at its largest.

29

The Controversy over Artifacts

Are Peking Man's stone artifacts so advanced in technique that they cannot be the earliest human tools? Or are they not advanced at all, making them the earliest tools and Peking Man the earliest *Homo sapiens*? This issue was hotly debated in 1961 and 1962, but it had all begun in 1957 when Jia Lanpo and his student Wang Jian published a short note (1100 words) in the *Science Bulletin (Scientia)*, No. 1, on their deduction that Peking Man's stone artifacts were too advanced to be representative of the earliest human industry, which therefore could only be found elsewhere. The authors used the title, 'Earlier Cradle of Man—the Nihewan Strata', and their intention was to break away from the shackle of old beliefs to extend the time interval of the earliest humans.

Nihewan is the name of a village in Yangyuan County, Hebei Province. The term 'Nihewan strata' is derived from an index, or standard cross-section of a rock sequence lying near Nihewan Village which for a long time had been dated back to the Late Pliocene. However, following the World Geological Conference held in London in 1954 at which the Villafranchian stage was determined as a major division of Early Pleistocene deposits and time (the Pleistocene Epoch began about 2 500 000 years ago and ended about 10 000 years ago), the Nihewan strata were redated as belonging to the same stage as the Villafranchian. When in 1974 a site at Xujiayao (Hsuchiayao) of

Nihewan structure yielded large numbers of artifacts, the scientists realized that the Nihewan stage includes sediments of younger age.

Professors Teilhard de Chardin and Pei Wenzhong shared the view that Peking Man's artifacts are not advanced, and the Soviet professor B. K. Nicholsky wrote that the stone fragments at the site look like tools only because of their natural accidental forms, and they were used for a general purpose. As a rejoinder to this last statement, Jia Lanpo and Wang Jian wrote:

As a whole, the stone artifact assemblage of *Sinanthropus* is somewhat advanced in technique. In fashioning a flake, for instance, [Peking Man] knew at least three ways: striking the material on a stone anvil, direct blow from a stone core, and the 'bipolar flake' method. At the secondary stage, he was able to refine the flake into a desired shape. The assemblage is quite diversified with the presence of hammer stones, chopper and chopping tools, disc-like implements, points and scrapers . . .

Had there been a stage at which early man used stones in their natural forms as tools? The answer is yes, certainly, but this early man cannot be *Sinanthropus*, but his more primitive predecessor. Without such a stage, there would not have been any such stone artifacts as those found in association with the remains of *Sinanthropus*. This is because things develop from simple to complicated and from a lower to a higher level and many facts prove that the earlier the stage of man, the slower the development of his culture. Therefore, it must have been a long evolutionary process before *Sinanthropus* could produce tools of such quality and diversity. From this we may safely deduce that man and his culture must have existed in the Nihewan stage which is close to the time of *Sinanthropus*.

This article met with silence until the publication of Pei Wenzhong's 'A Review of the Discussion on Eoliths' in a periodical published in Beijing.[1] In his review, Pei treated all the artifacts before the time of *Sinanthropus* as 'eoliths' and challenged the view that there had been a long evolutionary process before humans started deliberately to fracture rocks for tools. He stated:

> My view on eoliths is open and clearcut. I am against the theory that eoliths were shaped by man, as is believed by some. This has been my position since long ago. It all began in 1930 when I was in charge of the Zhoukoudian excavation. There, the large quantities of fractured quartz flakes and sandstone pebbles attracted my attention, as they could not have been a natural part of the limestone cave, but must have been transported there by *Sinanthropus*. He fractured the quartz and sandstone deliberately. My assertion had encountered fierce opposition from certain quarters . . .
>
> Under the circumstances, I began studying the differences between a human-flaked and a nature-flaked stone and the criteria by which the two can be distinguished. With the guidance of elder scholars, I made a series of experiments and surveyed the literature on the subject by European scientists. Later, in 1935-37, I wrote a paper on how to distinguish the two by the signs on a flake while I was at the University of Paris, and examined eoliths that occurred in France, Belgium and Britain which, as was impressed [upon me], were not human-flaked as a whole, and only very exceptionally would a specimen show otherwise.
>
> Some authorities held that early paleoliths, such as Abbevillian hand-axes and

stone artifacts of *Sinanthropus*, were already advanced in workmanship and that it must have been a long evolutionary process before man could use and produce stone implements like these. In the long transitional period, they believe, man had used very crudely manufactured tools; and before this period started there must have been a period of time when man knew only how to use stone implements but was not able to produce them. This assertion conforms seemingly to the law of the development of things, yet it is not [so], for the demarcation of man and other animals is not clear here.

> The tools of *Sinanthropus* came to several types, e.g. pointers, scrapers, choppers, hammers and anvils. Any of these would fulfil one of the three essential requirements of tools—being pointed, edged, or heavy, otherwise they would not be 'liths' but 'eoliths'. Based on this premise, I view the types of tools of *Sinanthropus* as primitive, not advanced.
>
> I also doubt the existence of manufactured tools prior to those of *Sinanthropus*. Loc. 13 is indeed of an earlier dating than Loc. 1, or the Peking Man site, but still the stone tools at Loc. 13 were made by *Sinanthropus*, and they were not tools that had been used by another earlier, more primitive human species . . .
>
> Concerning the statement that the Nihewan site (of Early Pleistocene) has human fossils or stone tools, we frankly say that so far no such evidence has presented itself. The problem here is the same—the eoliths, which for nearly a hundred years had been a point of controversy among the European scientists. The search for such evidence at Nihewan (equivalent to Europe's Villafranchian stage), has been fruitless.

Professor Wu Rukang, in a rejoinder entitled, 'On Eoliths and the Problem of Whether *Sinanthropus* Is the Earliest Man'[2] stated:

> I hold the view that Java Man is certainly slightly earlier than Peking Man, and he

[1] *New Construction*, No. 7, 1961.

[2] *Guangming Daily*, Sept. 6, 1961.

used tools and knew how to manufacture them.

Mr Pei obviously asserts that since Java Man could not shape tools, he is not a real human, and for that reason, "there is no proof that there had been another human species prior to *Sinanthropus*." In other words, a real human must know how to make tools, and *Sinanthropus* is the earliest human being.

The physical characteristics, the cultural quality, and the geological dating of the fossils of *Sinanthropus*, however, contradict this statement. The average cranial capacity of the species exceeds 1000 c.c. and he walked with an upright gait as his limbs were so well developed that they were similar to those of modern man. He knew how to use fire and make stone tools of several types as Mr Pei pointed out; the dating of *Sinanthropus* has commonly been determined as Middle Pleistocene, an age in which geological conditions permitted the presence of man. As a matter of fact, this has been borne out by the recovery of fossils of Java Man, *Australopithecus*, or Southern Ape, and other real humans or near humans. Therefore, I believe *Sinanthropus* is not the earliest man . . .

The cranial capacity of simians closest to man is only half of that of *Sinanthropus*. If there had not been more primitive humans on the evolutionary ladder, the cranial capacity of *Sinanthropus* would have been a sudden doubling from that of apes. Then the culture of *Sinanthropus* is such that the use of fire and tool-making were known to him. As his remains had occurred at Zhoukoudian, it would naturally lead to the conclusion that this site was the very place of man's origin. Since no creature prior to *Sinanthropus* knew the use or making of tools, according to the logic, Java Man, which is an earlier species as evidenced by morphological characteristics and geological context, should by all means be excluded from humans. If this theory can be established, literature all over the world on this subject would have to be re-written, including some of that by Mr Pei himself.

But in his article, Mr Pei does not provide any reliable evidence to back up his statement, which is, therefore, hardly convincing.

The issue remained a controversial one for five and a half years, counting from the publication of the first article by Jia Lanpo and Wang Jian in 1957 to the summing-up article, 'The Present State of the Discussions on Eoliths', in *History Teaching*, No. 8, 1962. There were more than twenty articles by various authors—Jia Lanpo, Wang Jian, Pei Wenzhong, Wu Rukang, Wu Dingliang, Liang Zhaotao, Xia Nai, Qiu Zhonglang, Zhang Senshui and others. One side represented by Jia Lanpo holds that human culture existed prior to *Sinanthropus*; the other represented by Pei Wenzhong refuted this view, holding that the culture of *Sinanthropus* was the earliest and that the species represents the earliest human being.

Bone implements were also a sharp point of controversy in this prolonged argument. Are they implements, or just pieces fractured by nature? The argument could be traced back to 1953 when a small display centre was built at Zhoukoudian for the finds. Jia Lanpo, who was in charge of the project, decided to include bone implements for display. Before the centre was formally opened, all researchers of the Institute of Paleontology were invited to the preview for a scrutiny of the exhibits. The idea of bone pieces being displayed there as implements met with opposition from Pei Wenzhong, so they were duly removed. But Jia Lanpo had never given up the belief that some of these bone fragments were once implements, and with his thoughts still unsettled, he wrote a paper entitled, 'On the Bone Implements of *Sinanthropus*',[1] which turned out to be a detonator. It reads, in part:

---

[1] *Kaogu Xuebao* (*The Chinese Journal of Archaeology*), No. 3, 1959.

The first foreign scholar who came to China for this scientific exploit was Professor H. Breuil of France. In the spring of 1931, he made a study trip to Zhoukoudian where he stayed for a few days. He was not only convinced of the validity of the stone tools and traces of the use of fire, but believed that among the bone pieces, many were man-fractured. At a geological conference held in the winter of the same year, he made a report giving a brief account of the significance of his findings. On his second trip to China, he made a special study on the bone and antler fractures that occurred at Zhoukoudian, and the resulting paper, 'Bone and Antler Industry of the Choukoutien *Sinanthropus* Site', had appeared in *Palaeontologia Sinica* in 1939.

In the book *Fossil Man in China* co-authored by Davidson Black, Teilhard de Chardin, Yang Zhongjian and Pei Wenzhong, a brief account is also given of bone implements found at the site.

The site has yielded a great number of deer antlers. Those of the thick-jawed deer appeared to have fallen off, the ones from Japanese deer were obviously knocked off. Most of these two kinds of antlers were, however, fractured into short pieces, some with tops, some stumps. The stumps of the thick-jawed deer antlers are generally 12-20 cm long, with branches clearly being cut off. The upper parts of some also show clear marks of being chopped off. The stumps of the Japanese deer were longer, with clear signs on some of being fractured at both ends, and their first branches usually being knocked off. Most of these antler tops were of the Japanese deer, and judging by the splitting parts, many were also deliberately cut off. Scars were often seen on thick-jawed deer antlers and furrows on Japanese deer antlers, indicating possibly their having been used by man.

The many furrows on big bones such as the humerus (upper-arm bone) of the rhinoceros show by their characteristics and distribution that the bones were once being used as anvils.

Deer limb bone fragments are the most numerous in this assemblage. They were usually split off along the long axis, and one end was made into pointed or edged tools. Moreover, many bone flakes show signs of being repeatedly struck along their edges.

The ways these bone fragments were fractured cannot be attributed to natural causes such as wave action, animal gnawing, or fallen rocks, and even cracking by man to get at the marrow would not be a cogent explanation, for in that case, he would not have to sharpen the ends or edges, and was even more unlikely to strike the flakes repeatedly. In addition, antlers do not have marrow, and such cracking by man would serve no purpose except for tool-making.

The truncated root part of a thick-jawed deer antler is hard and large enough to serve as a hammer, as H. Breuil observed. I agree. A pointed tine or a man-fashioned pointed limb bone was, in my view, used for grubbing.

Tools for grubbing were essential in the life of gatherers, especially prior to the hunting stage of human life. One example may suffice to explain: rodent fossils occurred in plenty at the *Sinanthropus* site, especially in the ash layers. They appear to have been burnt, indicating that the rodents were a part of man's diet. To run after and catch these creatures individually would have been inconceivable no matter how numerous they were, but to get at their burrows with grubbing tools would attain a better supply. The scratches and cracks on some may validate this inference.

Professor Pei Wenzhong replied subsequently in his paper 'On the Problem of the "Bone Implements" of the Zhoukoudian *Sinanthropus* Site',[1] as follows:

I would like to raise a question for discussion with Mr Jia. Let me begin with some fundamentals:

(1) My personal view is that although both stone and bone could be used for tool

---

[1] *Chinese Journal of Archaeology*, No. 2, 1960.

material, there was a great difference between the two. Stone at that time had no other use, while bones were left over from prey being consumed as food. As marrow in a long bone is edible, the bone was often crushed to get the marrow. This apart, there were carnivores, especially the hyena, which had the habit of chewing bones; and rodents, such as porcupines, which had the habit of gnawing bones. Moreover, bones are apt to be eroded by air and water, and fractured before and after being buried and during digging. Thus the problem of bone implements is considerably more complicated than [that of] stone tools.

(2) It is common sense in archaeology that the term 'implement' refers to an object that bears marks not only of being struck, but also of being used, or secondary working. Marks of being struck alone are insufficient to identify the object as an 'implement', but a mere flake, fragment, or bone bearing marks of being struck by man.

(3) Objects of the last kind are generally recognized as having occurred at the Zhoukoudian *Sinanthropus* site; they also serve as evidence of hunting. I myself shared this observation, as shown in the paper, 'Nature-fractured Bone Flakes' which I wrote in 1938. But the purpose of my writing was to stress the large quantities of nature-fractured bones at the site so that researchers on these objects would not mistake them for 'bone implements'.

(4) The focal point of the controversy lies in whether these bone objects bear marks of being used and of secondary working or not.

Antlers are more liable to be subjected to widely varied interpretations. One thing, however, should be affirmed. Among such finds at Zhoukoudian, one bears signs of being burnt and hacked by stone. It is a specimen of historical significance. So much so that P. Teilhard de Chardin took it to Paris to show abbé Henri Breuil, who confirmed the nature of these marks, and Teilhard, who was known for his conservative views on such matters, agreed . . . Thus the problem is not whether these man-made

marks are authentic, but whether the object is an 'implement' . . .

Teilhard de Chardin, however, made no inference that the object was an implement; rather he held that the reason that the antlers were hacked off was that it was inconvenient for man to carry the animal carcass with such large horns into the cave to eat, and burning would make hacking easier. Indeed, Teilhard believed, charred antlers give support to the view that they were discarded.

Pei Wenzhong carried the discussion further in his article entitled, 'The Eolith Issue in Retrospect':[1]

In historical perspective, bone and stone implements are in many respects different. It is generally agreed that human-fractured bones began to appear in the Mousterian stage, or the middle paleolithic age, and by the late paleolithic age, the articles made of bone were polished, perforated, or carved for ornamental purposes. This shows that the advent of the bone implement was later than that of the stone implement, but the workmanship of the former had made faster progress than the latter. According to this law of progression, if there had been an eolith period, it would have preceded the early paleolithic age, and the corresponding 'eolith' period of bone implements would have preceded the middle paleolithic time, or the early paleolithic age, namely the time of *Sinanthropus*.

Some authors did not share completely the views of either side. The following excerpt is quoted from a mimeographed paper written by Professor Liang Zhaotao of Zhongshan University, which Jia Lanpo received on January 17, 1962. It was entitled, 'The Background of the Eolith Controversy and *Sinanthropus* and the Nature of His Industry', and expressed the following views:

On the problem of the eolith, I disagree with Mr Pei. I believe that this endless argu-

_____
[1] *New Construction*, No. 7, 1961.

ment is derived from the controversy which prevailed in the West from the end of the nineteenth century to the early twentieth century between the two ideologies of evolution and counter-evolution (racism). We in China should not only keep away from the dispute, but should keep our discussion on *Sinanthropus* and his industry as a topic apart . . .

I also disagree with Mr Pei's view that *Sinanthropus* is the earliest human and his industry the most primitive.

Mr Jia's assertion that the 'bone implements' of *Sinanthropus* are implements is not convincing. I hold that the converse is true. Bone objects of the middle paleolithic age that have been unearthed so far are not such, for the strict criterion lies in 'making', not 'using'. The Mousterian bone tools show signs of having been used, but no clear trace of being made by man. Evidence that is singular and unclear is inadequate for drawing a conclusion. If 'marks of being used' were to be taken as the criterion to define an 'implement' or tool, all naturefractured objects that had been picked up at random by man, and that show signs of being used, would have been treated as tools or consciously made tools.

These discussions did not lead to consensus among the scientists, but the problem faded somewhat with time and with the later discoveries of large quantities of bone flakes at the Shiyu and Xujiayao (Hsuchiayao) paleolithic culture sites, Shanxi Province. More significant still, antlers bearing marks of being cut and scraped occurred at the Xihoudu site in southern Shanxi Province. The site is dated to be 1 800 000 years at least in antiquity by paleomagnetic testing.

30

The Predecessors of *Sinanthropus* —the Topic of a New Debate

Availing itself of the opportunity afforded by construction of the mammoth Sanmen Gorge Reservoir on the Huanghe (Yellow River), the Institute of Vertebrate Paleontology and Paleoanthropology of the Chinese Academy of Sciences sent a survey team to investigate the Quaternary paleoliths and mammals occurring there. The team covered a number of areas such as Shanxian and Lingbao in Henan, Tongguan in Shaanxi, and Jiankou, Ruicheng, Kehe, Tanguo and Dutou in Shanxi and found many paleolithic sites which yielded human-fashioned stone artifacts and a few fossils of animal remains. The result of the studies made on them by Jia Lanpo, Wang Zeyi, and Qiu Zhonglang was published by the Science Press in 1961 under the title *Paleoliths in Shanxi*.

In October 1959, a team of the Shanxi station of the Institute made another survey trip in the region, and, apart from stone artifacts, a maxilla of the thick-jawed giant deer was recovered from a gravel layer at Xiyang Village at the Huanghe riverbank.

The specimens collected in 1957 and 1959 were of major significance to the stratigraphic research of the Quaternary period and the study of the mammalian fossils and paleolithic artifacts. As a result, further investigation and excavation was soon carried out by the Academy of Sciences and the Museum of Shanxi Province. The team, under the leadership of Jia Lanpo, concentrated on the Kehe area and its vicinity. In the one and a half months of fieldwork, they collected a large number of specimens, which were studied by Jia Lanpo, Wang Zeyi and Wang Jian; the results were published in 1962 by the Science Press under the title *Kehe*.

In the concluding chapter of the book, the authors made an inference on the dating of the site that was to become controversial. They stated, in part:

> . . . although the identifiable or roughly identifiable animal fossils belong to only seven species, they provide sufficient information to lead the scientists to determine the deposits in which they occurred to be Middle Pleistocene, and a good many of these remains date back to Early Middle Pleistocene.
>
> In terms of variety and workmanship, stone artifacts of *Sinanthropus* are more advanced than the ones found at Kehe. The two assemblages are similar to, yet different from, one another, but they have more differences than similarities.
>
> By the same token, the Dingcun (Tingtsun, Shanxi Province) stone implements are more advanced than the Kehe ones, and the two industries are also related. The evidence already available has enabled us to make the inference that the Dingcun industry had evolved from the Kehe industry (just as the stone artifacts at Locality 15 of Zhoukoudian are closely related to *Sinanthropus*).
>
> Records borne by the liths, fossils and geological stratigraphy lead us to determine

the deposits that have yielded paleoliths to be Early Middle Pleistocene, while the industry itself dates back to the early period of the beginning of the paleolithic age.

Professor Pei Wenzhong was actually the first to deal with the Kehe site issue. In an article entitled, 'Is *Sinanthropus* the Most Primitive "Man"?—A Rejoinder to Wu Rukang, Jia Lanpo and Other Comrades',[1] he asserts:

> The problem posed by the so-called Early Middle Pleistocene stone implements occurring at the eleven sites in the vicinity of Kehe is essentially a problem of geological dating.
>
> The preliminary report reveals that the deposition at all these sites (especially Locality 6054) shows a dearth or absence of gravel layer at the base of the loess structure. As a general rule, loess deposits are present on all heights, hill slopes and mounts in the North China region, but at places near a river, a gravel or basal gravel layer would be formed. In this area, however, the sedimentary layers formed in the loess period do not show such a feature, except Locality 6054 where there is only a thin layer of loess at the top. Considering that many of these sites are very close to the Huanghe, they should be regarded as geologically different from the rest of North China.

In another article entitled, 'The Direction and Problems of Paleoanthropology',[2] Professor Pei said:

> On the evidence that the Kehe stone implements have occurred at the bottom of the gravel layer under the 'red soil' which is contemporaneous with *Sinanthropus* at Zhoukoudian, the authors draw the conclusion that the Kehe stone artifacts are earlier than the ones of *Sinanthropus*. But the question on which so far no agreement has been reached among the scientists is whether the 'red soil' here is the same red

soil referred to by geologists as equivalent in time with *Sinanthropus*, or is it 'yellow soil' later in age than *Sinanthropus* . . . The authors hold that the deposition is of the age equivalent to that of the lower layers at the Zhoukoudian site where a species of man of greater antiquity than *Sinanthropus* existed . . . On the stone artifacts the authors deem that there were three categories: (1) later than *Sinanthropus* in age, equivalent to the Dingcun industry, e.g., large triangular points, stone balls; (2) stone tools similar to those of *Sinanthropus*; (3) stone tools more primitive than those of *Sinanthropus*. There have been different views on the analysis made by the authors. Item (3) are actually eoliths, not human-fractured, and the other two kinds are not any earlier than *Sinanthropus*. In other words, there has been no convincing evidence to prove that Kehe stone tools are of earlier dating than those of *Sinanthropus*. As this problem is not yet resolved, it would be too rash to claim the existence of a Kehe tool industry that was earlier than *Sinanthropus*.

Later in 1962 Pei Wenzhong published another article, 'Man or Not Man',[3] in which he argued:

> With Engels' classic statements it should be clear to us that there is an insurmountable gap between man and 'not man', and the gap is men's ability to make tools, to work, and to organize themselves in social life. Yet there are different views on this criterion, hence the arguments . . .
>
> There had been a long process between the use of nature-flaked stone tools and human-flaked ones. Rocks are often fractured by natural causes and many look as if they were flaked by man. Such objects had given rise to the 'eolith' argument which lasted for more than a hundred years in the West. Monks of Europe were unhappy about Darwin's theory of evolution, which invalidated the Biblical story that it was God that created man. By using eoliths as evidence, they attempted to prove that man

---

[1] *New Construction*, No. 4, 1962.
[2] *Wenhui Daily*, June 24, 1962.

[3] *History Teaching*, No. 8, 1962.

had existed before what Darwin depicted as the time the human species came into being, so as to shake the foundation of his theory.

Another authority, Qiu Zhonglang, had also questioned the Early Middle Pleistocene dating of the Kehe stone artifacts. In his article, 'The Dating of the Kehe Site',[1] he stated:

> . . . For this reason, the deposits at Locality 6054 of the Kehe site, in which fossils of flat-antlered giant deer (*Megaloceros flabellatus*) and thick-jawed deer (*Megaloceros pachyosteus*) occurred in association, rank in time with the 10th, not the 13-11th layers of the *Sinanthropus* site. And the 10th layer was dated by the same authors as the Middle Pleistocene. Thus, even in the opinion of the same authors, the dating of the Kehe site should be Middle Middle Pleistocene instead of Early Middle Pleistocene.

> Neither the results of the studies made on the stone flakes and cores of the Kehe assemblage nor the types of the stone objects occurring at the site would give support to the conclusion of the authors that the "Kehe stone tools are more primitive than those of *Sinanthropus* . . ."

In their report on the Kehe finds, the authors have determined the date of the basal deposits at the *Sinanthropus* site to be earlier than *Sinanthropus*, for they regard the Kehe man as a "predecessor of *Sinanthropus*." On this point, however, the authors themselves actually differ. One of them had, in a paper entitled, '*Sinanthropus* Is Not the Most Primitive Man—Further Discussion with Mr Pei Wenzhong', expressed the view that man represented by the basal deposits at the *Sinanthropus* site "might be *Sinanthropus* (*pekinensis*), or perhaps a species slightly more primitive."

The eminent and foremost authority, archaeologist Xia Nai, in his general survey 'Archaeology in New China',[2] published in the Chinese Communist Party organ, had this to say:

> According to the scientists who found the stone artifacts at the Kehe site in Ruicheng County, Shanxi Province, these objects date earlier than *Sinanthropus*. We are thus able to trace the basic links of the evolution of man in China. There has been a persistent argument on the problem of the primitiveness of *Sinanthropus* recently. Judging by the fact that the species had already known the use of fire, the dating would have to be what Engels and Morgan termed the "middle period of the ignorance stage" in man's evolution, and cannot possibly be the earliest and most primitive. It is possible too that the paleoliths occurring at the Kehe site are of greater antiquity than *Sinanthropus*.

After the article, 'Dating of the Kehe Lithic Industry'[3] by Jia Lanpo, the debate seemed to have died down, although actually many of the participants were engaged in collecting more evidence to buttress their arguments.

Human fossil remains and artifacts of much earlier dating than *Sinanthropus* have been found at sites in various countries as well as in China in recent years. The following is a list of those unearthed in China. The dating was obtained by paleomagnetic testing administered by the Institute of Geodynamics of the Geological Sciences of China.

Teeth and artifacts, Yuanmou Man: Near Upper Nabang Village, Yuanmou County, Yunnan Province. Dating: 1 700 000 B.P.

Lithic industry, Xihoudu: At Xihoudu Village, 3.5 kilometres from the Kehe site, Shanxi Province. Dating: 1 800 000 B.P.

Skullcap and lithics, Lantian Man: At the Gongwangling site, Lantian County,

---

[1] *Journal of Vertebrate Paleontology and Paleoanthropology*, Vol. XI, No. 3, 1962.

[2] *Red Flag*, No. 17, 1962.

[3] *Wenhui Daily*, Oct. 7, 1962.

Shaanxi Province. Skullcap found in 1964, liths the following year. Dating of skullcap: approximately 1 000 000 B.P.

Mandible of Homo erectus: At the Chenjiawo site, Lantian County, Shaanxi Province. Dating: upwards of 500 000 B.P.

An absolute dating of the Peking Man site at Zhoukoudian was conducted in 1979. Various methods were applied to the rock series in accordance with the characteristics of each layer. The results and methods used were as shown in Table 30-1.

Table 30-1
Dating at Peking Man Site (1979)

Sequence of Rock Layers	Age (Years B.P.)	Method of Testing
10th	460 000 (approx.)	Fission track
10th	610 000	Thermoluminescence
4th	290 000	Thermoluminescence
8-9th	420 000 (approx.)	Uranium series
1-3rd	230 000 (approx.)	Uranium series
11th	460 000	Amino acid
8-9th	390 000	Amino acid
1-3rd	370 000 (approx.)	Amino acid
13th down, deposits overlaying basal gravel	710 000	Paleomagnetic
7th	370 000- 400 000	Paleomagnetic

Where, then, does the age problem of the Kehe site stand now? The answer is rather exciting.

The Museum of Shanxi Province had spent two years prior to 1979 digging at the site in search of an answer. In the autumn of 1979, archaeologist Wang Jian and his colleagues from the Museum led a team of the Academy of Sciences on a special trip to study the new finds from Kehe and other sites. The visitors, including the authors, were awed when they saw the array of specimens at the Museum in Taiyuan, capital of Shanxi. The objects filled two rooms. Both the mammalian fossils and the stone artifacts exceeded by far, in quantity as well as quality, what had been recovered in the past.

Most conspicuous among the specimens were a few teeth of the three-toed horse, a species that had before then occurred only in Pliocene and Early Pleistocene deposits. This may indicate that the dating of the Kehe liths is earlier than the original estimate. That is, the dating is not only earlier than *Sinanthropus*, but ranks in age with Lantian Man at the Gongwangling site.

31

Was Peking Man a Cannibal?

Charles Darwin in his *Journal of Researches into the Geology and Natural History of the Various Countries Visited by HMS Beagle, 1832-36* relates a similar account of cannibalism given by two persons on different occasions: in winter, driven by hunger, the islanders (West Indies) would kill their old women for food. Thomas Henry Huxley in his *Man's Place in Nature* (1863) draws attention in a note to cannibalism in Africa in the sixteenth century. And in modern times, John Gunther in his *Inside Africa* (1955) reports cannibalism in Rhodesia (Zimbabwe, etc.) and other areas. These are no random stories. Cannibalism has been "a widespread custom going back into early human history, [and] it has been found among peoples on most continents."[1]

In an article 'Did *Sinanthropus* Practise Cannibalism?', published around 1940,[2] Franz Weidenreich deduced from the disproportionate numbers of human skeletal bones at the Peking Man site that cannibalism prevailed in this early time. Judging from our present level of understanding, this inference is no fallacy but entirely credible. Of human fossil remains, there are far fewer limb bones than skullcaps, while with almost all other animals, the opposite is true, whether carnivores or herbivores.

[1] *Encyclopaedia Britannica*, Vol. II, pp. 511-12, 1981.

[2] *Bulletin of the Geological Society of China*, Vol. 19, No. 1, 1939-40.

The actual numbers of Peking Man skeletal remains so far recovered from the site are given in Table 31-1.

Table 31-1
Peking Man Remains Recovered (to 1982)

Skullcaps (only 6 relatively complete)	14
Facial bones (including maxillae, palates and zygomatic bone fragments)	6
Mandibles (mostly one side, only one nearly complete, many fragments)	15
Teeth: Single	122
Rooted in jaws	38
Humerus (upper arm, only one better preserved, the rest in fragments)	3
Clavicle (both ends absent)	1
Lunar bone	1
Femurs (thighbones, only one better preserved)	7
Shinbone (fragmentary)	1

They were recovered from more than 20 000 cubic metres of deposit in 15 areas at the site. They represent more than 40 individuals, some by only one tooth.

Human fossil remains always occurred in association with stone artifacts and vertebrate animal fossils, although more often than not, only the latter two kinds were found in large numbers, with no trace of human fossils.

In explaining this phenomenon, natural causes and human errors cannot of course be ruled out, but in Peking Man's case, they are unlikely. Assuming that nature destroyed the human skeletal remains, then why not other animals' as well? And we cannot attribute the anomaly to our own inability to find everything, either at the field or in the laboratory, because work procedures and the cautiousness of the workers do not bear it out. During the digging, scarcely an object, not even the tiniest fragment, would be discarded unless its nature had been made clear. When the specimens were shipped to the laboratory in Beijing, they were sorted over and sifted to the last splinter, and chances of even one specimen's being overlooked was practically nil. Indeed, nearly all the limb bones listed in Table 31-1 were the fruits of the lab workers' labour, evidence of the fact that it was hardly possible for a piece of human fossil to escape their trained eyes.

How were these human bones brought into the cave? Studies made by Weidenreich led him to conclude that they could not have been washed into the cave by water, as there were no signs on the ground to give such proof; nor could they possibly have been carried in by non-hominid animals, as there were no claw or tooth marks in the bones. The only possibility, he asserted, was that Peking Man did it.

Weidenreich also identified the damage on the skullcaps. The skullcap found in 1929 in Locus E (the very first one found by Pei Wenzhong) shows damage to the two parietal bones, caused by heavy blows. Another which was found in 1936 in Locus L bears a 1.5-centimetre depression, round, shallow, and uneven at the bottom, in the left parietal bone, with three cracks radiating out from the depression. The third skullcap, also from Locus L, shows a deep cut in the right parietal, nearly 3 centimetres long, with its end shaped like an arrowhead. There are also slight damage around the hole between the two parietals (foramen magnum) and a conspicuous scar in the left brow ridge of the same skullcap. Similar specimens unearthed at

some other loci also show such signs of damage.

No doubt, Weidenreich held, the injuries were inflicted when the skullcap owners were still alive, as some of the depressions appear to be characteristic of wounds that are commonly discussed in medical jurisprudence. Some appear to be the result of a heavy blow made with a pointed weapon; or, in the case of lengthwise cuts, with an edged tool, or, in the case of large, round depressions, with a stone or stick. From such evidence, it can safely be said that cannibalism prevailed in the Peking Man community. Traces of the custom have been found among peoples of later ages, such as in the middle and late paleolithic age. As Weidenreich has pointed out, cannibalism is indicated in the Neanderthal Man assemblage of the last Ice Age and for 'Ehringsdorf' Man near Weimar, East Germany.

How can we interpret the disproportionate occurrences of Peking Man's skull and limb bones? The answer, in our view, is that the base of a skull forms a good container for water, being as useful for this purpose as the many deer skull bases that occurred at the site. They were deliberately fashioned for the purpose. Using human skullcaps as containers has been a practice even during recent years, as the authors have witnessed in a lamasery.

When dealing with the characteristics of Australian skulls, in his *Man's Place in Nature*, Huxley reports that he saw Aborigines in Australia using skullcaps as water containers. "The majority of skulls possessing these characteristics, which I have seen, are from the neighbourhood of Port Adelaide in South Australia, and have been used by the natives as water vessels; to which end the face has been knocked away," he says.

Friedrich Engels also refers in his works to the custom of cannibalism in ancient society.[1] He noted in *Anti-Dühring* that up to the time when prisoners of war acquired a value, "one had not known what to do with prisoners of war, and had therefore simply killed them; at an even earlier period, eaten them." In another of his works[2] he observes, "The tribes which figure in books as living entirely, that is, exclusively, by hunting never existed in reality; the yield of the hunt was far too precarious. At that stage [Engels refers to the Middle Stage that begins with the utilization of fish for food and with the use of fire—*Tr.*], owing to the continual uncertainty of food supplies, cannibalism seems to have arisen and was practised from then onwards for a long time."

Such incredible savagery is most startling, yet there were indeed many cannibals in history, a fact which, to some scholars, partly explains the extremely low level of the production forces of early human beings.

---

[1] The translation of Engels' *Anti-Dühring* was made from the third German edition (1894), Foreign Languages Publishing House, Moscow, 1954, p. 250.

[2] *The Origin of the Family, Private Property and the State*, Foreign Languages Press, Beijing, China, 1978, p. 25.

32

The Exhibition Hall at Zhoukoudian

Since the discovery of Peking Man fossils at Zhoukoudian, this once obscure village has become a centre of attention for people in the profession the world over and attracts large numbers of visitors each year. Yet, for a long time, there was no place to display the finds; only the sites themselves were available for observation. All specimens unearthed here, whether human or non-human, original or reconstructed, before or after assessment and study, could be seen only at the exhibition hall in the city. A local display centre was desirable, especially for the benefit of the general public, yet there was none.

The excavation which had been suspended for twelve years was resumed promptly after the founding of the People's Republic in 1949, much to the surprise of the old staff members of the Zhoukoudian project, who were now entrusted with carrying on the work. Funds were made available without delay. Everybody was so overawed that for a time no one even thought about erecting a display centre on the site. Nonetheless, a makeshift three-room structure was built later, using the ingenuity and labour of the project's staff and manual workers so that the cost was minimal. As it turned out, only one room was used for exhibition, and it served the purpose well until a formal hall came into being. In the beginning, the fossils and artifacts were laid on two doorboards—rather like merchandise displayed

on the street—and one of the staff members would serve as a temporary guide. Indeed, though devoid of the splendid galleries, rows of shining showcases, and complex organization typical of a large city museum, this Zhoukoudian exhibition displayed its specimens in the larger context of the excavation area, giving visitors a perspective that no distant museum could provide. It did not take long for the relevance of this display to become obvious. In the winter of 1951, Zhu Kezhen, the celebrated meteorologist and Deputy Director of the Chinese Academy of Sciences, came to inspect the work in progress. It was he who suggested, while taking his leave, that it would be a good idea to build a formal display centre.

Thus inspired, the staff started tree planting in April 1952 to reforest the area and had a rail built along the edge of a steep slope leading to the Peking Man site. The next year, fruit trees of diverse species were planted. By then, the funds for the construction of a formal display centre had been made available by the Academy. In July 1953, the building of a modest structure of some 300 square metres in floor space was completed. The place was partitioned into two sections, one the display centre proper, the other an office and a reception room. The exhibition centre was opened to the public on September 21, 1953. At the preview the day before, the then Director of the Institute of Vertebrate

Paleontology, Professor Yang Zhongjian, had this to say in his speech:

> All the specimens unearthed here are the property of the people, and the significance of the displays lies in that they provide evidence of evolutionary processes of ape to man and of other species of the biological world, and the general public should be educated to acquire such a knowledge . . .

These words aptly stated the motives of our staff in preparing the exhibition.

The fossils and artifacts were divided into three sections and displayed in three rooms. The first room contained those of humans with the first half showing copies of Peking Man's fossil bones and related artifacts, including stone and bone tools, and evidence of the use of fire. The second half was devoted to Upper Cave Man, showing copies of a fossil skull and stone and bone tools and ornaments.

The display in the second room consisted of faunal fossils found in association with Peking Man and Upper Cave Man. The Peking Man assemblage contained many species which are extinct, for example the Chinese hyena, saber-toothed tiger, Merck's rhinoceros, woolly rhinoceros, Sanmen horse, Lydekker's wild pig, thick-jawed deer, and straight-tusked elephant. Their living in the age of Peking Man indicates that the environmental conditions of the region were quite different then from those of modern times.

Most of the species that made up the fauna of the Upper Cave Man age can still be found on the Mongolian plateau. Southern species are few in number, and only three are extinct, namely the cave hyena, cave bear and giant ostrich. The Upper Cave collection of fauna fossils attests that the environmental conditions of that age were not quite the same as those we have today.

There are more than twenty sites within two kilometres of Zhoukoudian at which fossil mammals of the Lower Pliocene and Upper Pleistocene have been found. The more significant of these were displayed in the third room. The objects in this room also showed the entire process of the geological, paleontological and human development of the Zhoukoudian area since the Upper Cenozoic.

The display was an immediate success. It attracted visitors from China and abroad. By 1955 their numbers had increased to such an extent that part of the floor space used for reception and offices had to be converted into show rooms. There were seven rooms instead of three. The objects, too, had grown wider in range and were divided into seven groups displayed in the seven rooms as follows:

1. Peking Man—human fossils and artifacts

2. Upper Cave Man—human fossils and artifacts

3. Objects from sites in other parts of China and from all over the world, comprising copies of fossils representing all stages of human evolution

4. Rock specimens and models showing the geological conditions of Zhoukoudian and adjacent areas, and charts and models in corresponding geological sequence showing the evolution from 'fish to human'

5 & 6. Fauna from sites of Zhoukoudian other than the Peking Man site

7. Faunal fossils found in association with Peking Man

The expanded exhibit centre opened in October 1955; in 1956 alone, it received 100 000 visitors, some 2000 from foreign lands. In the few years that followed, more human fossils were unearthed in the country, such as Changyang Man of Hubei Province, Maba Man of Guangdong Province and Liujiang Man of Guangxi; these were added to the exhibit, but the basic patterns of the display remained without major change.

Soon after the start of the 'cultural revolution', however, things took a tragic turn. The research, the digging, and of course the display were all suspended until 1972, when a new, larger exhibition hall was built with the objects arranged in sequences that bore the marks of the ideological bent of the times. The 1000-square-metre floor space, three times the size of its predecessor, was divided into three parts showing (1) the evolutionary process of vertebrates 'from fish to human', with the focus on the 'incubation of the human species'; (2) the development of the hu-

Top: A large, new exhibition hall was built in 1972. The old display centre was demolished in 1975. (*Photo by Wang Zhefu, 1972*)
Bottom: The exhibition hall reopened in October 1979 after the exhibits were rearranged. (*Photo by Wang Zhefu*)

A bust made by Wu Rukang and assistants. The reconstruction is based on a female skullcap unearthed at the Peking Man site. Weidenreich and Gerasimoff had made an earlier reconstruction of Peking Man in this form.

scene. This view was shared by many authorities, including the then Director of the Academy of Sciences Guo Moruo, who, after inspecting the preview of the exhibition, remarked: "A Zhoukoudian centre should focus on the Zhoukoudian finds." And Yang Zhongjian, then Director of the Institute, repeatedly urged before his passing away, that the set-up be changed. We agreed too, on the common sense ground that it is impractical to have a dentist function as a general practitioner.

The change was not effected until the winter of 1978; the new centre was formally opened on December 6, 1979, on the fiftieth anniversary of the discovery of the first Peking Man skullcap.

man species, focusing on the theme that 'labour created man'; (3) major finds in paleontological and paleoanthropological fields since the founding of the People's Republic. Some people held at that time that the old sequence was 'too specialized' so it 'served only the experts', and the new one was meant for the general public and was 'closely related to politics' to 'serve the workers, peasants, and soldiers'. Of course educating the general public is undoubtedly desirable, yet the new pattern made the display such a commonplace show that the centre lost all its characteristics as a specialized museum reflecting the Zhoukoudian

The new arrangement had four sections under four headings, namely, 'The Zhoukoudian area', 'The Peking Man site', 'Other sites at Zhoukoudian' and 'From ape to man'.

The first section was a window offering a panoramic view of the local geological and topographical features, as well as of the discovery of and the diggings at the sites. The objects consisted of valuable photographs, a sand model of Dragon Bone Hill, and rocks representing geological ages.

The second section was devoted to the most significant part of the entire exhibition, featuring objects showing the physical characteristics of Peking Man; the industry of Peking Man (toolmaking, gathering and hunting and the use of fire); and the environment of their time (the forming of the cave home and cave deposits, the fauna and flora of that period, and the dating of the period). Seen here were copies of Peking Man's fossil skullcaps, limb bones, and teeth; their stone implements; hackberry seeds that they had gathered; and bone fragments belonging to animals that had fallen prey to them. Charts and pictures were added to help the viewer to understand the exhibit.

The third section featured specimens, models and charts about Localities 14, 15 and 4, the roof deposits and upper gravel layers, and the Upper Cave site, which provided the visitor with a general idea of the geological, paleontological and human development since the Upper Cenozoic.

The fourth section displayed copies of fossils of some forerunners of human beings, including members of the genera *Dryopithecus*, *Gigantopithecus*, and *Ramapithecus*. Copies of specimens from China and abroad representing each stage of man's evolution—*Australopithecus*, *Homo erectus*, and finally, *Homo sapiens*—were presented. It was a review of the entire human evolutionary process and a summing up of the exhibition.

The contents of the displays remain much the same today. Their validity has been substantiated, especially with the new data gathered in recent years on the environments of Peking Man's time and the new dating of various sites.

Upper Cave Man reconstructed by Gerasimoff. Some modification was done by Wu Xinzhi and colleagues.

33

Anniversary Celebrations

Three anniversary meetings have been held so far to mark the finding of the first Peking Man's skullcap—the twenty-fifth held in 1954, the thirtieth in 1959 and the fiftieth in 1979. They were all held in Beijing in December, the month the first discovery was made. Each gathering has in fact been an opportunity to review not only the Zhoukoudian project and materials, but all significant paleoanthropological finds in China. Each was thus an occasion for looking back on what has been achieved, and for looking forward by giving fresh impetus to all concerned.

The significance of the event in 1954 was enhanced by the long list of participants, including Marshal Chen Yi (who was at the time in charge of the Academy of Sciences on behalf of the Central Committee of the Communist Party of China), leading personages of all units related to the Zhoukoudian project, well-known scientists, representatives from cultural circles, and some foreign friends in Beijing. At the opening session, the Director of the Academy, Guo Moruo addressed the meeting by saying, in part:

> The discovery of human fossils dating back a half million years is, as an important scientific event, worthy of commemorating . . .
>
> The first period of digging at Zhoukoudian, the ten years from 1927 to 1937 prior to the invasion of the Japanese, had not suffered interruption.
>
> According to incomplete statistics, at the

Peking Man (*Sinanthropus*) site, 1873 days of digging have been accumulated. This figure would come to 178 965 in terms of man-days. The time used in research and lab work is not counted. And in terms of the volume of work done, indicated by the rock and earth removed, it has been some 20 000 cubic metres at the *Sinanthropus* site, and another 4200 cubic metres at other sites in the area.

In fossil hunting, such a scale is certainly unprecedented. But the efforts were richly rewarded with the following results:

Specimens recovered filled 1221 boxes, or 375 cubic metres of materials (before being sifted). Human fossils occurred in quantity at the *Sinanthropus* site after the first skullcap was unearthed there. Counting the ones that came to light after 1949, the human remains represented some 40 individuals, consisting of 5 relatively complete skullcaps, 9 skull fragments, 6 facial bones, 14 mandibles, 152 teeth, fragmented limb bones, 1 collar-bone, 3 humeri (upper-arm bones), 1 lunar bone, 7 thigh bones and 1 shin bone. Some 100 000 pieces of paleoliths and worked stone flakes and cores were found in association, with evidence of the use of fire collected in the meantime.

Two fossilized plants and 118 faunal fossils were found. Of the latter, 94 mammalian species were identified, 30 of them extinct. Fossils of certain species were especially profuse. For instance, thick-jawed deer and hyena remains each represent more than 2000 such animals . . .

The more than 20 years of research done

Deposits at the main part of the site and at the Pigeon Hall section were opened to each other in 1958.

Top: The Chinese Academy of Sciences and archaeological specialists from the Department of History of Beijing University co-operated in the excavation at the Pigeon Hall area in August 1958.
Bottom: The President of the Chinese Academy of Sciences, Guo Moruo, visited the Peking Man site on September 23, 1958 and joined the students at work.

Top: Block R-1 near Pigeon Hall yielded a Peking Man lower jaw with both sides attached on July 6, 1959.
Bottom: Work in progress at the Peking Man site in 1960.

on the Zhoukoudian finds is reflected in the 72 volumes of monographs totalling 4310 pages. The figure does not include papers of a general nature or popular writings on the subject . . .

Guo also dealt with the new fossil finds in various parts of China in the five years since the founding of the People's Republic and concluded his speech with full confidence in the future:

China is not only rich in resources and

has an exceptionally bright future in its socialist construction, it is also rich in paleovertebrate and paleoanthropological fossil remains; and the research on this branch of science has an extremely bright future as well.

After this speech, five papers were delivered:

Yang Zhongjian, 'Research in China on Human Fossil Remains—Past, Present and Future';

Right: The 30th Anniversary Meeting held in Beijing, December 21-24, 1959. Professor Pei Wenzhong is shown addressing the audience. (*Photo by Wang Zhefu*)

Bottom: One frontal, one occipital bone and a tooth of Peking Man were unearthed in 1966. These new finds fit with two temporal bones previously excavated (one in 1934, the other in 1936), making the skullcap almost complete. The picture shows the finding of the bones.

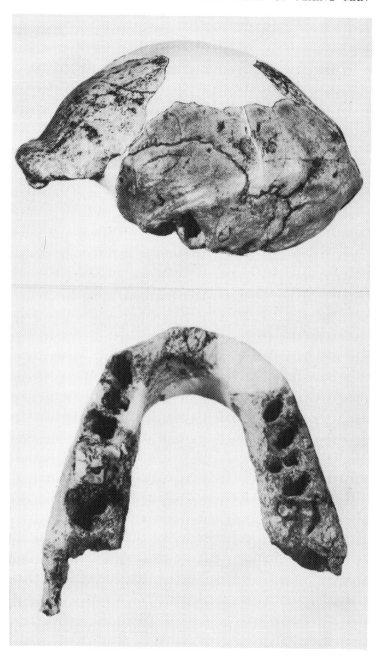

Top: The skullcap of Peking Man, reconstructed by fitting together the finds of 1934, 1936 and 1966, all of which belong to one individual.
Bottom: Lower jawbone of a female unearthed in 1959.

Zhou Mingzhen, 'The Environs of *Sinanthropus* as Indicated by Vertebrate Faunal Fossils';

Pei Wenzhong, 'The Significance of the Human Fossils Found in China in the Context of Man's Evolution';

Wu Rukang, 'Paleolithic Industries in China'; and

Jia Lanpo, 'A Brief Report on the Human Fossils and Paleoliths Unearthed at the Dingcun (Tingtsun) Site in Xiangfen County, Shanxi Province'.

These papers summed up work accomplished in the five years since 1949, the most significant of which was the resumption of excavation at the Peking Man site in 1949 and in 1951 after the twelve-year interruption brought about by the War of Resistance Against Japan. In those two operations, five Peking Man teeth were found at the site, and two limb bones (humerus and shin) were sifted out later in the laboratory. With the addition of the limb-bone finds, the number and variety of this category of specimens had enabled the scientists to deduce that Peking Man's arm bones are morphologically closer to those of a modern human than the lower limb bones, as the only primitive feature surviving in Peking Man's humerus was the small medullary cavity and thick walls of the canal.

Another important achievement was the excavation at the Dingcun site which yielded human fossils and quantities of paleoliths. Situated on the banks of the Fenhe, the site was first known to scientists in 1953, and systematic digging began in 1954. The site proved to be the most significant of its kind, besides Zhoukoudian, excavated since the founding of the new China. It has yielded 3 human teeth, 27 non-human mammalian fossils, and 1566 stone artifacts.

Actually the site is an area that includes a number of sites, so the dating turned out to be a knotty problem, but it is assumed to be of a later dating than the Peking Man time, approximately the Early Upper Pleistocene.

The stone artifacts consist of heavy triangle points, stone balls, choppers and scrapers, which represent a characteristic tradition in North China other than the Peking Man industry. Since 1976, scientists working for the provincial institutions, headed by Wang Jian, have been exploiting the area and

Top: The 50th anniversary of the finding of the first Peking Man skullcap was commemorated December 6-12, 1979 in Beijing. Zhou Mingzhen, paleontologist and Director of the Institute of Vertebrate Paleontology and Paleoanthropology, addressed the audience. (*Photo by Wang Zhefu*)
Bottom: Professor Pei Wenzhong addressed the 50th anniversary meeting in high spirits. He was 76 at the time. (*Photo by Wang Zhefu, December 7, 1979*)

have achieved impressive results. The number of sites grew from 13 to 24, and the area as a whole, which had stood at 11 square kilometres, was doubled. Along with this expansion of scale, the range of time periods has been widened to cover the entire paleolithic age instead of the middle paleolithic as before.

The thirtieth anniversary was a much larger gathering than the twenty-fifth, indicating the vigorous advancement in the realm of paleoanthropology. At such meetings in the past, as a rule, only those who were in Beijing were invited to attend. This time, there were 141 persons from 16 provinces and municipalities representing research units, colleges, related cultural and educational institutions, and industrial establishments. Among them were anthropologists, archaeologists, paleontologists, geologists, and other scholars in related fields. At the twenty-fifth anniversary, only five papers had been delivered, but this one received 28 papers covering a wide range of subjects in the fields of paleoanthropology, paleolithic industry, *Gigantopithecus blacki* (giant ape) and geopaleontology. Even the problem of the 'snow man' was made a topic. An on-site meeting was held at Zhoukoudian, where the participants inspected the sites and the display centre, at which they held a discussion.

Well-known scientists Yang Zhongjian, Xia Nai, Pei Wenzhong, Jia Lanpo, Zhou Mingzhen, Wu Rukang, Wu Dingliang, Feng Hanji, Lin Yaohua and Liang Zhaotao, were on hand at the anniversary gathering, and some of them made reports on their finds. In the course of the occasion, representatives from various regions of China conferred on the programme for the country's anthropological projects.

A number of finds had been made since the last anniversary, and two categories of simian fossils were of special significance. The first were the five fossil teeth unearthed successively in 1957 and 1958 in Upper Miocene coal-measure strata at Xiaolongtan, Kaiyuan County, Yunnan Province. To these Professor Wu Rukang gave the name *Dryopithecus kaiyuanensis* (Kaiyuan Oak Ape), but further studies resulted in grouping the 1957 Kaiyuan finds under the generic name *Ramapithecus punjabicus* (Punjab Rama Ape). This ape is believed to be the nearest precursor of *Homo sapiens*, indicating a promising future for Chinese scholars in their studies on the emergence of human beings. The second was the discovery of a gargantuan mandible and teeth by the Dutch paleoanthropologist von Koenigswald at a Hong Kong herbal medicine shop over the period 1931-52. The fossils belonged to an extinct genus to which the Dutch scientist gave the name *Gigantopithecus blacki*. These were single teeth, massive in size, but possessing characteristics very close to those of humans. For this reason, Franz Weidenreich reclassified them under *Gigantanthropus*. It had been certain that the fossils were from southern China, but the sites were unknown until 1956 when Pei Wenzhong and Jia Lanpo led a study group exploring lime caves in Guangxi. Here they dug up three teeth of the genus, and that settled the problem of the site. Then Pei Wenzhong bought from a villager a mandible of an aged female, and at 'Gargantuan Cave' at Liucheng, another two male mandibles and a number of single teeth were unearthed. The site also yielded, in association, mammalian fossils of pigs, tapirs, rhinoceroses, horses, straight-tusked elephants, and giant apes (*Gigantopithecus*). With such faunal evidence and more mandibles and teeth of the genus itself, the scientists now had a more solid base for dealing with the problems of its dating, environment and position on the evolutionary ladder.

Discoveries had also been made with

regard to human fossil remains. These included a mandible of Peking Man; a skullcap of Maba Man (at Maba, Shaoguan, Guangdong Province), and fossils of Changyang Man (in Changyang County, Hubei Province), both representing humans of the paleoanthropic stage; fossils of Liujiang Man (in Liujiang County, Guangxi) and Qilinshan Man (Laibin County, Guangxi), both representing humans of the neoanthropic stage. More specimens had been found of Ordos Man fossils at the old site of Sjara-osso-gol in Inner Mongolia.

Of paleolith sites, 55 new ones were found in Shanxi Province alone, representing all stages of the paleolithic age. Some other such sites were discovered elsewhere.

The fieldwork at Zhoukoudian was suspended in the period 1952-57 during which major excavations were made in other sites. But work resumed in 1958 under the supervision of Jia Lanpo. Digging was conducted in three areas at the Peking Man site, exploring the depth of the deposits in one area, while hunting for more materials in the other two. The first stage of work had the co-operation of the Archaeological Section of the Department of History of Beijing University.

Taking stock, the year was rewarding. The digging led to a clearer understanding of the stratigraphical condition of the site and the mammalian fossils unearthed furnished new evidence for defining the rock sequence. For instance, the discovery of the remains of flat-antlered giant deer proves that the basal deposit at the site ranks in time with Locality 13, where the same remains had occurred. The chert flake found at the basal deposit, like the stone artifact found at Locality 13, is one of the earliest tools the Zhoukoudian area has yet yielded.

In the year 1959, two younger scientists, Zhao Zikui and Li Yanxian, directed the operations, with digging centred on the western section of Pigeon Hall. Apart from a few mammalian fossils and unrepresentative stone artifacts, a significant find was made on July 6 at Layer 10: a fairly complete Peking Man mandible, which Wu Rukang and Zhao Zikui determined to be that of an old female. The same layer yielded remains of both thick-jawed giant deer and flat-antlered giant deer, indicating that the deposit was formed during the transition from early to middle Peking Man time.

Basing his view on the stone artifacts at the site, Pei Wenzhong had on the twenty-fifth anniversary stated that the rock sequence could be divided into two main stages, with the demarcation line placed between Layer 5 and Layer 6. The new evidence of 1958 led Jia Lanpo to believe that a three-stratum demarcation would be more valid:

1. Layers 11-13, ranking in time with Locality 13, characterized by few stone artifacts, devoid of identifiable Peking Man remains or fossils of thick-jawed giant deer contemporaneous with Peking Man. What occurred here were only remains of *Myospalax tingi* and flat-antlered giant deer, both of greater antiquity.

2. Layers 4-10, containing approximately the same mammalian fossils and stone artifacts.

3. Layers 1-3, yielding mammalian fossils of newer genera, indicated by the remains of 'ultimate spotted hyena', and stone artifacts of more advanced characteristics, such as a chert point that looked like an awl.

On the thirtieth anniversary, however, Huang Wanpo proposed a further division into six periods.

Zhao Zikui and Dai Erjian were in charge of the fieldwork in 1960. They carried on digging at the western basal section of the deposits at Pigeon Hall, reaching Layer 13 before the season closed on October 16. The discovery of a mandible of *Myospalax tingi* at this layer indicated that it is of the same dating as Locality 13. The same layer yielded a sandstone artifact showing that human beings were active here during the formation of these basal deposits in the cave.

The dig at Zhoukoudian was now suspended for a few years for more important tasks elsewhere. When work resumed in 1966, Pei Wenzhong directed the operations with the participation of archaeologist Qiu Zhonglang and the veteran technician Chai Fengqi. Because of the 'cultural revolution', however, the year's fieldwork was short-lived (March 15 to July 4), and the paper on the finds was not published until September 1973.

In spite of all this, the results were impressive. The area under excavation was the top of the southern fissure at the entrance to the Upper Cave where Peking Man remains had been found in 1934. The new finds included a Peking Man frontal bone, an occipital, and a single tooth. It was of great interest that these two skull fragments fitted exactly with the two temporal bones already recovered, one in 1934, the other in 1936. They belonged to the same individual, and were part of the skull with the serial number 5. Research done on the specimens collected led to the conclusion that this skull possessed more advanced morphological features than any other Peking Man skull fossil. This indicates that during the long interval of the formation of the cave deposits, humans had been making progress in terms of morphology, though not in step with their advancement in cultural matters.

No unusual mammalian fossils occurred this time, except for a short stump of red deer antler, which was new at the site. Red deer was a common species in North China in the Upper Pleistocene. Remains of the animal had occurred at Locality 15 and were now at the top level deposit of the Peking Man site, indicating its Upper Pleistocene dating.

The fiftieth anniversary was held on December 6-12, 1979 in Beijing, and the participants came with eagerness and excitement. These gatherings were supposed to take place every five years, yet this was the first since 1959. Besides, the year 1979 was also the thirtieth anniversary of the founding of the People's Republic of China.

The joy and scale of the gathering were both unprecedented. Every province, municipality and autonomous region, with the exception of Taiwan, had sent delegates, and the number of papers reached 109, covering subjects ranging from paleoanthropology, paleontology, ancient cultures and environments, and stratigraphy, to the dating of sites. They mirrored not only the new achievements in Zhoukoudian research, but also many significant discoveries in the realm of paleoanthropology elsewhere in China, including the Xihoudu hominid site (Shanxi Province), of 1 800 000 years' antiquity; the Yuanmou Man teeth and artifacts (Yunnan Province), of 1 700 000 years' antiquity; the Lantian Man skullcap and artifacts at the Gongwangling site (Shaanxi Province), of 1 000 000 years' antiquity; the *Homo erectus* mandible recovered at the Chenjiawo site, Lantian, Shaanxi Province; the *Homo erectus* teeth found in Yunxi County, Hubei Province; the paleolith site of Xujiayao Village, Shanxi Province, which had yielded early *Homo sapiens* remains and artifacts; the complete early *Homo sapiens* skull and artifacts from Dali, Shaanxi Province; the *Dryopithecus* (ancient ape) remains recovered at Lufeng, Yunnan Province; and the significant finds at the Dingcun site as mentioned earlier.

During the meeting, tribute was paid to Professor Yang Zhongjian, who had passed away on January 15 of the year. He had dedicated his entire life to paleontological work and had for a long time directed the project at Zhoukoudian. In his last days he had concerned himself with preparations for the fiftieth anniversary and had planned to make a joint speech with Jia Lanpo for the occasion.

Everyone was delighted with the presence of Professor Pei Wenzhong at the gathering. It was he who had discovered the first Peking Man skullcap. Jia Lanpo addressed the assembly at its opening session, expressing feelings shared by all and providing a historical appraisal of the Zhoukoudian project. He said, in part:

> December 2, 1929 was a memorable day in the history of paleoanthropology. The complete skullcap and artifacts of Peking Man and evidence of his use of fire, discovered by Professor Pei Wenzhong, had like a spring thunderbolt awakened those who were shackled by traditional bias and compelled them to admit that in the dawn of the history of man, there had been a stage of *Homo erectus* bearing features of its own in morphology, cultural characteristics, and social set-up. Every piece of fossil occurring at the Peking Man site convinced people of the existence of *Homo erectus*, and an increasing number of people believed that he was the descendant of *Australopithecinae*, or Southern Ape, and the precursor of *Homo sapiens*, which emerged after him. The fossils, implements, and evidence of the use of fire found at the Peking Man site have enabled us to have a better understanding of man's past, thus providing an important missing link in evolution . . .

The Zhoukoudian project has trained at least two generations of specialists in paleoanthropology, paleolith archaeology, and vertebrate paleontology. The project in its early days was under the direction of the Cenozoic Research Laboratory of the Geological Survey of China, which was the predecessor of the Institute of Vertebrate Paleontology and Paleoanthropology of the Chinese Academy of Sciences. It is said that Yang Zhongjian and Pei Wenzhong were the men who laid the cornerstone of these branches of science in China. I deem this an apt evaluation of the two scholars, borne out by history itself. Recent discoveries of human fossil remains and paleoliths across the country have been made possible by the Zhoukoudian project, with its training of specialists and provision of facilities. And of course the more fundamental factor is the change in the social system, which facilitates the advancement of scientific work. With the superior social system and fuller academic democracy, it is certain that the disciplines will advance with even greater strides.

There have been many Chinese and foreign scholars of the older generation who have contributed directly to the Zhoukoudian project. These include the geologist Li Jie of China, paleontologist Yang Zhongjian, anthropologist Davidson Black of Canada, geologist Johan Gunnar Andersson of Sweden, paleontologist Birger Bohlin of Sweden, paleontologist Otto Zdansky of Austria, anthropologist Franz Weidenreich of the United States, and paleontologist Teilhard de Chardin of France. Many of them have passed away, but our memory and veneration of them shall never fade.

Major leaders of the Academy of Sciences attended and spoke at the meetings, marking the importance of the occasion. These included Director Fang Yi, Deputy Director Qian Sanqiang, and Director of the Academy's Division of Earth Sciences, the well-known geologist Yin Zanxun, who made the closing speech.

34

Research on Zhoukoudian Continues

The Peking Man site has been under scrutiny for over a half century now, and the human and material resources that have been poured into the research and excavation are in proportions rare for a project of its kind in any country. Scientists from at least seven countries besides China have worked for it, and for many among them, Zhoukoudian has meant a lifelong career. Through their endeavours and their outstanding work, this once unknown site has been shedding a brilliant light on the realms of paleoanthropology, paleontology, and studies of Quaternary strata. Can we then say that the subject has been exhausted? Certainly not. In the first place, the profusion and complexity of the finds prevent the problems from being readily solved. And in the second, the scientific approach to the work changes with the prevailing level of science and technology. For instance, many of the methods commonly used today for dating and for the study of environments of the distant past were non-existent some years back. Therefore, either in range or in depth, studies at and on Zhoukoudian must be upgraded.

Digging and related work at Zhoukoudian have been interrupted twice, once by the War of Resistance Against Japan, and again for ten years by the 'cultural revolution'. The display centre at Zhoukoudian was reopened in 1972, but digging and research were not resumed. When Huang Weiwen, a younger member of the staff of the Institute, was entrusted with the work at the site, he planned to explore the mystery of Peking Man's origin and development, but the obstacles were so many that he had to give up the plan in the end. In 1976, in celebrating the one-hundredth anniversary of the publication of the article, 'The Function of Labour in the Transition from Ape to Man', by Engels, the Institute, with the co-operation of many other units, carried out a programme to determine the dating of some early human sites in China. Only then did the Zhoukoudian area become a little more alive again.

In December 1977, a comprehensive study on the Peking Man site was listed as one of the major projects of the Chinese Academy of Sciences, the plans to be developed in 1978. Subsequently, a working conference was held at the county seat of Fangshan, with Professor Wu Rukang representing the Institute and acting as chairman of the meeting. Many related units also participated. A programme for the 1978-84 period was worked out at that conference; the following major activities were included:

1. continued excavation at the Peking Man site, with further studies on Peking Man, his industry and faunal fossils found in association;

2. research on the late Cenozoic strata and paleoglaciation of Zhoukoudian;

3. research on the Peking Man cave and general laws of karst formation;

4. research on the characteristics of ancient earth and deposits at the Peking Man site and the environs in which they were formed;

5. sporopollen analysis of the Peking Man site;

6. research on the sedimentary environs in Peking Man's time;

7. dating of the Peking Man site and other sites of the kind in the Zhoukoudian area;

8. drawing of 1:250 topographical maps of Dragon Bone Hill and its vicinity; and

9. production of documentary films and recording of relevant events.

These tasks and subjects were taken up by 17 allied units in various regions of China, and more than 120 people were directly involved in either the fieldwork or office duties. They produced ample results in the two years that followed, reports of which were presented at the fiftieth anniversary of the Zhoukoudian project in December 1979.

There are still many problems requiring the attention of the researchers, but which are the most compelling? In our view, they are the dating of Peking Man, the ecology in Peking Man's time, and the origin and development of this Zhoukoudian cave dweller.

Significant headway has been made in recent years on the dating of Peking Man. The Pliocene dating assumed by Andersson and Zdansky had been invalidated by Teilhard de Chardin and Yang Zhongjian at the end of 1929, chiefly on the strength of faunal evidence which showed the age to be Middle Pleistocene—later than the Nihewanian age but earlier than the Loess age. In a book entitled *Fossil Man in China* published in 1933, co-authored by Black, Teilhard, Yang Zhongjian and Pei Wenzhong, this assertion was restated, and the time of Peking Man was equated with the end of the Mindel glacial stage. No one has

since challenged this view. Even if there have been some sceptics, they have not yet come up with credible evidence to prove their point.

The fossil-bearing deposition at the Peking Man site is more than 40 metres thick. Though it has been defined as 13 layers on the basis of rock records, the sediment as a whole is an uninterrupted series without detectable break. We have thus been confronted with the problem of the time span over which the deposition accumulated. Was it the entire Middle Pleistocene, or only a part of that epoch? If only a part, was it Upper or Lower Middle Pleistocene? The question has been left unanswered.

In a discussion that took place in 1957 on the geographical distribution of Quaternary mammals, Pei Wenzhong believed the fauna associated with Peking Man should be contemporaneous with Britain's Forest Bed series, France's Abbeville period, Italy's Val d'Arno period, and Germany's Mosbach period. He placed the fauna at Lower Middle Pleistocene, equivalent to Europe's Gunz-Mindel Interglacial Stage. His view found no support from some scientists such as German paleontologist H. D. Kahlke and Chinese paleontologist Hu Changkang, who upheld the earlier view of Black and his colleagues. They attributed the fauna to the broadly defined interglacial period of the Holoarctic realm (Mindel-Riss interglacial stage), ranking in time with the end of Europe's Mindel glacial stage or early Mindel-Riss interglacial stage.

The subsequent discoveries of human remains in the reddish clay at the Chenjiawo and Gongwangling sites in Lantian County, Shaanxi Province, in 1963 and 1964, have furnished new evidence for relative dating of Peking Man fossils. Paleontologist Wu Rukang observed that the Chenjiawo mandible is "generally in close proximity", morphologically, with the Peking Man type, but the Gongwangling

skull clearly shows features that are obviously more primitive than that of either
Peking Man or Java Man from the Trinil
deposits. Rather, it shows affinity with
Homo erectus robustus recovered earlier at
the Djetis bed in Java.

The paleontologist Zhou Mingzhen, basing his conclusion on a study of the mammalian fossils at the Gongwangling site,
has stated that the dating of that site
should be Lower Middle Pleistocene,
equivalent to the Djetis bed in Java, Europe's Gunz-Mindel, or Cromerian interglacial stage, while the Zhoukoudian remains
are of Upper Middle Pleistocene, ranking
with the Trinil bed in Java, and the Mindel-
Riss interglacial stage in Europe, or the
moderate period (interstadial) that separated the two periods of glacier advance in
the Mindel glacial stage. Jia Lanpo shared
this view at the time.

In 1966, a stump of red deer (*Cervus*

New excavation at the Peking Man site is underway at the east slope of the site. (*Photo by Yuan Zhenxin, winter 1979*)

elaphus) antler and remains of the 'ultimate hyena' (*Crocuta crocuta ultima*) occurred in the deposits in the top level at the Peking Man site. They represent species which were common in the late Pleistocene deposits in North China. Their occurrence confirms the latter half of Middle Pleistocene dating of Peking Man and seem to indicate the time of the deposits that yielded the fossil remains.

All the above was of course only relative dating based on rock record. Prior to the 1960s, absolute dating had not been extensively practised in China, hence the wide margin of error. We have stated that Peking Man's time was roughly 400 000 to 500 000 years ago, but when challenged, we are at a loss to clarify the issue. For example, human skull remains found in Kenya in 1975 were dated back to 1 500 000 years by radiometric dating. As that specimen is morphologically close to Peking Man skulls, the latter's dating on record has of course been questioned. Some Chinese embassies have received enquiries on whether the dating of Peking Man is perhaps too conservative. On May 21, 1975, an early man survey group from the United States visited China and raised the same question. The head of the team, F. Clark Howell, had even made a bet that the dating of Peking Man would prove to be at least 700 000 years, or much earlier, as the potassium-argon method has redated the Java Man to be 710 000 years old, and faunal evidence has shown that Peking Man is equivalent in time to, or a little later than, Java Man.

Relative dating by the traditional method of fossil-based stratigraphic geology is no longer valid in terms of precise answers to the dating of Peking Man and related problems. Since 1976, the Chinese Academy of Sciences and the Chinese Institute of Geology have been engaged in determining the precise age of the Peking Man site by radiometric dating, using the following methods: paleomagnetic tests, fission track, thermoluminescence, uranium-series disequilibrium, and amino acid testing.

The figures vary with the methods applied. However, there has been an area of agreement—the interval over which Peking Man lived at Zhoukoudian was half a million years, or from approximately 700 000 years to 200 000 years ago. This conclusion roughly tallies with the result obtained through fossil-based stratigraphy which indicates the dating to be the latter half of Middle Pleistocene.

The environmental problem of Peking Man has always been a focus of attention for the scientists. One of the authorities who stressed the point was the late geologist Li Siguang, Deputy Director of the Chinese Academy of Sciences. He pointed out that an understanding of the climatic conditions under which early humans lived and developed, the changes they had confronted, and the distribution of the population is a matter of great significance for research in paleoanthropology, for such an understanding of our past may guide our work in the future.

Much work has been done since the founding of the new China with regard to the Quaternary strata of the Zhoukoudian area, including landforms produced by glaciation. A considerable portion of the comprehensive research programme, which started in 1978 is centred on the subject of Peking Man's environs. As we gain depth in research, answers may be found to questions that are still unsettled, resolution of issues that are still debated.

The 'coming and going' of Peking Man may prove even more interesting. This genus of human being came from nowhere, left a record at the Zhoukoudian colony for us to trace, and then, after a half million years, disappeared mysteriously. What had happened?

In the compendium *Fossil Man in China* published in 1933, the question was left open. But thanks to the work done over the last thirty years across China, significant finds relevant to the problem have turned up one after another; scientists are now able to trace the cave dwellers after their disappearance from Zhoukoudian.

The most important evidence so far has been the human fossils of 100 000 years' antiquity dug up in 1974 at Xujiayao, Yanggao County, Shanxi Province. Though fragmentary, the specimens show clear affinity with Peking Man in many respects, especially in dentition, which bears a striking resemblance to that of the Zhoukoudian forerunner. In addition, the stone artifacts found in association belong to the same tradition in style as those at the Peking Man site. These facts led to the conclusion that they were related in some way.

Yet some features of the Xujiayao Man fossils are more advanced than those of the Zhoukoudian specimens. For example, the occipital torus is much weaker and more pronounced, and the muzzle of the maxilla does not protrude as much. Then, the more recent dating of the fossils and the more advanced culture all add up to make it a certainty that the specimens represent a branch of Peking Man's descendants.

Xujiayao Village lies 200 kilometres in aerial distance to the west of Beijing, and there are high mountain ranges between the two places. How was it possible for the primitive Xujiayao Man to have made this migratory journey? A glance at a map may reveal the answer.

Xujiayao is nestled in a vast region marked by several intermontane basins referred to as a whole as the Datong Basin or the Datong Lake Bed and covering the northern parts of the two provinces of Shanxi and Hebei. The region is so tilted that it gives the Sanggan River its general direction across the area from southwest to northeast to converge with the Yanghe in the Huailai Basin north of Beijing. From that point, the river is called Yongding and flows into the Hebei Plain where Beijing and Zhoukoudian are situated. The valleys of the two rivers actually formed a corridor which in Pleistocene times could have provided a passageway for both man and lower animals in their migration. It is quite possible that descendants of Peking Man followed this route in journeying northward to Xujiayao. Apart from the human fossils, which are direct proof, there has also been faunal evidence to bear out this hypothesis. Andersson found fossil remains of thick-jawed deer in the red clay deposits of Huailai Basin in 1918. Fossils of this genus have occurred at Zhoukoudian by the thousands, and no doubt the animal was the chief target hunted by Peking Man. In the Sanggan River drainage area, fossils of other animals have been recovered, and many among them are the same as those found in the Zhoukoudian area. Of course we are not saying that Xujiayao Man represents the only descendant of Peking Man, or that Xujiayao is the only area to which these descendants had gone. But we expect that the problem of Peking Man's 'coming and going' will come into clearer perspective as we go along.

35

Zhoukoudian and Beyond

It was hardly possible to carry out paleoanthropological research on a nation-wide scale prior to the Liberation of China in 1949. Research was restricted to Zhoukoudian for both financial and personnel reasons. In the approximately thirty years since the first discovery of paleoliths at the Qingyang site in Gansu Province, only a few other sites had come to light. These were the Shuidonggou site in the Ningxia Hui Autonomous Region; the Sjara-osso-gol site in Inner Mongolia; Locality 1 (Peking Man site), Localities 13 and 15, and the Upper Cave site at Zhoukoudian; and some lesser ones in Shanxi Province. From materials which these sites had yielded, the paleolithic age in China seemed to have been divided into the three stages—Peking Man, Sjara-osso-gol Man, and Upper Cave Man—until the discovery of Dingcun Man and his culture in 1954 shook the old conceptions and traditional beliefs.

In the ensuing years, after Liberation, investigation in this realm has been so extensively carried out that fossils and artifacts identified as of paleolithic dating have been found in 24 provinces, municipalities and autonomous regions. Major sites alone have come to 100, and the grand total is upward of 265 if minor ones are counted.

In some provinces, however, there are only traces seen at sites yet to be explored, while Fujian Province and the Xinjiang Uygur Autonomous Region have remained a blank page. Of special interest is Shanxi Province. In 1954, with the co-operation of scientists from local institutions, the Academy of Sciences discovered and excavated in succession the Dingcun, Kehe, Xihoudu and Shiyu sites, while a survey was conducted at the Emaokou neolithic site. And in recent years, the Xujiayao site has been a focus of attention. The result is that a creditable chronology can be constructed of the paleoculture in North China, in which finds from Shanxi Province alone and those specimens of stone artifacts typical of each stage may also serve as evidence for correlating liths found elsewhere.

Other significant discoveries during recent decades were the five Rama ape (*Ramapithecus*) teeth unearthed in coal seams at Xiaolongtan, Kaiyuan County, Yunnan Province in 1957; an almost complete mandible of Lufeng ape (*Ramapithecus lufengensis*) in an Upper Miocene coal seam in Lufeng County, Yunnan Province, in 1976; and three skullcaps found in succession at the same site in 1980. These are valuable evidence for the study of the origin of man.

In an article entitled, 'Some Problems of Human Origin',[1] the author Jia Lanpo stated:

> The westernmost site which has yielded *Ramapithecus* remains, if *Kenyapithecus* is

---

[1] *Vertebrata Panasiatica*, Vol. 12, No. 3, 1974.

included, is Fort Ternan (0.12S, 35.21E), Kenya; the Hari Talyangar (31N, 77E) site in India is in the centre, and the easternmost site is at Xiaolongtan, Kaiyuan County, Yunnan Province, China. Connecting these three points, we get a triangle of unequal sides, with its central area in southern Asia.

The sites yielding Lower Pleistocene human remains and cultural relics are located around this triangle. These were Sterkfontein (26.03S, 27.42E) and Taung (27.32S, 24.45E) in South Africa on the southwesternmost side; Menton (43.49N, 7.29E), France, on the northwesternmost side; Nihewan (114.41E, 40.15N), Yangyuan County, Hebei Province, China, on the northeasternmost side; and Sangiran (7S, 112E), Java, Indonesia, on the southeasternmost side. Connecting these points, we get a quadrilateral of unequal sides, and the central area of the triangle is positioned approximately in the middle of the quadrilateral, which roughly corresponds with the area to which early man had radiated out.

Lower Pleistocene cultural sites have been found across China. The earliest one to date is the Xihoudu site in Shanxi Province, which yielded stone artifacts, antlers with marks of being hacked and scraped, bones that appeared charred, and quantities of mammalian fossils that date back 1 800 000 years (by the paleomagnetic method). Three human teeth of about the same antiquity, mammalian fossils in association, and three stone artifacts occurred at a site in Yuanmou County, Yunnan Province.

In their book *Xihoudu* (1978), Jia Lanpo and Wang Jian state:

Lower Pleistocene stone cultures of more than one million years' antiquity are very widely distributed in the world and seem to have been centred in South Asia, from where they radiated outward, reaching Africa in the southwest, southern Europe in the northwest, China (Xihoudu, Shanxi Province) in the northeast, and Java in the southeast. We believe that there is only one ancestral tree of man, and if the hypothesis that South Asia was the home of man can hold, it must have been ages before his culture could be brought to the various sites. The paleolithic industries at Xihoudu and Olduvai, moreover, exhibit a higher level in technique indicating two different traditions, which would also require a great length of time to develop. Thus the paleoliths that have come to light at these two sites are not specimens of man's earliest tools. For all their primitiveness and crudeness, man could not have acquired the skill to produce them at that stage of his development. We have yet to get to sites of even greater antiquity in the search for man's 'first stone knife'.

Quite a few sites in North China have yielded human remains and paleoliths of Middle Pleistocene dating. Apart from Zhoukoudian, there have been Gongwangling and Chenjiawo, both in Lantian County, Shaanxi Province; Zhangjiagou, Tongguan County, also Shaanxi Province; Kehe, Ruicheng County, Shanxi Province; Sanmen Gorge City, Henan Province; and Jinniushan, Yingkou County, Liaoning Province. In addition, Xujiayao Man and his culture in Shanxi Province, and Dali Man and his culture unearthed in Shaanxi Province, may be dated back to the last phase of the Middle Pleistocene period.

Before the 1950s, no paleolithic site had been known in the vast region south of the Changjiang (Yangtze River) except one that had come to light in the Guangxi Zhuang Autonomous Region, dating back to the mesolithic period. In addition to the Yuanmou Man site discovered in 1965, there have been two more recent findings —the Guanyindong site in Guizhou Province, equivalent in time to Locality 13 of Zhoukoudian, and Shilongtou Cave in Hubei Province, probably a little later than Locality 1, or the Peking Man site.

Equally numerous are human remains

(1 X 100,000 y. B.P.)

Layers of the Fossiliferous Deposits in the Cave	Thickness (m.)	The Methods Used				
		Fission Track	Thermolumine- scence	Uranium Series	Amino Acid	Palaeomagnetic
1–3	7			$23^{+3.0}_{-2.3}$	37	
4	6		29 31			
5	1					
6	5					Brunhes
7	2					37~40 Epoch
8–9	6			$42^{+>18}_{-10}$	39	
10	2	46.2± 4.5	52 61			
11	2				46	
12	2					
13	2					70
Unnumbered Layers	?					Matsuyama Epoch

Dating of the Peking Man site

and artifacts of middle and late paleolithic dating.

Human remains in South China dating back to the middle paleolithic period are Maba Man, Guangdong Province, and Changyang Man, Hubei Province. Of late paleolithic dating are Liujiang Man and Qilingshan Man, both of Guangxi; and Zi-yang Man, Sichuan Province.

Lithic sites in North China include: of earlier discovery, the Sjara-osso-gol in Inner Mongolia and Shuidonggou in Ningxia; of more recent finding, the Dayao lithic worksite in Inner Mongolia; Dingcun, Shi-yu and Xiachuan sites in Shanxi Province; and the Hutouliang site in Hebei Province. The relationship of these cultures has been discussed in a paper by Jia Lanpo, Gai Pei and You Yuzhu.[1]

The authors observed:

It has been 50 years since the discovery of the Sjara-osso-gol site in 1922. The materials that have been unearthed over this period testify that the paleolithic cultures in North China have at least two traditions. First, the Kehe-Dingcun tradition characterized by big chopping tools made on large blades with heavy triangle points that are typical of the culture. Small tools occasionally occurred, but were limited in number and diversity. The Kehe site, the Sanmen Gorge area (Henan Province), and Emao-kou (Datong, Shanxi Province) belong to this tradition. The second is Locality 1 of the Zhoukoudian-Shiyu series, or the keeled scraper-burin tradition characterized by microliths fashioned on irregular blades. At each site, a large proportion of microliths is found among the assemblage, and the tools show a great diversity of fine workmanship. The following sites belong to this tradition: Locality 1 and Locality 15 of Zhoukoudian; Hougeda Height, Shuo-xian County, Shanxi Province; Sjara-osso-gol, Inner Mongolia; Shiyu, Shanxi Province; Xiaonanhai, Henan Province. This was a

very rich culture developed in the period from Lower to Upper Pleistocene and is widely distributed in North China, predating the microlithic culture of the neolithic period of the region. The significance of the Shiyu site lies precisely in its being the link between the Peking Man culture and the microlith industry . . .

We had considered giving a new term to the small tools of Middle and Upper Pleistocene, but the designation of microlith had already been established. In order to avoid confusion in this paper, we refer to the small tools of the Loc. 1-Shiyu tradition as microliths in the broad sense, and to the microliths of the neolithic period as 'developed microliths' which are commonly accepted as microliths.

Microlith sites had mostly been found north of the Great Wall, giving rise to various speculations: that the culture had its source in Europe and had come to China via Siberia; or that the earliest site is on the upper reaches of the Yenisei in the Soviet Union; or that it had originated in Mongolia. The Shiyu specimens have provided evidence for a systematic understanding of microlith development, leading to the hypothesis that North China was the source area of microlithic culture —a hypothesis that has been buttressed by the discovery of the Xiachuan cultural site in Shanxi Province.

Microliths occurring in China are characterized chiefly by tools made on long and narrow blades or flakes struck from specially prepared cores that in shape can be classified as prismatic, conical, wedge-like, fanlike, or keeled. Indeed, these cores have become a key to correlating the microlithic cultures in China, Mongolia, Siberia, North America and Japan.

Microliths in China appear to be of two traditions. The first tradition is found at Locality 1 (Peking Man site) and Locality 15 of Zhoukoudian, Xujiayao, Sjara-osso-gol, Shiyu and the Xiaonanhai sites, in

[1]*Acta Archaeologia Sinica*, No. 1, 1972.

order of succession. The other is found in the Xiachuan and Hutouliang cultures, in sequence. The neolithic cultures in China, Siberia, North America and Japan are all closely related, and the Xiachuan-Hutouliang tradition might have been a successor to the Peking Man culture.

It has been more than sixty years since studies on paleoliths in China began. Scientists have made tremendous strides in this field, especially since 1949. Still, there are a number of questions yet to be tackled:

1. Where is the earliest home of human beings, and from which genus did they evolve? Hypotheses and deductions are many, but more evidence is needed before any of these can be validated.

2. Is the *Ramapithecus*, a late Miocene-Pliocene genus, the lineal ancestor of the primates ancestral to humans? If *Australopithecus*, a Pleistocene form, is to be recognized as the species that evolved into *Homo*, which genus or genera are to be considered the 'missing link', in the long interval between *Ramapithecus* and *Australopithecus*?

3. In China, there are still some areas in which no paleolithic industry has been found. Fujian Province and the Xinjiang Uygur Autonomous Region belong to this category. Does this mean that nothing exists there? Both Taiwan, which is adjacent to Fujian, and Afghanistan, which shares borders with Xinjiang, have reported findings of the paleolithic period. The Zuozhen Man skullcap of 30 000 years' antiquity and artifacts representing the Zhangbin culture have been unearthed in Taiwan, while microliths of the North China tradi-

tion have come to light in Afghanistan. All indicate that Fujian and Xinjiang are by no means barren lands for paleontologists.

Available materials show some similarities and obvious differences between the paleoliths of North and South China. It is doubtful whether they are of the same tradition. Even within the North China assemblages, the present division into two traditions is being questioned—should further subdivisions be made under the main series according to the location of the sites?

It is possible to hold that the microliths unearthed in Japan, Siberia and North America are of Chinese origin. Quite a few specimens have been found in Ningxia, Inner Mongolia and the vast northeastern region of China, yet most of them have been picked up on the ground, and hence are undatable and of little use for correlation. It is essential that more work be done in the above areas and in coastal provinces such as Jiangsu and Shandong.

There are similarities as well as diversities between the microliths found in Europe and in China. It is no easy task to trace their origins and the history of these two broadly defined traditions.

No single institution, which is bound to be limited in resources, can undertake the kind of large-scale, multi-purpose investigation that is needed if these and similar questions are to be resolved. The authors firmly believe that only by international co-operation will we ever know, with certainty, how humankind evolved, or trace its incredible journey through prehistoric time and place.

Appendices

1. From the Evolutionary Origin of Humans to Significant Discoveries in China in Recent Years

Early Discoveries in Europe

Everything has a history. Every country has a history. Human beings have a history. But because there are no written records of the earliest history of human beings, we have to look for evidence from under the ground. We will never know the history of biology until the surface of the earth has been opened, for the 'file' of creatures, including humans themselves, is hidden beneath the surface of the earth. It is written in a special language on stones and in the fossils of primitive creatures. Fossils are 'epitaphs' left behind by living things after their death. Without such evolutionary evidence, we can neither trace human history nor construct the family trees of other creatures.

In the past, our outlook was limited; the history of humankind was considered to be only several thousand years old. After the discoveries of shell mounds and remains in peat beds in Denmark and Swiss lake-dwellings, scientists began to realize that there were cultures older than they had previously thought—but surely not earlier than the neolithic age, which is 10 000 years old.

By the end of the eighteenth century flint tools used by primitive people had been discovered in Europe, but scientists were puzzled by them. Although a collection of flint implements was discovered in a stratum 3.5 metres deep at Hoxne, Suffolk, in Great Britain and were purported to belong to "a remote age and people who lived before metal was produced," yet it was not until 1859, half a century later, when J. Evans saw the finds at Abbeville in the north of France, that these artifacts of greater antiquity were acknowledged. They proved that the history of humankind was even longer than previously suspected.

During the 1830s research on ancient civilization developed further. Many papers were published on the discovery of flint tools with signs of having been worked on and about the remains of extinct animals.

The most exciting discovery was the one in Neanderthal Cave, near Düsseldorf, Germany, in 1856, where portions of a human skeleton—fourteen pieces in all, with cranium, were unearthed. After an anatomical examination, Professor D. Schaaffhausen of Bonn concluded that they bore anthropoid characteristics and that they may be regarded as 'the most ancient memorial of the early inhabitants of Europe.' Not everybody agreed with this conclusion. In 1864 Professor W. King acknowledged that the Neanderthal fossils were remains of an extinct human group and named it *Homo neanderthalensis* in spite of opposing opinions.

Because of jealousy, or for some other reason, every important discovery provoked controversy. In 1891 Dutch biologist Eugene Dubois found a well-preserved skullcap in a village on the bank of the Solo River in Java. It represented, in both size and shape, a species between man and ape. A femur was found a year later, its features indicating that the creature had an erect posture and was capable of walking bipedally. In 1894 Eugene Dubois named this strange creature that had never been seen before *Pithecanthropus erectus*, or *Homo erectus*, commonly known as Java Man. When he returned to Europe, he became the centre of a bitter controversy, and was soon led to retract his opinion, saying that what he had found were in fact the remains of a great ape. When the mandible of *Homo heidelbergensis* was found in 1907 in a sandpit in Mauer, 10 kilometres southeast of Heidelberg in West Germany, it did not attract public attention. But on December 2, 1929, Professor Pei Wen-zhong found the first skullcap of Peking Man, followed eventually by the discovery of large numbers of stone and bone artifacts, and traces of the use of fire. Only then was the case of Java Man, who was a contemporary of Peking Man, settled.

Regarding the birth of humankind, most people in old China, like those in other countries, believed in a divine origin. But there was opposition all the time. In the Spring and Autumn Period (770–476 B.C.) a Chinese politician, Guanzi, pointed out that "water is essential to everything and the foundation of life. The essence of water coagulated to become the human figure. The human body and heart developed from water." A little later Greek philosopher Anaximander (611?–574? B.C.) pointed out more rationally that human beings developed from fish. He said that originally scaled animals crawled out of the water and became land animals, which in turn changed into people. What an amazing statement! The conclusion was almost the same as that which modern vertebrate paleontology has arrived at. Science has proved that if anthropoids are regarded as our 'cousins', then fish are surely related to our ancestral stock in some respects.

In the past, Europe was believed to be the birthplace of humankind not only because at one time what was believed to be the earliest culture had been found there, but also because the chronology of the paleolithic age was first established in Europe. Scientists from many European countries searched everywhere for remains and sites of ancient people, but evidence earlier than the million-year-old stone tools unearthed in Romania and France has never been found. Few people now believe that Europe is the birthplace of humankind.

Southern Asia as the Cradle of Humankind

It seems safe to assume that human beings could not have originated in Antarctica, Oceania, or America. A large segment of Antarctica is covered by ice, with yearly mean temperatures between -55°C and -57°C. Although people constantly go there for exploration, it has no permanent residents or genuine land animals. The only plants growing there are bryophytes, algae and seed plants.

Oceania became separated from Asia about 150 million years ago. Local animals include primitive species such as platypus, kangaroo, banded hare and echidna, which do not exist on other continents. In recent years scientists have found remains belonging to an age earlier than we had thought, but no older than 40 000 years.

America is a new land. It was dominated by Indians before Europeans set foot on it.

But the history of Indians in America is not long. Evidence found in North America is no older than 50 000 years. Originally, adventurous Asians went from Siberia to Alaska to hunt for large animals such as mammoths, and they settled down to become the first residents in America. These people must have arrived in Latin America still later. Some scientists have suggested that civilization was brought to North America 100 000 or even 200 000 years ago, but this point of view does not hold water—people would not have been able to survive the cold weather if they did not know how to make fire and sew skin clothes.

What about Africa? Because chimpanzees and gorillas, which are closely related to humans, still live on the African continent, Charles Darwin was of the view that Africa was the birthplace of humankind. French paleontologist Teilhard de Chardin, who worked in China for many years, shared Darwin's opinion. Pertinent evidence has been found in Africa in recent years. More fossil evidence of apes dating back more than 10 million years B.P. has been found in Africa than in any other place. According to the rearranged name list of fossils of *Australopithecus africanus* (literally southern ape of Africa), which was able to create stone tools,[1] about 98 per cent of such *Australopithecus* fossils were found in Africa. Stone tools nearly 4 million years old were also found here. Fossil evidence of human beings living at almost the same time as Peking Man has been discovered in Tanzania, Algeria and Morocco.

After Java Man was found, many people considered Asia as the birthplace of humankind. In the 1920s H. F. Osborn, an American paleontologist, put forward his influential theory that only Asia had the right to be called the cradle of humankind. He hypothesized that life on the Asian highland was more difficult than that on the lowland, and that reaction to such stimulation had helped to shape the human being. Mongolia has been a highland since ancient times. Its weather was always bleak and its living conditions hard. Food could not be obtained without great effort. Thus, according to Osborn, Mongolia provided perfect conditions for the formation of the human race.

We agree that Asia is the birthplace of humankind, except that not the Mongolian Plateau but the south of Asia is the more likely spot. The reason is that among all the fossil evidence of apes, the most significant is *Ramapithecus*, which lived between 15 million and 8 million years ago and which many scholars throughout the world classify as a hominid. The first fossil evidence of *Ramapithecus* was found in northern India and Pakistan and similar evidence has been found in Hungary, Turkey and Kenya. But the greatest number of *Ramapithecus* fossils have been found in China. Apart from the five teeth found at Xiaolongtan, Kaiyuan County, Yunnan Province, many other fossils were unearthed from a late Miocene coal seam in Lufeng County of the province from 1975 to 1983. They include 3 skulls, 5 mandibles, 4 fragmentary skulls, 19 fragmentary upper and lower jaws, 22 rows of teeth, and 329 separate teeth. From the same layer, remains of *Ramapithecus* were excavated, including 2 skulls, 5 mandibles, 2 fragmentary skulls, 22 fragmentary upper and lower jawbones, 7 rows of teeth, and 321 separate teeth. These *Ramapithecus* remains were distributed in a radial pattern with northern India and China's Yunnan and Tibet at the centre. Human fossils and culture remains of the early Pleistocene Epoch (more than 1 million years ago)

---

[1] Since it was able to create stone tools, it should be called *Homo*. But scholars are inclined to call it 'southern ape'.

were especially distributed in such a way.

Today Tibet is high and cold. It is characterized by high mountains and deep valleys and is covered by snow in winter. This was not the case during the period of transition from ape to human. In investigating Jilong Basin (4000-4300 metres above sea level and situated between the central Himalayas and the northern slope of Mt Xixiabangma), geologists and paleontologists from the Institute of Vertebrate Paleontology and Paleoanthropology of the Chinese Academy of Sciences found fossils of the three-toed horse (*Hipparion*) and the chilotherium 8 million years old, suggesting that the climate there was once warm. After studying the geology of the place, they concluded that 8 million years ago the Himalayas had an average height of about 1000 metres, the southern and northern slopes alike being moistened by the warm and humid monsoon from the Indian Ocean. This leads us to believe that the Qinghai-Tibet Plateau, barren as it is now, might well have been the birthplace of the human being.

Human Fossils of the Early Pleistocene in China

Besides the Late Miocene fossils of *Ramapithecus*, which is considered the direct ape ancestor of human beings, human fossils and culture remains of the Early Pleistocene (more than a million years ago) have been found in China. One of the most important sites is Xihoudu, which is 1 800 000 years old according to the paleomagnetic method.

This ancient culture was found in a sand-gravel bed 60 metres beneath the surface of the earth in Xihoudu Village, Ruicheng County, Shanxi Province. The remains were centralized, with a vertical range of about one metre. They included stone tools, antlers with cut marks, and burnt bones. Thirty-two pieces of more obviously human-made stone artifacts were selected as a target of study. Except for one stone tool of igneous rock and three of vein quartz, the other tools were made of quartzite in various colours. They included cores, flakes, choppers and chopping tools, scrapers, and a heavy triangular point.

Besides stone tools, antlers with marks of having been hacked were found along with a deer skull with two antler stumps. A deep furrow on the left stump and a scar on the furrow appeared to have been cut with a sharp implement. Although no bone implements that were obviously improved by humans were found at the site, the antlers bearing signs of having been cut were evidence that people of the Xihoudu culture used bone and antler implements. Mammal ribs in shades of black, grey and grey-green, as well as horse teeth were also found in Xihoudu. The grey-green horse teeth had cracks similar to those on charred bones and teeth found at the Peking Man site. Laboratory testing proved they had been burnt by fire.

Just when human beings began using fire is a question of great interest, because the ability to use and control fire is one of the characteristics that distinguishes human beings from animals. Years of work have produced a breakthrough on this question. That Peking humans had made progress in the use of fire is an indisputable fact, though there is no evidence that they were able to make fire. Perhaps they had merely learned to keep a naturally caused fire going. Heaps of ashes at the Peking Man site showed that they could control fire well and prevent it from spreading.

Another important discovery was the remains of Yuanmou Man. Two fossil teeth were found by geologists from the Chinese Institute of Geology in the stratum of Early Pleistocene in Shangnabeng Village, Yuanmou County, Yunnan Province. After a careful study paleontologists from the geological museum of the Ministry of Geology and Minerals of China identified the teeth as belonging to *Homo erectus* and named the species *Homo erectus yuanmauensis*. After several explorations and excavations at the site, scientists discovered more than ten pieces of stone flakes and other stone tools, many charcoal crumbs, Mollusca, and fossils of mammals, including *Hyena licenti, Megantereon nihowanensis, Stegodon zhaotungensis, Equus yunnanensis, Rhinoceros sinensis*, and *Axis shansius*. The features of these mammals showed that they had lived in the Early Pleistocene and a paleomagnetic test has revealed the dating to be 1 700 000 ± 100 000 years or between 1 630 000 and 1 640 000 years.

Not many stone tools were recovered at the Yuanmou Man site. Three scrapers were found in the brown clay bed where the teeth of Yuanmou Man were discovered. They were made of light yellow quartzite and all showed signs of having been improved by humans.

In the summer of 1981 a large cultural site of the Early Pleistocene was found in Donggutuo Village, Yangyuan County, Hebei Province. It was located four kilometres southwest of Nihewan which was long regarded as the centre typical of Early Pleistocene finds in North China. The quantity of stone artifacts found here was unequalled except by those from the Peking Man site and the Xujiayao site in Yanggao County, Shanxi Province.

The cultural remains were hidden in deposits of the Nihowan period 45 metres beneath the earth's surface. Thousands of stone artifacts, most of them small, had been carefully made, and the distinction between different types was clear. They seemed to resemble the Peking Man remains but were much earlier—1 million years old according to ancient terrestrial magnetic dating. From the features of the Donggutuo culture it is evident that the culture of Peking Man was descended from that of Donggutuo, while the culture of Xujiayao (about 100 000 years old) was descended from that of Peking Man.

The discovery of these culture sites of the Early Pleistocene has extended the history of man in China further into the past. No earlier evidence of the use of fire has been found anywhere in the world. Stone tool culture (more than 1 million years old) seems to have been centred in South Asia, from where it radiated outward, reaching Africa in the southwest, southern Europe in the northwest, Xihoudu in China in the northeast, and Java Island in the southeast. If South Asia was indeed the birthplace of humankind, it must have been ages before these stone tools were distributed in so vast an area. The stone tools of Xihoudu and those of Olduvai (Africa) exhibit a higher level in technique and different traditions, which also suggests a long lapse of time. It seems that the stone tools found so far are not specimens of man's earliest tools. We have yet to get to sites of even greater antiquity to search for man's 'first stone knife'.

How long is the history of humankind? In the past, authorities estimated 3 million years, but today we believe it is longer than that—probably 4 million years. Some scholars have suggested that we must search in the stratum of the Pliocene which precedes Early Pleistocene to find the earliest traces of humanity and the first stone tools. Their argument is quite reasonable.

2. My Views on the Human Fossils Unearthed at Jinniu Hill

(*Jia Lanpo*)

In recent years, more fossils of the human species have been discovered in China. The fossils found at Jinniu Hill have aroused much attention. Newspapers both at home and abroad have reported the find; the *Beijing Wanbao* (*Beijing Evening Newspaper*) reported it in instalments under the title, 'Excavation of Fossils of the Human Species at Jinniu Hill'. And I myself have often been asked for my views on the fossils.

This significant find was made on October 2, 1984, by postgraduate students of the Archaeology Department of Beijing University, when they were practising excavation under the instruction of Associate Professor Lü Zune and teacher Huang Yunping.

I first saw these fossils after their arrival in Beijing. Most of them were still covered with clay, and only some teeth and hand and foot bones were exposed. Judging from the pattern of the teeth and the clay adhering to them, they do not belong to recent humans. Moreover, fossils of extinct animals were also found in association, and the absolute dating of the layer, as measured by Beijing University, is more than 200 000 years old. So I believed that these fossils were an important discovery and was excited.

Numerous fossils can be found there, especially those of rodents. When I and Huang Weiwen visited Jinniu Hill on October 7, 1981, I brought back a piece of reddish clay, the size of an apple, which I gave to paleontologist Li Chuankui. This clay was mixed with numerous mouse bones, the density of the bone distribution in the clay being comparable with that in some parts of the fourth layer (ashes) at the Peking Man site.

Zhao Zhongyi undertook to repair the skull unearthed at Jinniu Hill, a job involving the fitting together, with enormous skill, of 200 broken pieces of bone into the original shape of the skull. On the morning of February 5, 1985, Lü Zune, Huang Yunping, and Zhao Zhongyi invited me to view the nearly completed skull. This time I got the following impressions:

1. The maxilla is nearly orthognathous, the line which links the base of the anterior nasal spine and the prosthion is almost a vertical line. It shows the lips not so projecting as those of Peking Man, but quite similar to those of Neanderthal Man.

2. The palatal surface is rugged, which is similar to recent humans.

3. The incisive foramen lies close to the alveolar margin as in recent humans.

4. The nasal spine is developed like that of recent humans.

5. The torus occipitalis is oval, while that of Peking Man grows as a wide ridge extending to the external auditory meatus.

6. The cranial bones are thin, as in recent humans.

Judging from the above features, I believe the skull discovered at Jinniu Hill is quite different from that of Peking Man, but closer to that of Dali Man. The feature of the nasal bone alone would seem to bear this out.

As for the dating of the skull, I believe it to be 200 000 years old (late Middle Pliestocene), because it occurs not only with fossils of the sabre-toothed tiger, but also, it is said, with thick-jawed deer. Therefore, it is impossible that the era is later than Middle Pleistocene. I have said that it is a significant discovery because the skull is quite complete. Moreover, this is the first time in China that so many other bones have been unearthed, such as hipbone, rib bones, ulna, and hand and foot bones, all of which are very important materials for studying the body structure of humankind at that time. This discovery has also raised a question about whether the creature whose fossils were unearthed at Jinniu Hill might have existed in the same era as Peking Man of a later period, for the latest

Peking Man might also have been alive 200 000 years ago.

3. Davidson Black— the Man Who Forgot his Nationality

In the spring of 1934, when the excavation at Zhoukoudian was progressing smoothly and the materials of Peking Man were gradually being brought to light, Davidson Black, Honorary Director of the Cenozoic Research Laboratory, died of a heart attack. His death was a great loss to the work of Zhoukoudian.

Davidson Black was born in Toronto on July 25, 1884. His father was a Queen's Counsel, and his mother was a descendant of the royal family. Young Black studied very hard and kept forging ahead. As a boy he often travelled to the Kawartha Lakes in southern Canada, where he became an expert dugout canoeist. While still in middle school Black spent his summers carrying supplies for the Hudson Bay Company, covering thousands of miles by canoe, to northern Ontario. Navigating his loaded canoe through rapids, he faced the risk of capsizing. He made friends with Indians and learned their language during his trip. The Indians liked this clever young white man and gave him the friendly nickname 'Mushkemust Kemit' (the little white muskrat) on account of his quick, agile movements. Once, he was caught in a forest fire from which he only escaped alive by standing up to his shoulders in a lake for a day and two nights.

One summer, Black worked at the Canadian Geological Survey Bureau. Through fieldwork, he gained a practical knowledge of structural geology and stratigraphy, creating a solid foundation for his later work in organizing the excavation at Zhoukoudian and for his excellent research on the Cenozoic Era.

Black graduated from the University of Toronto in 1906. He got his B.A. in medical science, but he was more interested in biology and went back to school to study comparative anatomy. He began his teaching and research career in 1909 as an instructor in anatomy at the Medical Institute of Western Reserve.

In 1914, he was granted a half-year sabbatical leave and went to G. Elliot Smith Research Laboratory in Manchester, England, where he studied under the guidance of Professor Elliot Smith. At the same time he worked at the Dutch Central Institute for Brain Research under Professor Ariens Kappers. Smith was the top nerve specialist in England and was at that moment engaged on the reconstruction of the Piltdown skull. Academic circles at that time were sharply debating the subject of evolution, and Black's attention was strongly drawn. This new interest in exploring the theory of evolution changed the course of his career and was later to make him one of the most famous anthropologists in the world.

In 1915, Black went to the Museum of Natural History in New York and paid a visit to Professors H. F. Osborn and W. D. Matthew, who allowed him to study some of the valuable models of mammalian cranial cavities stored in that museum. This trip also had a deep influence on his later career. His view that Central Asia had been the birthplace of human beings was obviously influenced by the two senior paleontologists.

Black's change of direction was described by his colleague Paul H. Stevenson, who worked at the Peking Union Medical College, as follows:

> Here was the call from the unknown for which his restless spirit had been waiting. A call that came at once as a challenge and an opportunity; one of those rare opportuni-

ties that come only to those prepared . . . All of his previous interests and experiences immediately and naturally fell into their self-appointed places in this broad foundation of correlated qualifications that guided his approach to the new problem now uppermost in his mind.

Black was invited to China by Professor Cowdry of the Peking Union Medical College in 1919. A professor of neurology and embryology, Cowdry was appointed Director of the Anatomy Department two years later.

Not long after he came to Beijing, Black and Johan Gunnar Andersson became partners in scientific research. They were in charge of the neolithic fossils discovered by Andersson in Liaoning, Henan, and Gansu provinces.

At the end of 1922, Black wrote a letter to Henry S. Houghton, head of the Peking Union Medical College, detailing a plan for exploring the birthplace of human beings. He wrote: "All available evidence points to the conclusion that the dispersal area for mankind and his forerunners is to be sought somewhere in Central Asia." He systematically described his viewpoint in the article, 'Asia and the Dispersal of Primates' (*Bulletin of the Geological Society of China*, Vol. 4, No. 2, 1925).

Since the summer of 1925, Black and Andersson had been preparing a plan to explore in Central Asia, with Xinjiang as their principal target. In autumn 1926, when the plan was about to be implemented, news came from Sweden that two tooth fossils of Peking Man had been discovered. This changed Black's original plan. He was determined to organize the Zhoukoudian excavation as one of the 'supplementary projects' of the Central Asia exploratory plan, which was to be carried out first. With the enthusiastic support of Ding Wenjiang, Weng Wenhao, and others, Black finally got funds from the Rockefeller Foundation in the United States, and in February 1927 an agreement was reached between the Geological Survey of China and the Peking Union Medical College for the co-operative excavation of Zhoukoudian.

In the spring of 1927, Black and Weng Wenhao speeded up their preparations. They chose people to take part in the fieldwork, made observations at the Zhoukoudian site, drew up plans for the excavation, and made arrangements with the Peking Union Medical College for storage of specimens and for office space. He put his heart and soul into every detail, down to the trunks for the transportation of specimens. Through careful preparation, the excavation work started on April 16.

In the last few years, at the beginning and end of every fieldwork season, Black would come to Zhoukoudian to provide directions himself, so the excavation always went smoothly. He never claimed credit for himself or became arrogant, but always commended others, particularly those scientists who worked at the site.

As a leader of the Anatomy Department of the Peking Union Medical College and the Cenozoic Research Laboratory, Black had a lot of work to do. But still he continued the important study of human fossils at Zhoukoudian and made great contributions to it. At the end of 1927, he established the new genus *Sinanthropus pekinensis* (Peking Man). At that time, many specialists thought that his decision was too hasty, because a few teeth were the only evidence on which it was based. If he had called it *Homo* sp., more people might have accepted the designation. However, Black did not back down from his brave decision. Only when more and more Peking Man fossils were discovered later was his conclusion finally accepted by the academic world.

Black's devotion to science was very

moving. To reduce the possibility of damage to the Zhoukoudian fossils during their repair, he often reconstructed them himself. He did not wear a mask while working; after his death some people said that his lungs had been damaged by the dust he breathed in from the fossils. But Black had congenital heart disease. As a medical doctor, he knew clearly the danger of his condition, but he put all his efforts into the work and gave no thought to himself. To avoid interruptions, Black often worked at night. When others had gone home, he would enter his office, lock the door, and start another 'working day' undisturbed. Many of his important works were written in the dead of night and in this empty building. From one of his own progress charts we can get a general picture of his schedule:

Original draft:
Pages 1-3   Jan. 9-12 (6 a.m.)
Pages 3-6   Jan. 12-13 (finished 3.30 a.m.)
Pages 6-8   Jan. 14 (6 a.m.)
Pages 9-11   Jan. 15 (5.30 a.m.)
First draft: Jan. 16
Second draft: Jan. 22
Final: Jan. 29

Hospitalized from overwork, but always concerned about the work at Zhoukoudian and the Cenozoic Research Laboratory, Black wrote a letter on March 5, 1934 to G. B. Barbour [his last letter]. With much regret, he wrote:

> The last six weeks has been most out of the ordinary. I have had to lay up in the hospital for a rest and did not get to the laboratory all through February.

When his health improved somewhat, he engrossed himself in the work again. But his illness was soon to take his life. According to the recollection of his assistant, Hu Chengzhi:[1]

> Dr Davidson Black passed away on

[1] From a letter to Jia Lanpo, March 4, 1977.

March 15, 1934 at his office desk. He often worked at night and rested in the daytime. You know all about this. The previous day, while I was repairing the radius of Upper Cave Man, I broke the picking pin. So I went to ask Dr Black for another one. Through the door I heard him talking with Yang Zhongjian very animatedly. It was already 5 p.m., so I did not walk in, but went home instead. The next morning after I got to the office, the first thing I heard was that Black had passed away during the night from congenital heart disease.

Black was the author of many brilliant academic works. From 1913 to 1934, a total of 56 articles were published, including, 'On the Discovery, Morphology and Environment of *Sinanthropus pekinensis*', published before his death.

On May 8, 1934 the Committee of Professors of the Peking Union Medical College issued a memorandum in memory of Davidson Black. It said that because of his death, the college had unfortunately lost an outstanding colleague. His brilliant achievements in science had done credit to the College. His research on Peking Man, which had made him world famous, would continue to be a great contribution to the historical research on the early stages of mankind.

Black was a person of excellent character greatly respected by his Chinese colleagues and the people who knew him. Ding Wenjiang expressed a colleague's appreciation in the following words:

> The last point which I should like to touch is a delicate one, but I am going to touch it nevertheless. It is frankly admitted that sometimes we find co-operation between Chinese and foreigners in scientific work rather difficult. The reasons I think are not difficult to seek. Firstly, many foreigners suffer from a superiority complex. Subconsciously they think somewhat like this: here is a Chinese, he knows something about science, but he is a Chinese

nevertheless—he is different from a European, therefore we cannot treat him in the same way. At best his manners become patronizing. On the other hand, their Chinese colleagues suffer from an inferiority complex. They became self-conscious and supersensitive, always imagining that the foreigner is laughing at them or despising them. Ninety per cent of the troubles between Chinese and foreign colleagues working together comes from these two factors. In my dealings with Davidson Black, and I think Black's colleagues will bear me out, I never found him to be suffering from such a complex and his Chinese colleagues also became freed from theirs. In politics, Black was a conservative, but in his dealings with his Chinese colleagues he altogether forgot their nationality or race, because he realized that science was above such artificial and accidental things.

4. Father Pierre Teilhard de Chardin and I

In Commemoration of the Hundredth Anniversary (1881-1981) of the Birthday of the Great Scholar

My first encounter with Father Teilhard de Chardin took place in the spring of 1931. I was a trainee at the Geological Survey of China, assigned to Zhoukoudian to take part in the excavation. It was in May 1931, that Bian Meinian and I, led by Pei Wenzhong, arrived at the site. A few days later, three leading personages of the Cenozoic Research Laboratory, Teilhard de Chardin, Davidson Black and Yang Zhongjian, came in a taxi to Zhoukoudian to give directions for the jobs to be done in the field. My age (23) and my position prevented me from feeling comfortable in their presence. Naturally I did not have much to talk to Teilhard about in the beginning. But this scientist of towering

stature quickly put me at ease with his amicable manner and his patience and tirelessness in educating the young learner.

My year at that time was divided between Zhoukoudian and the Laboratory office in the city, where I would see more of Teilhard. In the winter of 1931, we shared a two-room suite in the Geological Exhibition Hall building. He occupied the back room, where he studied stone artifacts from Zhoukoudian, and I the front, where I sifted fossils and assigned serial numbers to the artifacts. One day I had just glued a few antler fragments together and had put the piece on my desk, when the Father walked in. Seeing the specimen, he was about to pick it up for a closer examination. I wanted to warn him that it could not be moved yet, but in my limited English could only say, "Hands up!" With a hearty laugh, he put up both arms as if to surrender. I was very much embarrassed as he pointed out my mistake and told me the right expression to use in that situation. After this first lesson, the scholar was to teach me much more on scientific matters, while in return I became his assistant, helping with the measurement of specimens that he was studying. As adviser and specially commissioned research fellow of the Cenozoic Research Laboratory, Teilhard had three more offices elsewhere in the city. He spent more of his time in Room 106 of the Lockhart Hall of the Union Medical College, where he studied mammalian fossils from various sites in China and also edited many of our papers. This was a large studio room where Pei Wenzhong, Bian Meinian and I had also worked.

In 1937 when the Japanese aggressors started their all-out war against China, work at Zhoukoudian was suspended. Research was, however, carried on in the city while it was still possible. Teilhard, after conferring with Yang Zhongjian, assigned

French paleontologist Father P. Teilhard de Chardin (1881-1955) in 1929 (*left*) and in 1936 at Zhoukoudian (*below*). (*Photos by Jia Lanpo*)

me to work on the Yin Dynasty horse fossils unearthed at a site in Henan Province. I was instructed to identify the number of horses in the assemblage, their ages, their sex and whether there were any fossils of mules or asses. That was an awesome job for me, but I accepted it in spite of my uneasiness. When eventually I handed in my twenty-page paper, which was written in English, he went over every sentence, making comments in his fine handwriting between almost all the lines —certainly a more painstaking job than if he had written the paper himself. But Teilhard spared no effort in educating the young. Because of the war, the paper was lost before it was published. The regret still lingers with me, for it would have been a significant memento if it had been preserved.

I remember that in 1935, when Pei Wenzhong left for France to study and

Bian Meinian was engaged elsewhere, I was put in charge of the Zhoukoudian dig, and my contact with Teilhard became more frequent. He came to the site several times to give directions for the work. When he came alone, he would always travel by train and get off at the station 15 kilometres away from Zhoukoudian; from there, the only transportation available was by mule. I would be notified by phone or by mail from his office before he came, and would be on hand to greet him at the railway station. I could see how at home he was on muleback. He had even learned to give commands to the beast in the fashion of a Chinese cart driver. All along the way, he would yell, "Da Da . . . Jia Jia . . . Wooh . . . ," and his orders were obeyed! He had indeed travelled extensively in North China and was used to the inconveniences that a fieldworker had to put up with in those days.

It was a moving experience to see how many hardships the man could bear. Every time he came to Zhoukoudian, he shared our food and asked for nothing special. Once I went to the railway station with him to see him off to Beijing, but we missed the train and had to wait for the next one, due that night. We had supper towards evening at one of the two or three none-too-clean restaurants in the village. I was worried that he would have no appetite for such fare, but he ate heartily. The meal over, he picked up a dead cricket from under the table and said that he had found it in his rice. He had thrown it under the table furtively for fear that the sight of it might spoil my appetite. Some legs were missing, and I suspect they had found their way into the scientist's stomach.

On an investigation trip to Ningxia in 1980 with members of the team, I paid my respects at the little inn where the two Catholic Fathers, Emile Licent and Pierre Teilhard de Chardin, had stayed when they were digging at the Shuidonggou site, which they had discovered in 1923. Nothing remained of the inn except dilapidated walls to evoke memories of the past. We were told that the building used to be partitioned into three rooms, the western room serving as the living quarters of the owner and his wife, the middle one as the kitchen, and the third one for guests. In that remote area, Europeans were a novelty at the time, so the French Fathers attracted great attention and left a deep impression on the populace. The innkeeper and his wife had long since passed away, but some of the old-timers still had vivid recollections of the two foreigners. In my heart, the remains of that inn are a monument to the dedicated spirit of two great scientists.

Teilhard felt deeply for the sufferings of the Chinese people during the war. When he was informed of the tragic death of three Zhoukoudian workers at the hands of the Japanese aggressors in 1937, shortly after the war broke out, he immediately stopped typing; his face turned pale, his lips trembled, and his eyes stared at me. He sat motionless for a while, then slowly stood up, and with his head bending low, began to pray. I had known him for a few years by then, but this was the first time I had ever seen him in prayer. That over, he solemnly stalked out of the room, uttering not a word. The spontaneous grief he manifested for his fellow men at that grim moment moved me so much that I can see it in my mind's eye to this day.

In the wake of the Pearl Harbour attack of December 1941, the Japanese military seized the Peking Union Medical College, and the Cenozoic Research Laboratory affiliated with it ceased to exist. But Teilhard carried on his work, at an institute of geological and biological studies. It was two years before Pei Wenzhong and I went to see him. We had a lengthy talk about the war, our work, and life at the time. That was the last I saw of Teilhard de Chardin. When we were taking leave, he produced a book, his newly published *Fossil Man*, inscribed it with his signature, and gave it to me as a keepsake. I immediately added the date to his signature: December 20, 1943. The book was to evoke many happy memories of my life with this dedicated scholar.

Index

L

Q